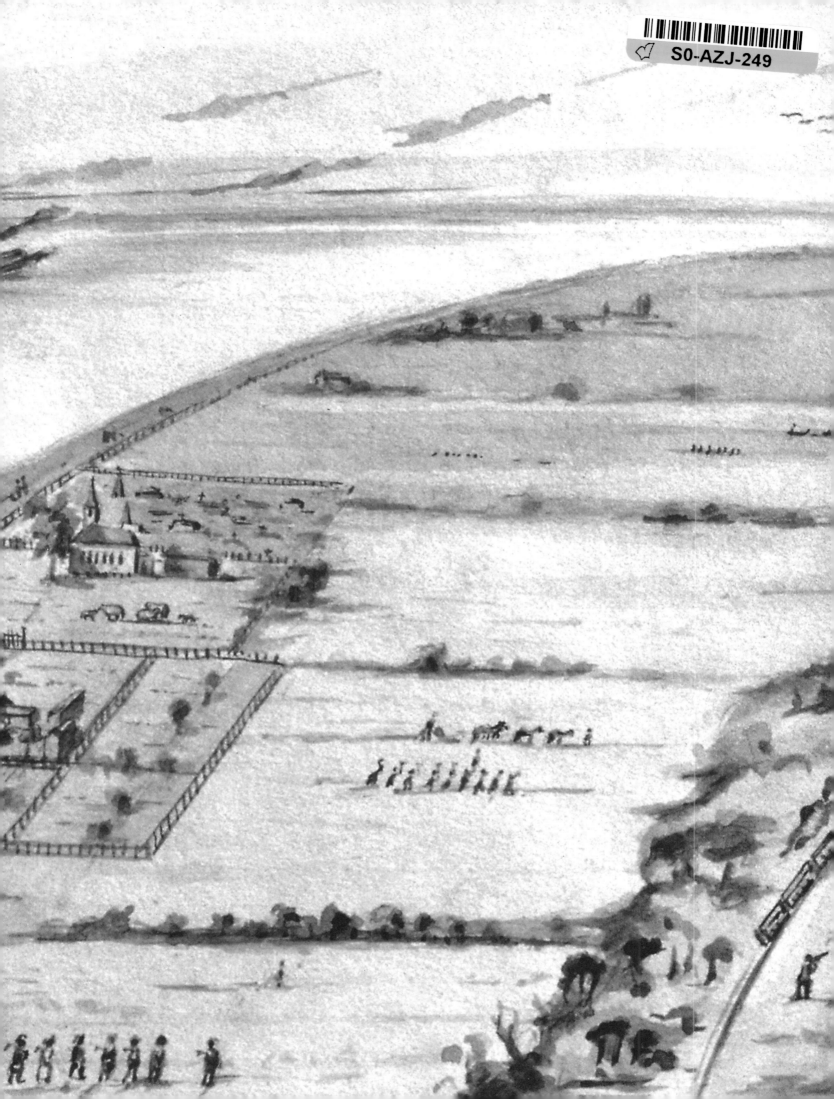

To: Patsy Distefano

Thanks for helping us to "capture" history!

Joan Weaver Becnel

Suzan Bent

Marilyn Mayfall Leekour

St. Charles "Parish of Plenty"

"Parish of Plenty" created in 1807 from the County of the German Coast. Sketch by Janis Blair.

St. Charles Parish

Louisiana

A Pictorial History

The St. Charles Historical Foundation wishes to gratefully
acknowledge and thank the following sponsors whose generous
support made possible this limited edition pictorial history as an
official bicentennial project of St. Charles Parish.

"Let us, before we die, gather our heritage and present it to our children."
Author Unknown

Taking Possession of Louisiana and the River Mississippi, in the name of Louis XIVth, *by Cavelier de la Salle by Bocquin, ca.1860, color lithograph, THNOC.1970.1 In 1682, René Robert Cavelier, sieur de la Salle claimed the lands drained by the Mississippi River for France. Passing through St. Charles Parish on his return trip upriver, LaSalle presented his blue serge coat to the Quinapissa Indian chief in present-day Hahnville in honor of this special occasion. (Courtesy of The Historic New Orleans Collection)*

St. Charles Parish
Louisiana
A Pictorial History

by Joan Weaver Becnel, Suzanne Friloux, and Marilyn Mayhall Richoux,
with contributions by Fay Walker Louque

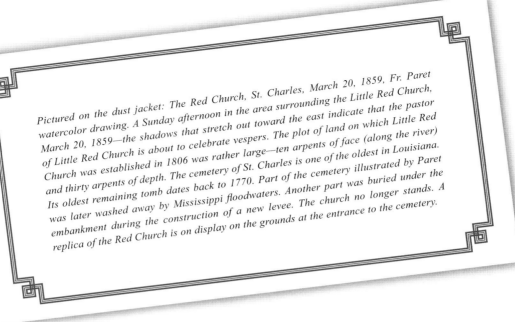

Pictured on the dust jacket: The Red Church, St. Charles, March 20, 1859, Fr. Paret watercolor drawing. A Sunday afternoon in the area surrounding the Little Red Church, March 20, 1859—the shadows that stretch out toward the east indicate that the pastor of Little Red Church is about to celebrate vespers. The plot of land on which Little Red Church was established in 1806 was rather large—ten arpents of face (along the river) and thirty arpents of depth. The cemetery of St. Charles is one of the oldest in Louisiana. Its oldest remaining tomb dates back to 1770. Part of the cemetery illustrated by Paret was later washed away by Mississippi floodwaters. Another part was buried under the embankment during the construction of a new levee. The church no longer stands. A replica of the Red Church is on display on the grounds at the entrance to the cemetery.

The Donning Company Publishers
184 Business Park Drive, Suite 206
Virginia Beach, VA 23462

Steve Mull, General Manager
Barbara Buchanan, Office Manager
Anne Cordray, Editor
Tonya Hannink, Graphic Designer
Derek Eley, Imaging Artist
Cindy Smith, Project Research Coordinator
Tonya Hannink, Marketing Specialist
Pamela Engelhard, Marketing Advisor

Neil Hendricks, Project Director

Library of Congress Cataloging-in-Publication Data

Becnel, Joan Weaver, 1943-
  St. Charles Parish, Louisiana : a pictorial history / by Joan Weaver
Becnel, Suzanne Friloux, and Marilyn Mayhall Richoux ; with contributions
by Fay Walker Louque.
    p. cm.
  Includes bibliographical references and index.
  ISBN 978-1-57864-638-8
1. Saint Charles Parish (La.)--History. 2. Saint Charles Parish
(La.)--History--Pictorial works. I. Friloux, Suzanne. II. Richoux, Marilyn
Mayhall. III. Louque, Fay Walker. IV. Title. V. Title: Saint Charles Parish,
Louisiana.
  F377.S124B43 2010
  976.3'33--dc22
                              2010023635

Printed in the United States of America at Walsworth Publishing Company

Dedication

To our lead author, parish historian, friend, and former schoolmate

Fay Ann Walker Louque
1939–2008
and
To the Pioneers, those First Families of St. Charles
(Names from 1724 Census)*

Simon Lambert, Conrad Friedrich, Johann Georg Troxler, Johann Georg Bock, Wilhelm Ziriac, Johann Callander, Stephan Kistenmacher, Jeremias Wagner, Leonhard Magdolff, Andreas Schantz, Johann Georg Betz, Johann Adam Matern, Caspar Dubs, Ambrose Heidel, Jacob Ritter, Michael Vogel, Sebastian Funck, Michael Horn, Balthasar Monthe, Johann Georg Raeser, Johann Jacob Bebloquet, Johann Cretzmann, Balthasar Marx, Bernard Wich, Johann Rommel, Catharine Weller, Anna Kuhn, Magdalena Fromberger, Margarethe Reynard, Catherine Hencke, Christian Grabert, Andreas Necker, Jacob Oberle, Andreas Schenck, Marcus Thiel, Moritz Kobler, Karl Friedrich D'Arensbourg, Andreas Traeger, Jacob Lueck, Andreas Hofmann, Mathias Friedrich, Bernhard Reusch, Paul Klomp, Adam Schmitz, Johann Rodler, Anton Distelzweig, William Pictot, Friedrich Merkel, Peter Muench, Andreas Struempfl, Johann Adam Riehl, Jacques Poche, Joseph Wagensbach, Sibylla Heil, Johann Adam Edelmeier, Philipp Zahn, Johann Jacob Foltz, Bernhard Anton

*J. Hanno Deiler, *Settlement of the German Coast of Louisiana and the Creoles of German Descent*

*The St. Charles Historical Foundation
proudly presents its bicentennial project.*

Contents

Foreword

The history of St. Charles Parish reaches back to the earliest settlements in the Louisiana territory, that vast expanse of land later known as the Louisiana Purchase. France's claim to this huge amount of territory hinged on colonizing it and developing the riches of the land. Few Frenchmen of substance were willing to leave the relative comfort of 18th Century France. However, they were happy to accept concessions of land in what was then called "the Mississippi", but were unable to obtain settlers needed for colonization. Forced emigration of undesirables was the first remedy of the French government. But Sieur de Bienville, governor of the territory, complained so bitterly about the quality of these immigrants that the practice was stopped within a few years.

In the early days, after the founding of New Orleans in 1718, only seven concessions upriver from the capital were in operation. The Dubrueil concession was the most successful of these, where the land had been cleared, levees built, and canals dug to drain the land into the swamp. Dubrueil's large house was said to be the nicest in the entire colony. He also had planted his fields with indigo, the crop demanded by the French government for export. Those plantations that functioned grew tobacco as well as indigo, cash crops to supply the French controlled market for the commodities.

In 1721, a small group of German-speaking settlers arrived. They had been recruited by John Law to work his concessions along the Mississippi River. Estimated at 3,000 in number, only a tenth lived to reach their final destination. Abandoned by a bankrupt John Law, they were left to languish on the beaches of the Gulf Coast, where the local Indians helped them survive until resettlement. After much suffering and death, Governor Bienville finally had them transferred to an area along the Mississippi River, now part of St. Charles Parish. There, these hardy Germans were given small plots of land that they could farm. But they had neither enough land, slaves, nor draft animals to grow crops for export. They were limited to cultivating grain and vegetables, to raising poultry for eggs, and to keeping a few farm animals. Nevertheless, while still under French rule, these colonists were able to produce enough surplus to supply the New Orleans market. It is said that the residents of the capital would have starved without the weekly shipments of supplies from the *Côté des Allemands* (German Coast).

After the Louisiana territory was acquired by Spain in 1762, the German settlement continued to prosper. The large plantation holders, however, were adversely affected by the new Spanish trade policies, which permitted the sale of their products only to other Spanish-held colonies or to the mother country. Revolution resulted, led by the large concessionaires but supported by the small farmers of the *Côté des Allemands*.

By 1775, the land upriver from New Orleans was divided into two ecclesiastical districts named after the two churches of the area, the parishes of St. Charles and St. John the Baptist. They operated as two separate governmental districts, each with a commander appointed by the governor. Both banks of the down-river section, now part of St. Charles Parish, became known as the *Primera Costa de los Alemanes* (First German Coast).

At this time, St. Charles Parish could boast over 70 large concessions with well over 800 slaves. These large-scale plantations had horses, plows, and both Negro and Indian slaves to supplement the white workers and overseers. They were able to cultivate enough land to produce indigo for export as well as staple food for their own use. Ten years later the census reported 561 whites, 69 free men of color, and 1,273 slaves. While indigo still remained the principal export crop, corn and rice were also widely grown. Because the Spanish supply ships were unreliable, St. Charles Parish became the principal supplier of rice to the inhabitants of New Orleans and to the garrison stationed in the city. Corn was used to feed the cattle and slaves. Both indigo processors and rice mills dotted the river banks of St. Charles Parish. Additionally, a considerable number of dairies produced milk, cream, and butter.

However, the large concessions were endangered by the unpredictable harvests due to fluctuating weather conditions, and most changed hands several times. Frequent flooding by the river was an additional hazard. The plantation owners were obliged to build and maintain ever stronger levees. The technology needed to build such levees was brought by an influx of Acadians to the area, in 1764, who possessed engineering expertise acquired in French-held Canada.

Hurricanes devastated St. Charles Parish in both 1770 and 1780. In 1784, a terrible drought destroyed the corn crop and greatly reduced the amount of rice that could be harvested. A severe frost in 1786 killed much of the indigo while the droughts increased the amount of insects feeding on the plants. From this point on the indigo crop became unpredictable. The final blow was produced by the arrival of an insect called the clamp bug, which caused crop failure year after year.

Finally the cultivation of indigo was replaced by sugar cane. Sugar mills and sheds for bagasse began to appear in the landscape. Lumbering became the next most important export produce. Wood was easily transported from the cypress swamps through the canals to the river. Logs were bound together and sent in rafts down-river to New Orleans. By 1782, free trade was permitted under Spanish rule as it had been during the French colonial period, and a thriving trade developed with the islands of the West Indies and Havana.

Sporadic Indian attacks had to be dealt with in St. Charles Parish throughout the colonial period. The male settlers all bore arms and were good shots. A fort where soldiers were stationed was built by the government on the German Coast for protection and to insure the staple food supply. Further danger to the status-quo of the parish came from the English at Bayou Manchac and the Americans settling in Baton Rouge. In 1791, Don José Pontalba was given command of a militia to defend the colony against these encroaching British and American interests.

From 1770 on, French ships were permitted to bring Negroes. Slavery was wide spread in St. Charles Parish by this point. The misuse of slave labor was rare. The laws of the *Code Noir* of 1724 continued to be observed throughout the colonial period. Small plots of land were given to the slaves where they grew corn, rice, sweet potatoes, and vegetables. The slaved could sell whatever portion of their harvest went beyond their own needs. These regulations remained unchanged until the Civil War.

By 1795, sugar cane had replaced indigo as the export crop in St. Charles Parish, although some indigo was still grown along with rice, corn, cotton, and vegetables. St. John Parish up-river, however, was less prosperous and grew primarily cotton and rice. *The richest concessions of the colony were in St. Charles Parish, where three-fourths of the population and seven-eights of the wealth of all Louisiana were concentrated.* At the time of the Louisiana Purchase, in 1803, St. Charles Parish was described by several observers as follows:

"Plantation touches plantation. I have seen in no part of the United States such a rich and highly cultivated tract." Other observers described the landscape as delightful: "The houses up and down the river are separated by plantations and orange groves. Their barnyards are full of hogs, cattle and foul of all kinds." "The individual concessions appear to be small villages. The sugar works, slave quarters, and overseer's house all lie next to each other. Somewhat set back from the river front area is the home of the plantation owner."

With the Louisiana Purchase the American government took over the plantation system with its associated slave practices. So prosperous was St. Charles Parish that it was known as the Gold Coast. Only with the Civil War was this economic and cultural development ended. Still today remnants of this great prosperity can be seen in the plantation homes and sugar cane cultivation of the parish, monuments to the great social and economic success of the antebellum period of St. Charles Parish.

Ellen C. Merrill
Professor, historian, and author

Preface

The St. Charles Historical Foundation's idea to develop a pictorial history surfaced at the December 2003 board meeting when several members discussed the notion of producing a publication, which would capture, primarily with pictures, the history of St. Charles Parish. A proposal was developed and presented to the St. Charles Historical Foundation board at a subsequent meeting. The board agreed that exploratory work should begin.

As deliberations progressed, it was decided to seek the endorsement and support of parish government. A meeting was scheduled with Parish President Albert Laque and Administrative Assistant Timothy Vial. During the course of the meeting, the St. Charles Historical Foundation members emphasized that 2007 would mark the two-hundredth anniversary of the formation of the civil parish of St. Charles. It was determined that in addition to the pictorial history publication there should be an organized parish-wide effort to celebrate the parish bicentennial. St. Charles Historical Foundation members proposed the formation of a bicentennial committee comprised of delegates from organizations across the parish and committed to be part of the group. In the interim, the book project continued to move forward. The St. Charles Historical Foundation contracted with the Donning Company Publishers. In order to finance the pictorial history project, the historical foundation initiated a fundraising campaign and all members of the community were invited to participate. A community call was issued for historically significant photographs, newspaper articles, and documents. Hurricane Katrina in 2005 and extenuating circumstances in 2006 delayed the project. In August of 2006 an authors committee was formed to continue the project. The pictorial history proposal was later presented to the bicentennial committee and unanimously accepted as an official project of the bicentennial celebration. In 2008, Hurricane Gustav further delayed the book project.

Members of the newly formed authors committee decided the history of St. Charles Parish needed to be presented in more than just pictures. This publication evolved from being just a pictorial history of St. Charles to an extensive review of history as characterized by timelines, first hand accounts, and legal documents, as well as maps, charts, graphs, and photographs. This publication is an historical recounting and pictorial history of St. Charles Parish, which begins before the arrival of early explorers and first settlers and progresses to the twenty-first century. Chronicling over three centuries of the diverse and rich culture of St. Charles Parish was a challenging and rewarding task. Our story is as deep and turbulent as the mighty Mississippi River, which continues to be the lifeblood of St. Charles Parish. The St. Charles Historical Foundation is proud to present this pictorial history as a 2007 bicentennial project albeit late in celebration of the two-hundredth anniversary of the parish.

Law's Recruitment Broadside. *(Courtesy of The Historic New Orleans Collection. Acc. No. 83-382)*

"Pamphlets and handbills were published, but the descriptions of Louisiana were not correct. They said that four crops could be raised each year; that the Indians were friendly and did most of the work; that there was plenty of game, including deer and bear. Many Frenchmen and other Europeans beleived these descriptions and came to Louisiana."—Edwin A. Davis, Louisiana: The Pelican State

⚜ ⚜ ⚜

Acknowledgments

Statue of Saint Charles Borremeo
(by Joe Schexnaydre)

The St. Charles Historical Foundation posthumously thanks and acknowledges our lead author, Fay Walker Louque, who very carefully and accurately guided us through our historical records.

The foundation was very fortunate to have the full support of Parish President Albert Laque; Parish Council Members Lance Marino, Clayton Faucheux II, Desmond Hilaire, Brian Fabre, Ram Ramchandran, Dickie Duhe, April Black, Barry Minnich, and Derryl Walls; Administrative Assistant Timothy Vial; and Economic Development and Tourism Director Corey Faucheux.

Special thanks to Neil Hendricks and Editors Kathy Sheridan and Anne Cordray Burns, and Tonya Hannink from the Donning Company Publishers, for their patience and guidance. Special recognition to LSU Professor Dr. Jay Edwards, artist Janis Blair, Dr. Ellen Merrill, and Editorial Assistants Winter Randall and Patricia Danflous. We appreciate the assistance of Professor Reinhart Kondert, The Historic New Orleans Collection, Center for Louisiana Studies, ULL, Gene and Pat Yoes, *St. Charles Herald Guide*, Leonard Gray, Triche Family, George Lorio Family, Maureen Downey, Norman Marmillion, St. Charles Parish Library System, River Road Historical Society, Nancy Robert, St. Charles Borromeo Church Staff, Rhitt Growl and St. Charles Parish Public Schools Satellite Center, Clarisse "Sis" Webb, United Way of St. Charles, Lily Galland, River Region Arts and Humanities Council, CPA Nolan Schexnayder, Gerald Zeringue, Paul Hogan, Elizabeth Simoneaux, and Verna Simoneaux.

Thanks to those parish residents who enthusiastically opened family albums and attic boxes in search of historically significant items to enhance the project.

The foundation is grateful for past St. Charles Historical Foundation board members and advisors Darnell "Dee" Abadie, Joan Becnel, Carolyn Smith Boyd, John Campo, Rita Carlson, Joseph Catarina, Maureen Downey, Deirdre Faucheux, Suzanne "Sue" Friloux, Lorraine Gendron, Barry Guillot, Coleen Perilloux Landry, Don Paul Landry, Angela "Angie" Matherne, Michael Matherne, Gregory Miller, John Polk, Marilyn Richoux, Jara Roux, Garland Strother, Angie Wall, Harriet Williamson, Nancy Wilson, Percy Wilson, and Patrick "Pat" Yoes.

The St. Charles Historical Foundation again thanks each and every sponsor for the faith and trust placed in our project. The foundation is very grateful to all who assisted in assuring that the rich culture and tradition of St. Charles Parish would be captured and recorded for future generations.

We acknowledge and appreciate the support and assistance our family members provided during our countless hours of work: Warren and Kim Louque, Ralph Richoux, Roland Becnel and Sue's cats.

Prologue

In 1807, St. Charles Parish was named for the Ecclesiastical Parish of St. Charles, which served its parishioners in colonial times and in succeeding centuries at its present location in Destrehan. Charles Borromeo was born of noble birth on October 2, 1538, in a castle on Lake Maggiore in Italy. His father was Count Gilbert Borromeo and his mother was a Medici of Milano. While studying civil and canon law at the University of Paris, Charles acquired the reputation of being *a paragon of virtue and humility.* He earned his doctorate at age twenty-two. When his uncle, Cardinal de Medici, was named Pope Pius IV in 1559, he named Charles as cardinal-deacon and administrator of Milano or the secretary of state of the Vatican. In 1563, at the age of twenty-five, Charles was ordained a priest. Charles flourished in his new profession. He supervised the drafting of the *Catechism of the Council of Trent* and the reform of liturgical books and music. In 1566, he returned to Milano to reform the diocese and retained his reputation as *a paragon of virtue and humility.* He established the Confraternity of Christian Doctrine mandating that children be properly instructed in Christian doctrine. Thousands of children participated in this program during his lifetime and this mandate continues today. Charles died on November 3, 1584, at the age of forty-six. He was beatified in 1602 and canonized in 1610 (his feast day is celebrated on November 4).

The Church of St. Charles was founded on the east bank of the German Coast 130 years later. The name Borromeo surfaced later in church records. There is a statue of St. Charles enshrined in front of the church in Destrehan. The altar stone at St. Charles Borromeo rests on a massive walnut tree trunk imported from Arona, Italy. This tree was estimated to be four hundred years old, dating back to the time that Charles Borromeo walked the streets of Arona. As a tribute to his prominence in the parish's history, a statue of his likeness stands at the parish courthouse in Hahnville.

The Patron Saint of St. Charles Parish—St. Charles Borromeo.

Saint Charles Borromeo's Humilitas Badge.

Eighteenth *Century*

4,800 years ago—The Mississippi River creates the first delta lobe in the area.

1,300 years ago—The Mississippi River's present course is established.

1,000 years ago (approximately)—The earliest inhabitants of St. Charles Parish are part of the archaeological culture known as Tchefuncte.

1542—Spaniard Hernando DeSoto discovers the Mississippi River.

1662–1700—Age of Exploration (LaSalle, Bienville, and Iberville).

1682—Frenchman Robert Cavalier, Sieur de LaSalle, travels the length of the Mississippi River with his lieutenant, Henri de Tonti, camping in the vicinity of a Quinapissa village near present-day Hahnville. He claims the Mississippi River territory for France (King Louis XIV). It becomes known as *La Louisiane.*

1694—Karl Fredrick Darensbourg is born on January 25; later serves as first commandant of the German Coast.

1699—The mouth of the Mississippi River is discovered by the Iberville/Bienville expedition traveling north passing through St. Charles Parish.

1699—First settlement in Louisiana colony at Fort Maurepas, Old Biloxi (Ocean Springs).

1712—Frenchman Antoine Crozat is granted exclusive rights to settle the Louisiana Territory.

1717—Scotsman John Law assumes Crozat's charter to settle the territory and forms the Company of the West.

1717—Law enlists French, then German, settlers and imports African slaves.

1717—Law initiates his plan to finance the development of Louisiana, later referred to as the "Mississippi Bubble."

(Sktech by Janis Blair and authors.)

1718—New Orleans is founded by Bienville and the Company of the Indies.

1719—Law merges the Company of the West into the Company of the Indies.

1719—*Les Deux Frères* arrives at Old Biloxi with the first settlers who later establish *le premier ancien village allemand,* some 1.5 miles inland from the Mississippi River, 30 miles above New Orleans. The area becomes known as *la Côté des Allemands* (German Coast).

1720—Law's "Mississippi Bubble" bursts.

1721—The *Portefaix* arrives at Old Biloxi on June 4 with Karl Fredrick Darensbourg and three hundred Swiss and Alsatian families.

1722—In January, Darensbourg and the new German settlers are transported to the *Côté des Allemands* where they join settlers in the villages of Hoffen, Mariental, and Augsburg.

1722—Karl Darensbourg appointed first commandant of the German Coast by Governor Bienville. The homestead of Darensbourg is named Karlstein in his honor.

1722—*La Grand Ouragan* (hurricane) devastates the German Coast on September 12.

1722—Some of the German and French settlers move to the east bank area referred to as *L'Anse Aux Outardes* (Bustard's Cove) in present-day New Sarpy.

1723—St. Jean des Allemands Catholic Church is established at Karlstein (Trinity Plantation).

1724—German Coast settlement serves as the breadbasket for New Orleans.

1729—First Indian attack on the German villages.

1731—The charter of the Company of the Indies expires and the Louisiana Territory is transferred to France.

1732—First phase of the settlement of the German Coast draws to a close.

1734—Darensbourg begins recording the first official government acts, now referred to as "The Darensbourg Records, 1734–1769."

1740—Tradition says that St. Jean des Allemands Catholic Church was relocated to the east bank and called St. Charles or "Church of the Germans."

1743—Organized attempts to build protection levees for the Mississippi River begin.

1751—Louisiana successfully grows sugar cane brought from Santo Domingo by Jesuit priests. Sugar cane becomes the first cash crop of early Louisiana.

1762—France secretly transfers to Spain the Louisiana Territory west of the Mississippi River (Treaty of Fountainbleau).

1763—France transfers the Louisiana Territory east of the Mississippi River to England (Treaty of Paris).

1764—First Acadians arrive in the colony; more arrive in 1768.

1765—Jean LaBranche develops LaBranche Plantation (now Esperanza Plantation).

1766—Spanish Governor Antonio de Ulloa arrives in the colony.

1768—German Coast militia joins New Orleans citizens and leads a major revolt to defy Ulloa's Spanish rule of the colony.

1769—General Alexander O'Reilly arrives to secure Louisiana for Spain; he executes revolt leaders but spares Darensbourg and citizens of the German Coast.

1770—Governor Luis de Unzaga gives land grants to establish churches and cemeteries on the German Coast.

1772—St. John the Baptist Church is built on a Spanish land grant in present-day Edgard on the German Coast.

1776—Declaration of Independence of the United States of America is signed.

1777—Darensbourg dies on November 18.

1779—German Coast patriots join Governor Galvez in Louisiana's defense against British advancement.

1779—Bonnet Carré Crevasse floods vast areas on the east bank of the German Coast.

1787—Robert Robin de Logny begins construction of his plantation (Destrehan). De Logny's son-in-law, Jean-Noël Destrehan, acquires it in 1802.

1790—Pierre Trépagnier builds the plantation now known as Ormond Plantation (in Destrehan).

1790—LaBranche Plantation is built in present-day St. Rose.

1791—Home Place Plantation in Hahnville is believed to have been built at this time by Charles, a free mulatto, who also built Destrehan Plantation.

1792—The Catholic Diocese of Louisiana is established on April 25.

1795—Etienne Bore successfully granulates sugar cane; his research is partially funded by his brother-in-law, Jean-Noël Destrehan.

1796/1800—Spain secretly returns Louisiana to France.

Ancient Civilizations

Forgotten Cultures

Prehistory to AD 1500

American Indians

The first "Americans," nomadic hunters from Asia, crossed a land bridge from Siberia to Alaska in search of food. Eventually, as the climate changed and animals upon which they depended became extinct, those hunters became "hunter-gatherers" and then, eventually, "farmers." Those earliest settlers are now generally referred to as American Indians.

This transition to farming was necessitated by the extinction of the large animals they hunted. They began to observe that plants grew from seeds and roots. When they began planting their own food supply, this was the beginning of agriculture. Agriculture freed them from the constant search for food and allowed them to settle permanently.

They tended to build their family settlements where animals migrated or wild plants could be harvested. By 1500, when the Europeans arrived, there were a variety of different cultures, from simple hunters to advanced civilizations.

Archeological sites in the United States have exposed evidence of these early American peoples. Poverty Point, in north Louisiana, is a major national archaeological site.

Poverty Point

Around 1730 BC a great culture, named for the famous Poverty Point settlement in northeastern Louisiana, flourished. It was probably people from this culture that first entered into what is now St. Charles Parish. (The first residents of the parish were most likely the people of the Tchefuncte culture (ca 600 BC to AD 200). The remains of a village from this culture are located about halfway between LaPlace and Manchac. These people built temporary circular shelters covered with palmetto or grass, and consumed large numbers of brackish water clams and oysters that resulted in huge mounds of shell that can still be seen today in St. Charles Parish in the Lake Salvador area. These Native Americans are generally considered to be the people who introduced pottery into Louisiana.

In 1739, it was reported that the Washa, along with the Chawasha, had fallen in with the Acolapissa, Bayougoula, Houma, and two other nations (likely the Mugulasha and Quinapissa), and were living at Côté des Allemands, or the west bank of the German Coast. There is a record of a Choctaw village located between present-day Boutte and Paradis that is said to have existed well past the other tribes in this area. (Very little is known of the tribes of St. Charles Parish.) ⚜ ⚜ ⚜

Photo of Mississippian pot found by Daniel Deroche in St. Charles Parish. Piece measures approximately nine inches in diameter. (Photo courtesy of Maureen Downey)

Spanish explorer Hernando de Soto discovered the Mississippi River about 1542. After de Soto's death, Luis de Moscoso and the remaining men of his expedition traveled down the Mississippi passing through St. Charles Parish on their way to Mexico. They were perhaps the first Europeans to touch St. Charles Parish soil although others may have been here before them. (Sketch by Janis Blair)

Exploration and Discovery

After the discovery of the river, few explorers came to the Lower Mississippi Valley. Because of this, over 140 years would pass before the idea of settlement would arise. ❖ ❖ ❖

In 1682, Robert Cavalier, Sieur de LaSalle, a French fur trader and explorer who started his journey in Canada with his lieutenant, Henri de Tonti, traveled the entire length of the Mississippi River. As his expedition passed through present-day Hahnville, it was attacked by indigenous Quinapissa villagers. LaSalle went on to claim for France the Lower Mississippi Valley and called it *La Louisiane* (Louisiana) in honor of King Louis XIV. The Louisiana Territory, as it would be referred to, spanned more than half of the continent. It was a vast region that extended to the beginning of every river and stream whose waters flowed into the Mississippi River. Upon his return upriver, LaSalle presented the Quinapissa chief with a blue serge coat in honor of the special occasion. Tonti, on his return trip upriver, gave the chief a double glass bottle and left a letter for LaSalle when he returned. Several years later LaSalle returned, but failed in his attempts to colonize Louisiana.

Colonizing the Mississippi River Valley remained a priority for France as a result of LaSalle's fellow explorers and other French entrepreneurs who believed the colony would enrich the crown in many ways. As a result, King Louis XIV authorized the settlement and establishment of a military outpost near the Mississippi to deter England's interest in colonizing the Lower Valley and to take advantage of Spain's concurrent military decline.

The Mississippi River and its tributaries enabled the early explorers to enter what is now called St. Charles Parish. ❖ ❖ ❖

LaSalle and Tonti are the first known Europeans to set foot upon the soil of St. Charles Parish. ❖ ❖ ❖

Robert Cavalier, the Sieur de La Salle. (Sketch by Janis Blair)

Immigration and Settlement

In 1698, nobleman Pierre le Moyne, Sieur d'Iberville, a Canadian war hero, was selected along with his younger brother, Jean Baptiste le Moyne, Sieur de Bienville, to lead the expedition to establish a settlement and a French military outpost near the Mississippi River. Catholic priests were included in the Iberville party on his voyage. As the "Founder of Louisiana," Iberville successfully rediscovered the Mississippi River on March 2, 1699, and settled the area in the French colony that would become the Louisiana Territory. Iberville proposed the immigration of families and young women to make homes for the young settlers. He promoted agriculture as the colony's chief livelihood. Iberville made several trips to France, returning with new colonists and supplies.

Arriving on the Gulf Coast in early 1699, Iberville set up a temporary village at Ship and Cat Islands, consulted with the Biloxi Indians, and then began scouting the

*Founder of Louisiana
Pierre le Moyne, Sieur d'Iberville.
(Sketch by Janis Blair)*

*Father of Louisiana
Jean Baptiste le Moyne, Sieur de Bienville.
(Sketch by Janis Blair)*

"Indians adored Bienville while fearing him because they knew him to be always just though often stern."— The Louisiana Historical Quarterly, Vol. 3, No. 2. ❖ ❖ ❖

Antoine Crozat. (Sketch by Janis Blair)

Crozat imported Negro slaves from the West Indies, but most slaves would later come from Africa. ❖ ❖ ❖

land for a suitable place for a permanent settlement. Iberville, his brother Bienville, and about fifty Canadians and sailors (including Catholic priests), traveling in two large boats and two canoes, began pushing slowly southwestward, threading their way around the islands east of Lake Borgne, until they reached the Mississippi River. After rediscovering the Mississippi, they began traveling upriver and on the fourth day reached a large Bayougoula Indian settlement (in St. Charles Parish) at the river's intersection with a tributary at the site referred to as *L'Anse aux Outardes* (Bustard's Cove), or present-day New Sarpy. They found the Quinapissa had joined the Mugulasha and they later formed one village with the Bayougoula. Iberville discovered that the Mugulasha chief had a blue serge coat, and he was therefore probably the same chief LaSalle had met many years earlier. The glass bottle left by Tonti was discovered in the Bayougoula temple. Later Bienville was given the letter that Tonti had written to LaSalle. The Bayougoula called this letter the "speaking bark."

Iberville continued traveling upriver, passing the present-day Louisiana capital. When he saw a red pole with the heads of a fish and bear, he named it *Baton Rouge* ("red stick"). The Indians produced and used the red paint to mark and decorate. Iberville made his return trip to the Cat and Ship Islands, traveling east by way of Bayou Manchac, the Amite River, and Lakes Maurepas, Pontchartrain, and Borgne. Bienville traveled separately down the river to its mouth, then north to Cat Island. The two brothers arrived within hours of each other. Iberville's exploration determined the permanent settlement should be on the Gulf Coast. The French then constructed Fort Maurepas in Old Biloxi (near the present-day Ocean Springs, Mississippi).

The French made Louisiana a Crown Colony in 1699 and explored the Lower Mississippi River Valley and the Mississippi Gulf Coast for fifteen years, mapping the area and establishing Indian relationships to learn about crops, food, furs, skins, and other resources. Iberville's journal revealed this remarkable information on the early history of St. Charles Parish, focusing on the "traveling" historical items: the blue serge coat, the bottle, and the letter. ❖ ❖ ❖

Jean Baptiste le Moyne, Sieur de Bienville, "Father of Louisiana" and "Founder of New Orleans," who was chosen by the king of France to accompany his brother Iberville to Louisiana, remained in Louisiana for many years to help settle the colony. In 1718, Bienville founded the city of New Orleans. He served four terms as the French governor of Louisiana. He reportedly brought sugar cane and a few slaves with him. Governor Bienville is credited with establishing the first charity hospital with the Jean Louis Endowment. He failed, however, in his effort to prevent the transfer of Louisiana to Spain in 1762. He died in Paris in 1768 at the age of eighty-four.

By 1712, the French colony had a population of about four hundred and was permanently established. In 1712, under a Royal Charter obtained from King Louis XIV of France, Antoine Crozat was given a fifteen-year charter (or franchise) to settle and develop the Louisiana colony. Crozat, a Parisian merchant and one of France's richest men, was required to continue the laws of France in Louisiana and provide the colony with two shiploads of supplies and colonists each year. After several years of financial losses in this venture, Crozat petitioned the King in 1717 to revoke his charter.

John Law's Charter

In 1717, Scottish banker John Law, serving as finance minister to the duke of Orleans, was granted Louisiana in a charter almost identical to Crozat's. The duke of Orleans, regent successor to King Louis XIV, was desperate to help France recover from its financial woes following the king's reign. He readily accepted John Law's plan, historically referred to as the "Mississippi Bubble," to establish the Royal Bank of France using paper currency, with Louisiana and her riches to be used as collateral. Law's venture depended on the successful establishment of a colony able to pay interest on company shares.

In 1718, Law began recruiting French *engagés* to settle Louisiana. The early French colonists were not suited or prepared for the harsh conditions found in the colony. Failing in his initial effort, Law was forced to look for non-French colonists. In 1719, Jean-Pierre Purry, a company director with Law, proposed recruiting Germans and German-speaking Swiss farmers for Louisiana.

John Law visited farmers in the Rhineland with advertising pamphlets and broadsides presenting his plan to create a model community. Louisiana was described in posters as "a land filled with gold, silver, copper, and lead mines." Historians have not yet settled on the actual number of *engagés* that left their homeland for America, but it is possible that it could be in the thousands. Decades of horrible living conditions contributed to the exodus of people. The Thirty Years' War had left the Rhineland devastated. This was followed by the disastrous reign of King Louis XIV, which resulted in pestilence, famine, religious persecution,

John Law. (Courtesy of The Historic New Orleans Collection. Acc. No. 60-63RL)

In 1719, with a twenty-five-year charter, Law merged the Company of the West with his Company of the Indies. ⚜ ⚜ ⚜

Law's Recruitment Pamphlet. (Courtesy of The Historic New Orleans Collection. Acc. No. 83-382)

Law's Recruitment Broadside. *(Courtesy of The Historic New Orleans Collection. Acc. No. 83-382)*

and barbarous French generals. Many died even before leaving European shores. A small group of immigrants arrived in the Louisiana French colony in 1719 and were transported by waterways thirty miles west of New Orleans, to an area which would be referred to as the German Coast. The exact location is still unknown, but it is believed to be in the present-day Taft-Killona area of St. Charles Parish. One old record stated that the *le premier ancien village* was about a mile and a half from the river. *Le Compte France* (French records) indicated the first religious ceremony recorded was a baptism on September 20, 1719. In 1720, nine final rites, four baptisms, and one marriage were performed.

The *Deux Frères,* one of the first pest ships to depart for the Louisiana French colony carrying immigrants, left the French port of Lorient in 1720. It was followed by *La Garrone,* the *Durance*, and *Le St. Andre.* Some of these are referred to as "pest ships," because of the inhumane living conditions. Many passengers died as a

Ship List, 1719.

consequence of these conditions and others died after arrival on the shores of Old Biloxi (Ocean Springs) before moving inland.

Law and his company are credited with financing migration to Louisiana, resulting in settlement of the German Coast. Louisiana historian Edwin Adam Davis believes Louisiana owes John Law a great debt of gratitude. That would indeed be true of the German Coast, as the people of the German Coast were beneficiaries of Law's settlement plan.

Law's financial plan collapsed about 1720, but the Company of the Indies operated until 1731, when it returned its charter to France. Law disappeared into exile. France was not to recover for another ten years.

France's charter with John Law thus sets the stage for the marriage that would occur one hundred years later, in 1812, between the ecclesiastical parish and the civil parish of St. Charles, where they would become one in name and boundary (Louisiana Constitution of 1812). ❖ ❖ ❖

In 1721, the Louisiana Territory was divided into nine governmental districts, each under a commandant and judge. A year later, the province of Louisiana was divided into three ecclesiastical jurisdictions by the bishop of Quebec. New Orleans and the surrounding areas were given to the Capuchin Order of Clergy.

"With the help of perhaps eighty lumberjacks, carpenters, and other workers provided by the Company of the Indies, these Germans (Swiss and Alsations) built three villages modeled upon European towns in which houses were

John Law's Charter

There are different schools of thought regarding John Law's leadership. However, there can be no doubt that his contribution to Louisiana is legendary. Under Law's leadership and the Company of the Indies charter:

> *Population of the colony increased;*
> *Several towns were founded and settled, most notably the German Coast;*
> *Agriculture was firmly established, particularly along the German Coast;*
> *The German Coast became the breadbasket of the territory;*
> *New Orleans was established;*
> *The foundations for the establishment of the Catholic religion were laid.*

Article 53 of the company's charter provided for the building of churches and designating priests of the Catholic faith to serve the spiritual ministry of the inhabitants: "...the said Company shall be obliged to build at its expense churches at the places where it forms settlements; as also to maintain there the necessary number of approved ecclesiastics..."

The Company of the West considered this a serious mandate! This clause was responsible for the effort that established the Catholic Church on the German Coast. ❖ ❖ ❖

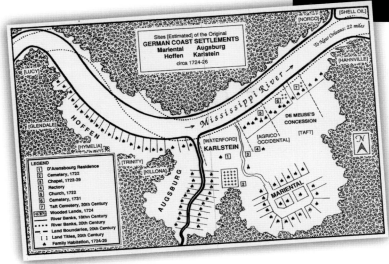

Map of early villages of the German Coast.
(Map by Norman Marmillion)

stretched out along the only road running through the village…Probably with the help of the eighty individuals who had assisted in the construction of the villages, the Germans began to clear, cultivate, and sow the lands around them with the grains and vegetables."—Reinhart Kondert, *The Germans of Colonial Louisiana: 1720–1803*.

In 2003, the St. Charles Historical Foundation, with funding from a Dow grant, conducted an aerial search for these early villages using thermal imaging photography to register temperature differences that might indicate where cultural activity took place centuries ago. "Hot spots" were discovered in the area of the Nelson Coleman Correction Center. ⚜ ⚜ ⚜

Karl Fredrick Darensbourg

Captain Karl Fredrick Darensbourg, a German-speaking Swedish soldier, left France on the *Portefaix* on March 7, 1721, bringing with him three hundred German-speaking Swiss and Alsatian colonists bound for Louisiana from the Alsace-Lorraine area. When they arrived in Old Biloxi on June 4, 1721, Bienville appointed Darensbourg commandant. On December 15, Governor Bienville issued an order decreeing all owners of longboats and flatboats to surrender their vessels to the colonial administration. In January 1722, these vessels would transport the colonists to the settlement on the coast, west of New Orleans, where they joined colonists already in the villages of Hoffen, Marienthal, and Augsburg. These *engagés* became

Changes in German Names

These early German settlers readily married into French families already living on the German Coast and adopted the French language and customs. They even accepted Gallicized revisions of their names. The French officials were well educated, served as scribes, and recorded the names of the Germans phonetically. The most common example is the German name Zweig, which sounded like twig. This became LaBranche in French. The spoken German language died slowly on the coast, but the written German faded quickly, as many of these first Germans had no formal education. ⚜ ⚜ ⚜

German Original	French Translation	German Original	French Translation
Dubs	Toups	Mayer	Mayeux
Engel	Hingle	Rommel	Rome
Foltz	Folse	Schaf	Chauffe
Heidel	Haydel	Scheckschneider	Schexnayder
Helfer	Elfer	Traeger	Tregre
Himmel	Hymel	Trischl	Triche
Huber	Oubre	Troxler	Trosclair
Kamper	Cambre	Wagensbach	Waguespack
Lesch	Laiche	Weber	Webre
Manz	Montz	Wichner	Vicknair
Matern	Mathern	Zehringer	Zeringue

concessionaires and were provided small land grants with no ownership rights. Darensbourg's concession was named Karlstein in his honor. This area became known as *Côté des Allemands* or the *German Coast*. Darensbourg brought the news to the colony that Law's plan had failed. This news was of great interest to residents of the colony. Historians have noted how ironic it is that the same settlers who brought the news of Law's company's collapse are the ones who were successful in settling the colony. They have also noted that the Swiss played an important role in the colonization of Louisiana in particular on the German Coast.

The new company had no accommodations for the arrival of the immigrants. They were without food, shelter, or any means of transportation. They had no horses or plows. These German pioneers faced unbelievable hardships in their new country. The land was a tropical to semi-tropical forest covered with thick underbrush. Using the indigenous trees and brush as lumber brought on the problem of stumps and their removal. Not until ten years after their arrival did they even have a horse in the settlement to lend assistance. Consequently, many succumbed to these early hardships. Professor J. Hanno Deiler believes many more would have perished had they not come from such hardy German stock.

In addition to those first families of St. Charles Parish, those pioneers listed in the 1724 census to whom the authors have dedicated this book, other German families not listed in the 1724 census were in the area and eventually came to the German Coast including: Jacob Huber (Oubre), Thomas Lesch (Laiche), Mueller, Johann Weber, Pierre Brou, Michael Zehringer (Zeringue), Schaf (Chauffe), Hans Reinhard Scheckschneider, Jean Zweig, Adam Trischl (Triche), and Johann Manz (Montz). Many of the descendents of these pioneer families remain today on the German Coast.

Early Death Certificate Registre d'état-civil Louisiana, f° 4: extrait des registres du R. P. Philibert Viauden…

Zweig (LaBranche) Family

Two Zweig families were listed as passengers on the pest ship *Deux Fréres* that arrived in Biloxi in March 1721:

a) Johan Adam, his wife, and daughter. Johan Adam is mentioned in the 1724 census as having died in Biloxi.

b) Johan, his wife, a son, and a daughter.

The surviving Johan became the progenitor of all the LaBranche families in Louisiana. His son Jean married Suzanne Marchand, an orphan living with the Ursuline sisters, and the official records of this marriage reflect the family's name change to the French LaBranche. "Legend has it that Johan Zweig could not write his name, but at his wedding he gave French officials an idea of what it meant: Zweig = twig = branch. Voila! LaBranche. So the French notary wrote 'Jean LaBranche.' Thus, family tradition says, the family name was born." (Dr. Isabel French, St. Charles Borromeo Church)

Bustard's Cove—*L'Anse aux Outardes*

In 1722, hurricanes devastated the German Coast and many Germans considered leaving. In order to prevent this exodus, Governor Bienville conceded lands to the Germans on both sides of the river. Later that year and in 1723, a few of the French and German concessionaires moved across the Mississippi River and established the first east bank settlement at a site near the confluence of several waterways connecting the river and Lake Pontchartrain. This area was already known as Bustard's Cove or *L'Anse aux Outardes*.

Bustard's Cove Historical Marker. Bustard's Cove was the site of the first east bank settlement near present-day New Sarpy at the confluence of the Mississippi River and Bayou LeSeur.

The Catholic Church

In 1723, *La Paroisse de St. Jean des Allemands* Catholic Church was established at Karlstein. The earlier German Coast settlers worshiped in New Orleans in an old abandoned warehouse that served as the predecessor to St. Louis Cathedral (Church Records of 1720–30).

CENSUS OF 1724 RECORDS: "The Chapel with house and kitchen. Garden. Cemetery of about one and a half arpents. It was at the completion of this new cemetery that the cemetery between the two old villages was abandoned."— *J. Hanno Deiler,* Settlement of the German Coast of Louisiana ⚜ ⚜ ⚜

The 1724 census reveals that a chapel had been constructed in a village on the German Coast, which, it appears, could have been there for several years prior to the census. This chapel has been described as "a miserable shed standing in a hole." It was built on land later referred to as Trinity Plantation. Church records indicate that visiting priests from New Orleans held services on the German Coast until a resident priest was appointed. Funeral records in Paris archives indicate that Father Philibert de Viander, a Capuchin Catholic missionary, was already ministering to the settlers at the end of 1722 and in early 1723. It is believed that the chapel was built as soon as the Germans settled the concession, because in 1727, Father Raphael pleaded for the Company of the Indies to build a new church. The colonial budget of 1729 makes provisions for a resident priest, Father Philippe de Lurembourg. The first book of sacramental records of this chapel (1739–56) is housed in the archives of St. Louis Cathedral in New Orleans.

French Prayer Book. (Photo courtesy of Abbey Simoneaux)

The 1723 chapel found in the second old village, Le deuxieme ancient village, about one-half mile from the Mississippi River, which neighbored the first village. (Sketch by Janis Blair)

J. Blair

In French Louisiana, the Roman Catholic religion was the universal religion. In fact, Catholicism was the only religion permitted. In Louisiana, the Church was supported by government subsidies and forced contributions and assessments. Every family had a pew rented by the year and the family's social position was usually indicated by pew location. The parish priest was closer to the families than the district commandant. There were more than twenty-five Holy Days a year, plus Sundays. Church bells rang for every occasion. Often the Blessed Sacrament was carried in the monstrance to the river levee to hold back floods. On the entire *Côté des Allemands* there were only ten Protestants. The Capuchins were relentless in their work for the Catholic Church. For example, in order to practice medicine, a person was first required to prove they were an upstanding Catholic. The Capuchins felt the Germans showed far more religious energy than the French, building their little chapel simultaneously with their settlement, rather than being content to worship in old stores or warehouses. It is believed that Father Raphael, an uncle of Jean-Noël Destrehan, opened the first parochial school in Louisiana in 1725, in New Orleans.

Louisiana's Code Noir or Black Code.

Negro Slavery in the Early Days

Apparently, history has not yet recorded the exact date when the first Negro slave was brought to Louisiana, although many believe Bienville brought a few West Indies slaves with him about 1708. A few more came during Crozat's charter period and many were imported by the Company of the Indies with slave ships arriving every year. In 1724, Bienville felt it necessary to enact a series of slave regulations called the "Black Code" or *Code Noir,* which codified relations between blacks and whites. It should also be noted that when Bienville had this special legislation passed, Article 3 of the code allowed "the exercise of the Roman Catholic creed only."

On the German Coast during the 1720s, houses were built on both sides of the Mississippi River. The first German settlers continuously supplied the markets of New Orleans. They used the river to transport their surplus produce in small boats or canoes, known as *pirogues,* returning home through Lake Pontchartrain into Bayous Trepagnier and LeSieur, and other tributaries to the Mississippi River.

Ellen Merrill, noted historian and authority on German Coast culture, reveals that in the 1724 census all of the German families were not only harvesting enough vegetables and grain for their families and cattle but were bringing their surplus to New Orleans markets. In addition to farming, they were constructing and maintaining levees where their property fronted the Mississippi River. It is apparent from these records that from the beginning of their settlement, German Coast farmers were a dependable source of food for the city of New Orleans.

The Gleaner *by Robert Fisher, a black American artist and educator at Destrehan High School.*

Pirogue. (Sketch by Janis Blair)

The first Indian attack on the German Coast occurred in about 1729, and although it was only a small raid, it left a lasting impression on the settlement and raised the level of concern regarding their safety. ✤ ✤ ✤

German Coast Settlement—Breadbasket of the Colony

In 1731, as the first decade of settlement on the German Coast ended, the Company of the Indies charter was retrieved by France and Louisiana again became a French colony. The land farmed by settlers on the German Coast technically belonged to the Company of the Indies until France retrieved its charter. Gradually, landholders began to petition France for ownership in order to sell the property and use the proceeds for economic improvement.

Land grants under French and Spanish rule were configured in arpents. The old French measurement for one arpent (superficial-square arpent) was 3.419 square meters or 4.089 square yards. An October 12, 1716, edict issued by King Louis XV mentions that land in the Province of Louisiana would be granted in modules two to four arpents wide along the river by forty to sixty arpents deep. Under Spanish rule, the modules were six to eight arpents wide by forty arpents deep. Generally, measurements of the grants were often stated in lieue (meters). In Louisiana, French and Spanish surveyors interpreted the lieue as 2500 toise de Paris (one toise equaled 1.95 meters or 2.13 yards) which equaled eighty-three and one third arpents de Paris instead of eighty-four. After the Louisiana Purchase, United States surveyors measured existing land grants, settling on an exact measurement of 191.994 feet per arpent. Today, many families in St. Charles Parish continue to own arpent tracts along River Road, particularly on the west bank.

In the following years, the colonists cultivated mainly grain and produce. Corn, rice, fruits, and vegetables were raised. They sold the excess in the markets of the capital (New Orleans). They also brought apples, plums, pears, figs, sweet potatoes, melons, artichokes, cabbage, and various greens. Cattle raising was developed as an industry. *Within the next decade, the* Côte des Allemands *developed into the second*

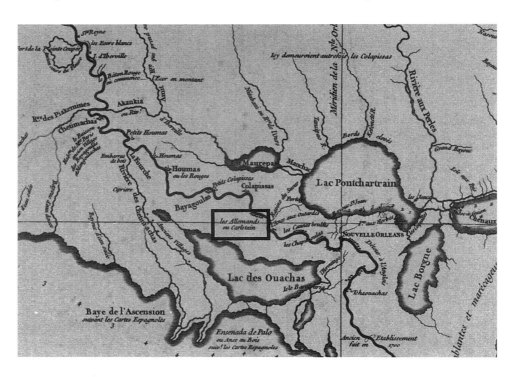

This 1732 map shows a route early settlers would have taken in their pirogues to reach markets in New Orleans, traveling downriver to the capital returning through Lake Pontchartrain into tributaries leading into Mississippi River. (Photo courtesy of The Historic New Orleans Collection. Acc. No. 1957.26)

largest settlement after New Orleans. Anytime there was a poor harvest it had a disastrous effect on the New Orleans market and caused turmoil through the delta region. The German settlement became the only dependable source of fresh foodstuffs. On more than one occasion, the German Coast farmers saved the city from starvation continuing to be the breadbasket of the colony.

Mississippi River Levees

Settlers along the river were required to build levees within a certain time period or lose the land. These levees were about two feet high and six feet wide, with both a foot and a horse path on top. Through the years, improvements and enlargements were necessary. Thus began two centuries of lingering threats of flooding on the German Coast from levee breaks, called crevasses. Not until after the first quarter of the twentieth century (with the construction of the Bonnet Carré Spillway) would residents of the German Coast be freed from such annual flooding threats. Levees were in place on both sides of the river as early as the 1730s from about twenty miles below New Orleans to the upper end of the German Coast. This was an impressive accomplishment for the small farm settlers of the German Coast who did not have the labor force of the large concessionaires downriver. Historians always emphasize this fact in their writings. However, levee construction would over the years contribute to wetland loss and rich land building sediment loss as man begins to tame the river.

In 1732, Louisiana Governor Etienne Perier issued a directive ordering every man who owned land along the Mississippi River to build a public road in front of his property and with that order, construction of the Mississippi River Road began. Even today, the State of Louisiana only holds tacit title to most of the land known as River Road. In 1990, with the passage of Public Law 10-398, the United States Congress created the Mississippi River Corridor Study Commission that resulted in the creation of Louisiana's Mississippi River Road Commission and the development of the Mississippi River Road Master Plan, a blueprint for the River Road's future. In 1991, the National Trust for Historic Preservation placed the historic Mississippi River Road Corridor between Baton Rouge and New Orleans on the nation's eleven most endangered historic properties. ⚜ ⚜ ⚜

French colonial laws and directives required landholders along streams and bayous to build roads and levees fronting the waterways. Stricter enforcement would be applied in the later eighteenth century under Spanish rule. ⚜ ⚜ ⚜

The Darensbourg Records. The earliest original acts of St. Charles Parish date from 1734, only three years after Louisiana became a crown colony. These historic documents are housed in the St. Charles Parish Courthouse. These first documents were recorded by Karl Fredrick Darensbourg, first commandant of the German Coast, and have been abstracted by Elizabeth Becker Gianelloni and published as Volume Three of the Calendar of Louisiana Colonial Documents, Part One, The Darensbourg Records, 1734–1769.

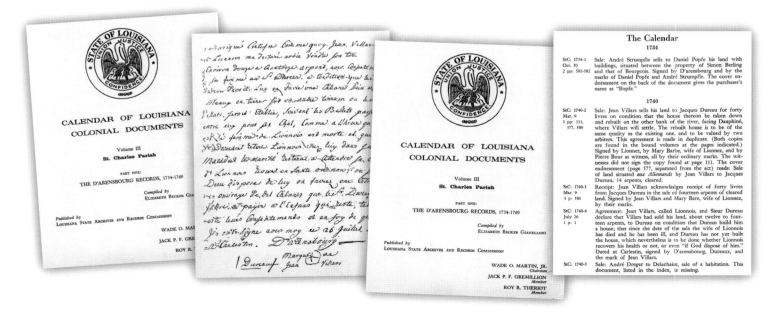

The 1740 chapel, named "St. Charles," was built in the area now known as Destrehan. (Sketch by Janis Blair)

St. Charles Church

Tradition says that in 1740, that first little chapel, St. Jean des Allemands Catholic Church at Karlstein (on what later would be referred to as Trinity Plantation in Taft), was replaced by a crude log cabin on the east bank and named St. Charles. That chapel continued to serve the spiritual needs of the French, Canadians, and Germans on both sides of the river on the German Coast until 1772 when St. John the Baptist Catholic Church was erected in present-day Edgard. According to historian Dr. Isabel M. French, "that it was built at the present site of the St. Charles Church at Destrehan is pinpointed by the wording in a 1770 grant of land to the Church." Early church records from 1739 to 1756 reveal the names of French and German families' baptisms, marriages, and deaths showing that those pioneers were blessed with very large families.

The St. Charles Church cemetery is today recognized as the South's oldest German cemetery. ⚜ ⚜ ⚜

Indian Unrest

In 1748, two savage Indian attacks of the east bank German Coast colony caused the settlers to abandon their fields, houses, and livestock and flee either to New Orleans or the west bank settlement near the St. Charles/St. John Parish line. Commandant Darensbourg's west bank militia lacked sufficient boats to cross the river and protect settlers. Louisiana's governor sent troops to shoot or capture the Indians but fear of more raids was ingrained in east bank settlers. Because of the Indian unrest and the impact on the lives of the German Coast settlers, food production was stifled. The lack of a food source for the people of New Orleans was profound. Most settlers refused to return to the unprotected east bank of the

Plate 4. Part of a 1772 copy of the 1765 Survey of the Mississippi River by Lt. Ross

A 1765 survey of the Mississippi River by Lieutenant Ross published in 1772 shows the old German fort, established on the east bank across from Karlstein in 1750 by Governor Vaudreuil, was still standing. The survey is published in the Encyclopedia of Forts, Posts, etc. by Powell A. Casey

German Coast. In 1750, a small military post of thirty men was established on the east bank to encourage settlers to return, but many still refused. The east bank post was located across the Mississippi River from Karlstein. The economy of the colony suffered for many years due to reduced food production from German Coast families.

In the 1750s, several waves of German immigrants from Alsace Lorraine arrived on the coast and as they joined existing colonists, the settlement's ability to supply the markets of New Orleans was strengthened. At this time, the German Coast was the second largest settlement, having a population of two hundred families. Only New Orleans exceeded this count, with a population of four hundred families.

Don Antonio de Ulloa. (Sketch by Janis Blair)

Health and Education of the Colony

The French government policy to provide a doctor for each settlement failed when they were unable to attract enough physicians. Priests treated diseases through prayer, novenas, and the application of reliquaries and relics. Diseases such as small pox, yellow fever, malaria, mumps, fevers, and other illnesses often became epidemic in the settlement. No regulations existed regarding wells, cisterns, or open privies. In 1736, sailor Jean Louis left the state a $2,500 bequest in his will allowing Governor Bienville to launch the charity hospital movement in Louisiana.

Education was not a priority for the average settler. Home and church schooling were very limited. Life was very difficult and all members of the family were needed and expected to work. The Catholic Church felt public education unnecessary and early on became an obstacle to any public education movement. Wealthy families sent their children abroad, but this privilege was usually reserved for family males.

Acadians Arrive

In 1764, a few Acadians, whose ancestors had settled the province of Acadia or Nova Scotia, arrived in the colony, and a few settled on the German Coast. However, the great Acadian migration to Louisiana started in 1765, when most settled above the German Coast on what would come to be called the Acadian Coast (St. James Parish). The Louisiana colony, attracted the Acadians because of the French influence that affected the religion, tradition, and language of the region.

General Alexander O'Reilly. (Sketch by Janis Blair)

In 1762, *La Côté des Allemands* becomes *El Puerto des Alemanes.*

France's King Louis XV gave Louisiana to his Spanish cousin, Charles III, in the formal Treaty of Fountainbleau signed on November 3, 1762. However, Spanish Governor Don Antonio de Ulloa did not arrive in Louisiana until 1766. Colonists preferred to remain under French rule and were very upset. Talk of rebellion began to grow, even on the German Coast. In 1768, Commandant Darensbourg and German Coast citizens were a part of this growing insurrection. Rumors and suspicion drew the newly arrived Acadians into the fray. German militia from

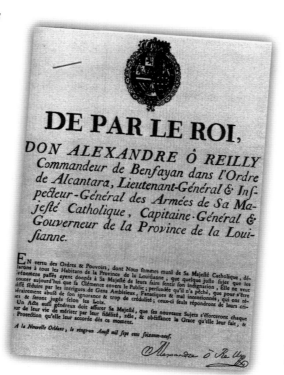

O'Reilly's Proclamation of Amnesty for the innocent citizens of Louisiana.

the coast joined Acadians and New Orleans Germans. Fearful for his life, Ulloa left New Orleans, but Spain later sent General Alexander O'Reilly to secure the colony.

General Alexander O'Reilly, a Roman Catholic Spanish officer of Irish origin, was sent to New Orleans to restore Spanish authority, set up a new government, and to punish conspirators involved in the rebellion. O'Reilly arrived in 1768 with 24 ships and 2,600 troops. He remained only seven months, but firmly established Spanish rule and granted clemency to Darensbourg. This clemency (Proclamation of Amnesty) was also extended to the citizens of the German Coast, the principal group involved in the rebellion.

Historians believe that O'Reilly's clemency could have reflected the economic importance of the German Coast to the colony, which O'Reilly did not want to disturb.

Prosperity on the German Coast under Spanish Rule

Louisiana prospered more under Spanish rule than under French. ⚜ ⚜ ⚜

Almost from the earliest years of Spanish rule, farmers of the German Coast prospered. It was during this time the livestock industry grew to the extent the German Coast cattlemen became almost the sole providers of meat for New Orleans. Cypress trade and grain production also increased on the west bank of the coast and small dairies spotted the landscape. Governor O'Reilly promoted the cypress trade. In 1776, French parliament members noted this prosperity in their comments, saying the German and French of the German Coast were the foundation upon which Louisiana had been established. Spanish rule allowed the unrestricted importation of slaves.

As early as 1776 Chavalier de Champigny wrote, "The area that is still today occupied by the descendents of the Germans and the Canadians is the most cultivated and the most populous in the colony. I regard the Germans and the Canadians as the foundation upon which Louisiana has been established."

1770 Land Grants at First and Second German Coasts of Louisiana

...in the year 1770, from Legajo 2357 of the Archives of the Indies at Seville. Grants were made by Luis de Unzaga, Governor General of the Province of Louisiana, from lands in his name, some of which had been formerly owned by others. Each grant is in the form of a Proces Verbal, in French, originally made in triplicate, with one copy for the Governor, one copy to the Clerk ("ecrivain") of the Cabildo, and one copy to the grantee to serve as his title to the land. Each is executed by Nicolas Francois Le Grand Chevalier de Bellevue as engineer and arpenteur, and by Mr. De Bellisle (who signs "Bellile"), Captain of infantry and Commandant of the Coste des Allemands.

Translated and edited by Mrs. S. J. Gianelloni, Jr., Longwood Plantation, Route 3, Box 114, Baton Rouge, Louisiana

CHURCH AND PRESBYTERE, dated 15 March; witnesses, LeMesle and Brazeau (who sign "fr. Lemelle" and "Brazeau"), inhabitants of the German Coast; 10 arpents on the left bank (of the Mississippi River), about 8 leagues distant from the city (of New Orleans); of land formerly belonging to Rousillon, bounded above by lands of De Livaudais fils (fils – son, or junior), below by lands of Brazeau.

CHURCH OF THE UPPER GERMAN COAST ("L'eglise d'en haut de La Coste des Allemands"), 10 April; witnesses, Antoine Himel and Jean Lamp? (Laub); 4 arpents, right bank, about 10 leagues from the city; being part of land of DuBroq, bounded above by Francois Lebrun, below by DuBroq. (Material extracted from Genealogical Register, Vol. VIII, No. 3, September 1961) ⚜ ⚜ ⚜

Spanish governors were lenient in allowing French and German settlers to continue their customs, traditions, and language. According to historian Edwin Davis, Spanish governors permitted the French to hold most local offices and to continue speaking French. When the Spaniards married French women, the children did not learn a word of Spanish. In this way, they were like the Germans, leaving few traces of their heritage on the German Coast. It should be noted that although the people of the German Coast enjoyed economic prosperity under Spanish rule, they were elated and rejoiced when Louisiana was returned to France at the end of the eighteenth century.

Under Spanish rule, the German Coast would continue to prosper for the next thirty-four years until the Americans purchased Louisiana from France in 1803. ✤ ✤ ✤

Because of England's continued interest in colonization, it instigated most of the Indian attacks on the settlements in the colony. With the arrival of Spanish Governor O'Reilly and his congenial relationship with the Indians, as well as his powerful display of troops, Indian raids lessened.

But through the Treaty of Paris signed in 1763, the English gained all of the land east of the Mississippi River from Baton Rouge upriver, putting them in close proximity to French settlements. Minor Indian attacks agitated by the English continued into the Spanish era, but Spanish forces had better equipped riflemen to scout and roam swampland and forests.

Revolutionary War Begins
A New Nation is Born

Thomas Jefferson's Declaration of Independence

In January 1776, Thomas Paine published his *Common Sense* pamphlet rallying American colonies to part with their British king. Thirty-three-year-old Constitutional Convention delegate, Thomas Jefferson, attorney and planter, drafted the words for the Declaration of Independence. Several months passed and on July 4, delegates to the Second Continental Congress signed Jefferson's Declaration of Independence and the Revolutionary War began. Their goal

THE LOUISIANA SOCIETY
OF THE
SONS OF THE AMERICAN REVOLUTION

ORGANIZED MAY 16, 1889
INCORPORATED JANUARY 8, 1897

NEW ORLEANS, LA.

From his service Record
Dated June 30, 1792

Alexandro La Branche was a 2nd Lieut. in Militi
He was 41 years old and and from St. Charles Paris
the German Coast. He volunteered Jan 1, 1770 a
took part in the engagements at Fort Bute, and
Baton Rouge in 1779 and Mobile in 1780

ALEXANDRO DE BRANCHE — Second Lieute—
nant —
Served in the German Militia 9 years,
5 months; in the Militia of Carabineers
12 years, 7 months and 11 days; in this
Regiment 8 years, 10 months and 19 days
Took part in the surprise of the Fort
or But, siege and taken of Baton Rouge
in 1779; siege and taken of Mobile in
1780.

Military records of LaBranche. (Courtesy of the Fortier Family Book)

1779
Bonnet Carré Crevasse

In 1779, German Coast Commandant Robin de Longy reported that serious repetitive flooding from a crevasse in the Bonnet Carré bend of the river, as well as a devastating hurricane, resulted in severe crop damage for the settlement. Another serious storm occurred in 1794. Both of these storms took the same path as the 1722 hurricane that destroyed the original German Coast settlement. ⚜ ⚜ ⚜

was a new republic, a nation in which citizens would elect representatives to manage the government.

The German Coast settlement in the Lower Mississippi Valley of the Louisiana Territory was not immediately affected when the Second Constitutional Convention representatives adopted the Declaration of Independence announcing to the world that British colonies in North America were separating themselves from England to become a new nation. But, less than three decades later with the Louisiana Purchase, it eventually would become a major player in the deal because America coveted the Louisiana Territory in order to control the Mississippi River and to take advantage of its prime agricultural resources. Thomas Jefferson believed the economy of America depended upon farms rather than factories where farmers would trade their products for manufactured goods. And Spain, happy to see England in trouble, began secretly shipping supplies from New Orleans to aid the Americans and become their ally during the American Revolution.

Bernardo de Galvez, distinguished Spanish soldier sent by Spain to govern Louisiana in 1777, was widowed and married Félicie (de St. Maxent) Destrehan as his second wife. Galvez aided the Americans in the American Revolution. Although originally neutral in the American Revolution, Spain declared war against Great Britain in 1779. Louisiana's Governor Galvez, assisted mainly by German Coast militia, launched a successful campaign against the British which is recognized as one of the most significant campaigns in American history. The militia was led by Don Jose' Pontalba and members included German Coast residents Pierre Trépagnier and Alexander LaBranche. This was the only American Revolution battle fought outside the original thirteen colonies. It was so successful, in part, because of the help of German Coast residents. Galvez left Louisiana in 1785 and died the next year.

Because of that successful campaign, Britain was not allowed to gain a foothold in the Lower Mississippi Valley, thereby paving the way for future American occupation. Galvez is often remembered as one of Louisiana's most popular governors. He emerged from the American Revolution as Spain's greatest military hero of that era.

After the Anglo-Spanish war, one of the most prosperous and peaceful periods followed. Spain allowed American immigration in Louisiana, even Protestants. This was a major policy change because all colonists were required to be Catholic, under both French and Spanish rule.

Old Spanish Trail

Legend holds that early Indians and Mexicans traversed through St. Charles Parish on the west bank enroute to points east along what might have been part of an earlier portion of the Old Spanish Trail. The trail was used by vaqueros (cowboys)

Bernardo de Galvez. (Sketch by Janis Blair)

to drive over nine thousand head of longhorn cattle to New Orleans. This beef was used to feed the Spanish soldiers during the American Revolution. Today Highway 90 in St. Charles Parish parallels the route of part of the Old Spanish Trail.

1777: *"Father of the German Coast"* Dies

Karl Fredrick Darensbourg, the first commandant of the German Coast, served for over forty-eight years. He was beloved by the people of the German Coast. Darensbourg was born on January 25, 1694, in Stettin, Pomerania (presently Poland, but was a Swedish possession at the time). According to historian Reinhart Kondert, Darensbourg's baptismal certificate from the Lutheran Castle Church in Stettin shows his name written as Carol Frideric Arensburg. He was a Swedish officer on the *Portefaix* and later became one of the leaders of the 1768 revolution against the Spanish takeover of the French colony. He married German-born Marguerite Metzer, had two sons and four daughters, and all of his children married into prominent French families. Darensbourg earned the respect of all of Louisiana's governors and was appointed *Chevalier St. Louis* in 1765 by the king of France. He died in 1777 at the age of eighty-four. Many of his descendants still reside on the German Coast where it is believed Darensbourg is buried.

*Karl Fredrick Darensbourg.
(Photo courtesy Tulane University, Special Collections, Kuntz Collection)*

The Culture of Sugar Cane

Indigo, the main crop of German Coast settlers for many years, had been brought to the colony from the West Indies in the 1700s. This tropical plant produced a lasting blue dye important to the European textile industry and the blue color remains very popular even today in cotton denim fabric of blue jeans. However, today almost all indigo produced is synthetic. According to census records, by the end of the eighteenth century, an unknown insect infested indigo plants to the extent that indigo no longer was harvested on the German Coast.

Tradition says sugar cane was planted between 1724 and 1726. Records from Bienville reveal sugar production as early as 1733. Other records credit the Jesuits with introducing sugar cane to this area, supposedly bringing it from Saint-Domingue about 1751.

Granulation technology was not fully developed until 1795. Before that time, cane was widely used to produce molasses. Until granulation began, Louisiana cane could not be processed into sugar. After 1766, the planting of sugar cane was largely abandoned. Future events and developments, however, would eventually reverse this trend.

"The farmers and planters of the coast engaged, until the end of the eighteenth century, in the production of indigo, corn, rice, and peas. It was not until the very end of the century that two events coincided to bring about the introduction of the sugar cane culture. In 1795, Etienne Boré, whose family had strong ties to the German

An indigo processor. (Courtesy of The Historic New Orleans Collection. Acc. No. 1979.128)

An indigo plant. (Courtesy of The Historic New Orleans Collection. Acc. No. 1980.205.40)

Coast (Destrehan family) grew a variety of sugar cane on his plantation near New Orleans, which matured sufficiently before cold weather killed it so as to allow for granulation. The man responsible for the actual granulation, Antoine Morin, was a chemist who had come from Saint-Domingue, settled on the German Coast, and married into the Troxler family.

"The second event that helped usher in the sugar cane culture was the black revolution in Saint-Domingue. Between 1793 and 1809, thousands of black and white Creole families from Saint-Domingue poured into Louisiana seeking refuge...Sugar cane, however, was, and is, definitely a plantation crop, requiring large tracts of land for growing, large labor forces for cultivation, harvest, and processing, and large investments of capital."—Glen Conrad, *Abstracts of the Civil Records of St. Charles and St. John the Baptist Parishes, 1804–1812* ⚜ ⚜ ⚜

Although Etienne Bore' was the first to granulate sugar, St. Charles Parish native son, Valcour Aime, the princely planter and the philanthropist of St. James Parish who owned the most magnificent sugar plantation of his time in Louisiana (LePetit Versailles de la Louisiana), is credited with being the first sugar refiner of the state. Aime studied methods of refining sugar in Cuba and Europe and is ranked with Bore'. He became one of the wealthiest plantation owners in the country. Aime was born in 1798 at Fortier Plantation (Home Place) on the German Coast, to Francois Aime and Marie Felicite Julie Fortier Aime. He died in 1867.

Sugar cane would gradually replace indigo on the large concessions but the small farms on the German Coast would continue to produce rice, corn, and other crops.

LaBranche Plantation

LaBranche Plantation was established in 1765 on the site of present-day Esperanza by descendents of Johan Zweig who is listed in the 1724 census.

Esperanza Plantation is presently owned by Judge Edward A. Dufresne and is the oldest, continuously operating plantation site in the parish.

Jean Baptist LaBranche was a wealthy sugar planter in the first quarter of the nineteenth century residing in New Orleans and owning plantations on the German Coast. Land records in St. Charles and St. John confirm family stories handed down for generations that most LaBranche plantations and land were lost after the Civil War to carpetbaggers. Jean Baptist was about sixty years old when he was killed in a duel in 1837. (LaBranche Family History and Genealogy, Marie LaBranche 2001)

Robin de Logny (Destrehan Plantation)

Robin de Logny served as commandant of the Second German Coast (St. John the Baptist Parish) appointed by Governor Alexander O'Reilly.

FPO: St. Charles Original Acts, 1782. No. 516-12-10-82. *SALE. Guillaume Guignon declares, in the presence of François Aime and Pierre Trépagnier, that he has sold some of his property to Robert-Antoine Robin de Logny, commandant of St.-Jean-Baptiste Parish. Among the items sold was a farm 20 arpents wide by depth to the lake, bounded below by the property of Jean LaBranche and above by that of the priest, located on the right bank of the river ascending. Guignon also sells Robin de Logny some slaves and animals. Price paid is illegible.*

On January 3, 1787, de Logny contracted with the free mulatto Charles to build his house on this property, now known as Destrehan Plantation. The plantation is listed in the National Register of Historic Places and is the oldest documented plantation house left intact in the Lower Mississippi Valley. De Logny died on his plantation in 1792 and his family inherited the property.

Jean-Noël Destrehan de Beaupré was the son of Jean Baptiste Honoré Destrehan de Beaupré, royal treasurer of France's Louisiana Colony. Jean-Noël was a wealthy planter and prominent merchant in the county of the German Coast and very active in local and state government. He was born in Louisiana in 1759 and married Marie Celeste de Logny in 1786, daughter of Robin de Logny, original owner of the plantation now known as Destrehan. In 1798, he was host to the Duc d'Orleans, later King Louis Philippe of France, at the family plantation which he later purchased in 1802. Jean-Noël died at his plantation in 1823 and was buried in St. Charles

Jean-Noël d'Estréhan de Beaupre (1759–1823). (Source: Louisiana Portraits, courtesy of Marguerite Larue de la Houssaye)

Borromeo Cemetery. His grave and many others have been lost to the ravages of time and the Mississippi River. Destrehan family members' tombs remain in Borromeo Cemetery.

Ormond Plantation

Ormond Plantation in Destrehan was built prior to 1790 and is believed to be one of the oldest French West Indies style Creole plantations on the Mississippi River. Pierre Trépagnier built the original plantation after having received the land from Louisiana's Spanish Governor Bernardo de Galvez as a gift for his valor against the English. Trépagnier received a tract that reached from the Mississippi River to Lake Pontchartrain. He then erected a two-story raised cottage with deep galleries and a cypress roof. Richard Butler purchased the plantation after the War of 1812 and named it "Ormond," after Ormond Castle in Ireland, the home of James Butler, Earl of Ormond. A major restoration took place in the mid-twentieth century by Mr. and Mrs. Alfred Brown of Brown's Velvet Ice Cream and Avery Island (McIlhenny) respectively. One of only three plantations remaining today in St. Charles Parish, the Ormond mansion sits on a sixteen-acre site and is owned by John Carmouche.

Home Place Plantation

Many believe that Charles, the same free mulatto who built de Logny's plantation (Destrehan), also built Home Place Plantation in present-day Hahnville in about 1791 for Pierre Gaillard. The Fortier family contends Home Place was built by their family after receiving a Spanish land grant. The ground floors still have imported Italian marble. As with many other plantations, indigenous material such as birch and cypress were used in construction of the house. It is described as a French Colonial raised cottage, is a National Historic Landmark, and is listed on the National Register. It is presently owned by descendants of the Keller family and others.

Valcour Aime was born at Home Place Plantation in 1798 on the First German Coast to Francois Aime and Marie Felicite Julie Fortier Aime. ⚜ ⚜ ⚜

The Eighteenth Century Draws to a Close

At the end of the eighteenth century, census records show that the majority of the residents of the German Coast settlement were German. Some were bilingual (French and German), and few traces of their German, Swiss, or Alsatian culture remained. Sawmills were everywhere, operating day and night. Cypress and other

Ormond Plantation.

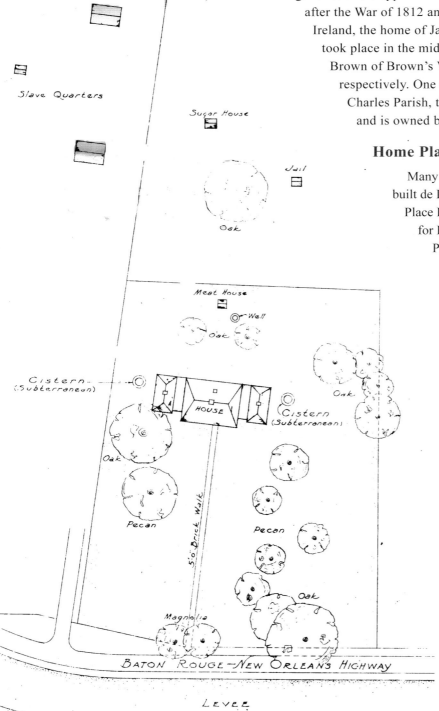

Slave Quarters

Sugar House

Jail

Oak

Meat House

Well

Oak

Cistern (Subterranean)

Oak

HOUSE

Cistern (Subterranean)

Oak

Oak

5'0" Brick Walk

Pecan

Pecan

Oak

Magnolia

BATON ROUGE-NEW ORLEANS HIGHWAY

LEVEE

Home Place Plantation, River Road, Hahnville was built in 1790. (Courtesy of Gene Yoes)

woods were being transported out of the swamps in exorbitant amounts. Traveling through channels and tributaries to the river, the wood was rafted and floated to New Orleans, the capital, for shipment to Havana and other places. The cattle industry was bustling. Sugar Cane was the main crop and plantations lined both sides of the river. In 1800, when news leaked that Spain had secretly returned Louisiana to France, German Coast residents were elated. Although the residents prospered and thrived under Spanish rule, they remained loyal to France and the Catholic faith. The Church of St. Charles on the east bank continued to be the only church to attend to the spiritual needs of residents of both banks of the river. Spain's liberal immigration policy in the last half of the eighteenth century laid the groundwork for an American Louisiana. The nineteenth century's Louisiana Purchase of 1803 legalized immigration activities, which had been occurring for decades on Louisiana's German Coast.

As under French rule, German Coast farmers continued to be the breadbasket of the colony supplying food to New Orleans through the entire Spanish era. The Mississippi River, which made all of this possible, remained the lifeblood of the settlement and the colony.

Although the role of the German Coast and its people have been marginalized or non-existent in most historical accounts of the colonial period in the settlement of the Louisiana colony, it should be noted that in this same obscure manner, the industrious citizens of St. Charles Parish have continued through the centuries to help the river region, the state and the nation prosper. ⚜ ⚜ ⚜

"We are the descendants of those Germans who turned the wilderness into a paradise such as Louisiana never possessed before."—J. Hanno Deiler, Settlement of the German Coast of Louisiana and the Creoles of German Descent ⚜ ⚜ ⚜

Nineteenth Century

1800—Treaty of San Ildefonso

1801—Thomas Jefferson becomes president of the United States.

1803—Louisiana Purchase—the United States pays France $15 million for the Louisiana Territory, 828,000 square miles of land west of the Mississippi River, which doubles the size of the nation and opens the way for westward expansion. Thirteen states are eventually carved from the Louisiana Territory.

1803–61—Rise of Louisiana plantations; period brings economic and cultural prosperity to the German Coast.

1804—Congress passes act prohibiting slave importation.

1804—An Act of Congress approved on March 25 divides Louisiana into two territories: the Territory of Orleans and the District of Louisiana. The County of the German Coast was in the Territory of Orleans.

1805—First legislation passed to establish a county seat.

1805—First courthouse is established.

1805—On February 17, a legislative act defines the County of the German Coast.

1806—Jefferson Document appoints Jean-Nöel Destrehan to Orleans Territorial Council.

1806—Original St. Charles log church burns and is replaced by a wood-framed church painted red (known as the Little Red Church). The Trépagnier family donates a statue of St. Charles Borromeo.

1807—St. Charles Civil Parish is established when Act I of the 1807 legislature divides

the Territory of Orleans into nineteen civil parishes on March 31.

1807—Pierre St. Martin is appointed first superior court district judge for St. Charles Parish.

1811—State appropriates funds for public schools.

1812—First steamboat arrives in New Orleans.

1812—War of 1812 begins.

1812—Louisiana's first state constitution is adopted.

1812—Louisiana becomes a state on April 30 by an Act of Congress.

1814—Captain Rene Trudeau's "Troop of Horse" participates in Battle of New Orleans.

1815—Prospect Plantation is established in New Sarpy.

1815—Battle of New Orleans

1824—New Orleans philanthropist John McDonogh envisioned using the Bonnet Carré Crevasse site for a future Mississippi River outlet.

1826—Second parish courthouse is erected.

1845—The Louisiana Constitution of 1845 establishes the Office of State Superintendent of Public Education and directs the legislature to establish free public schools.

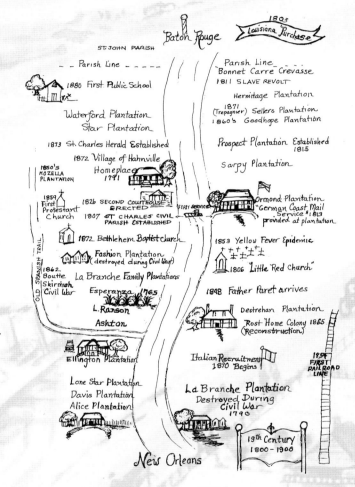

(Sketch by Janis Blair and authors.)

1848—Father Paret arrives on the German Coast to serve St. Charles (Red Church) parishioners.

1850s—Ellington Plantation is established. Later owned by F. A. Luling, for which settlement is named.

1850s—Mozella Plantation is established.

1850—St. Charles Parish is included in the

newly established New Orleans Archdiocese.

1852—First parish public school superintendent is appointed.

1852—Parish courthouse is enlarged.

1853—Yellow fever epidemic kills over eleven thousand in the New Orleans area including St. Charles Parish.

1854—First railroad line passes through St. Charles Parish.

1856—Unnamed hurricane devastates southeast Louisiana (Last Island).

1859—First Protestant church is established on Old Spanish Trail.

1860—Abraham Lincoln elected U.S. president.

1861—On January 26, Secession is approved at the Louisiana Secession Convention.

1861—After Secession, Louisiana becomes part of the Republic of Louisiana.

1861—The Confederate States of America is formed.

1861—On March 21, Louisiana becomes a part of the Confederate States of America.

1861—Civil War begins on April 12.

1861—On April 19, President Lincoln issues a Proclamation of Blockade against southern ports.

1862—St. James Methodist Church is established in Hahnville.

1862—New Orleans falls to Union forces without a shot. Skirmishes take place at Boutte Station, the courthouse, and Des Allemands. LaBranche Plantation (St. Rose) and Fashion Plantation (Hahnville) are destroyed by Union forces.

1863—President Lincoln issues the Emancipation Proclamation.

1864—Henry Allen is elected governor of Confederate-held Louisiana.

1864—Georg Michael Hahn is elected governor of Union-held Louisiana.

1864—A new Louisiana Constitution is adopted.

1865—Bethlehem Baptist Church is founded by African American missionaries near present-day Hahnville.

1865—Civil War ends; Reconstruction period begins.

1865—U.S. Freedmen's Bureau establishes Rost Home Colony at Destrehan Plantation.

1865—President Lincoln is shot on Good Friday, April 14 and dies on April 15.

1866—L'Englise Notre Dame du Rosaire (Our Lady of the Rosary) Chapel is established in Taft.

1866—Canaan Baptist Church is erected in Killona.

1866—"Carpetbaggers" and "scalawags" begin to arrive.

1868—Louisiana is readmitted to the United States.

1868—Louisiana Lottery Company is chartered.

1868—Louisiana Reconstruction Constitution is adopted.

1870—Italians are recruited for the agricultural workforce in the New Orleans region.

1870—Judge Othello Flagg establishes the Village of Flaggville.

1870—Carpetbaggers control most business in St. Charles Parish.

1871—Bonnet Carré Crevasse occurs and remains open until 1882.

1872—George Michael Hahn establishes the Village of Hahnville. Flaggville is subsequently absorbed into Hahnville.

1873—First issue of the *St. Charles Herald* is published. Georg Michael Hahn is rumored to be the owner.

1874—Mount Zion Baptist Church is established in St. Rose by Palmer Elkins.

1875—St. Charles is recorded as one of the top three parishes in rice production.

1876—Colonel Thomas J. Sellers purchases Trepagnier Plantation in present-day Norco. The plantation was later consolidated with Roseland and renamed Diamond.

1876—Alexander Graham Bell invents the telephone.

1877—Reconstruction draws to a close in Louisiana, ending longest-lasting Union occupation in the United States.

1877—St. Charles "Red Church" rectory fire destroys all records except the original register of 1739–55.

1880—First recorded parish public school is established.

1880—St. Charles Parish is site of the first and largest labor strike of cane workers for better wages.

1881—The Bethlehem Benevolent Society is incorporated.

1883—Parish ferry service provides seven landings.

1883—Telephone service begins in St. Charles Parish.

1884—Davis Crevasse occurs (Luling).

1885—Special delivery of mail begins.

1890s—Red Church interdiction begins due to church charter conflict.

1890—Rural delivery of mail begins.

1893—Unnamed hurricane devastates parts of southeast Louisiana.

1893—Louisiana Lottery ends.

1897—Internationally renowned twentieth-century artist Clarence Millet is born in Hahnville.

1897—Mount Airy Baptist Church is established on Old Spanish Trail.

1897—St. Matthew Baptist Church is established in New Sarpy.

1898—Spanish American War

1899—On October 10, State Senator Basile LaPlace, Jr., is murdered at Ormond Plantation.

Territorial Period

At the turn of the century, by the secret Treaty of San Ildefonso, Spain ceded Louisiana back to France on October l, 1800. The two countries kept the treaty a secret until Napoleon could organize a military expedition to protect the Louisiana Territory from American or British invasion.

Abstracts of Civil Records of St. Charles Parish, 1700-1803, Glenn Conrad Entry No. 1887, dated June 9, 1803, verify the passage of the treaty:

Notice Published by order of the Governor General and the Marquis de Casa Calvo regarding the cession of Louisiana to the French Republic (Printed Document). The document is dated in New Orleans, May 18, 1803.

The German Coast in the Early 1800s

This correspondence is translated from old German script and reveals life of a German Coast resident. Although rumors were rampant, it appears from this letter that settlers did not realize they were again a French colony.

Aux Allemans
March 1, 1802

Beloved Brother, And Remaining Relatives and Friends:

One thing I must let you know: that I am still alive, where I live and that (Thank God!) my present circumstances are very bearable. I live on the Mississippi, 13 hours over New Orleans, (Lat: 30 N, Long: 2:16 E Lod. (?)) Northside of the river, Cote des Allemans, paroisse St. Jean Baptist.

February 28, 1800 I was married to CATHARINA VICKNER, Widow MARCHAND, with two children: JOHANN BAPTIST, age 7 and CATHARINA, age 4 and a wealth of 15000, and what's more, we live in unity and happiness together. November 28 my daughter MAGDALENE CELESTE was born.

My wife's father, ADAM VICKNER, her mother MARGARETA TRAEGER, both are of two of the first and most numerous families here.

As I write this, we are subject to Spain, free from all taxes and tributes, and are bothered by nothing. All are a member in the militia. There is degradation of the human soul here: Slavery......We have only five slaves who till the fields, and four little ones. Some have hundreds.

The fields yield rice, Indian corn, Indigo, sugar, cotton. Fruit, as you know it in Germany, there is none. Only oranges, peaches and figs. Garden produce is available year-round. Caterpillars and other damaging insects are great inconveniences. The great heat in summer, the quick change of the weather, are dangerous to health and live, especially to foreigners.

All tradesmen are free; everybody does what he can.

What is called rightfully pressing poverty does not exist, thank God! Everyone can make enough to get by. Slavery is barbarical enough, but not as tyrannical as the unfortunate serfdom in the civilized Holstein by far. For the nights and the Sundays are for them, and necessary clothing and board have to be given them. Yet happy is the land that knows no slavery, for it is a pest for morals, insolence, stealing, and all shame and vice are rampant among the people. They are slaves and make their masters into slaves too, or relentless, unmerciful barbarians and avengers.

The main language is French, English, Spanish, German, Cathalone is spoken too.

I never did write, and I suppose I have been forgotten long ago, but I still mean to take a trip to Germany, but I am and will never be well at sea — so I fear my illness more than the sea, and my wife shows much reluctance. The other world will reunite us.

I have asked the Captain to write down your address for himself, too. His name is JOHANN OTTERSTAEDT. The ship's name is Anna Magtilda, both from Altona. Herr OTTERSTAEDT will make the return journey immediately. If there is any feeling of friendship left for me, one would let me have an answer. Let me know how it is with the friendship. Find me worthy of reply as to who is alive, who died and what else has changed. The Captain is my friend. He will not fail to do his utmost. He was with us last Christmas and knows my wife's relatives as well.

The strongest sensations of friendship, goods and blood connect me with the most heartfelt wishes for the true well-being of all of you without exception, and recommend myself to all of you for the renewal of your memory of me and the assurance of my true friendship.

Faithfully,
JOHANN HOALHIM LAGEMANN

Courtesy of: Hanna Edelglass, Gansevort, New York
German-Acadian Coast Historical and Genealogical Society
From *Les Voyageurs*, Vol. II, No. 3, September 1981

The Louisiana Purchase

"The day may come when the cession of Louisiana to the United States shall render the Americans too powerful for the continent of Europe.

"Let the Louisianans know that we separate ourselves from them with regret; that we stipulate in their favor everything that they can desire, and let them, hereafter, happy in their independence, recollect that they have been Frenchmen, and that France, in ceding them, has secured for them advantages which they could not have obtained from a European power, however paternal it might have been. Let them retain for us sentiments of affection; and may their common origin, descent, language, and customs, perpetuate the friendship."—Napoleon I, 1803

Fearing Napoleonic France's control of the mouth of the Mississippi River, and with a desire to preserve and expand the agricultural character of the United States, President Thomas Jefferson sent James Monroe and Robert Livingston to France in early 1803 to negotiate for the purchase of New Orleans and as much land east of the Mississippi River as possible. On April 29, 1803, Napoleon unexpectedly agreed to sell the *entire* Louisiana Territory for only $15 million dollars, which doubled the size of the United States. The U.S. Senate approved the purchase on October 20, 1803. President Jefferson instructed William C. C. Claiborne and General James Wilkerson to take possession of the territory.

The transfer took place on December 20, 1803. The Louisiana Territory proved to be one of the richest regions in the world because of its natural resources, timber, vast agricultural and ranching lands, and fertile soil.

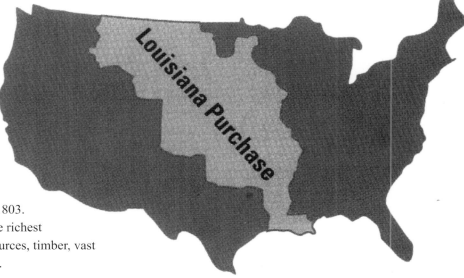

Louisiana Purchase Map. (Used with permission from the Department of Culture, Recreation, and Tourism, State of Louisiana Bicentennial brochure.)

Jean-Nöel Destrehan. (Photo courtesy of Destrehan Plantation)

President Thomas Jefferson signed what is now referred to as the Jefferson Document appointing four men to the legislative council. One of the four was Jean-Nöel Destrehan of the German Coast. These men were carefully selected and charged with the task of planning the new provisional government. The original Jefferson Document can be viewed at Destrehan Plantation on River Road.

General Horatio Gates told President Jefferson on July 18, 1803, "Let the land rejoice, for you have bought Louisiana for a song,"

Many historians believe that, with the exception of the Declaration of Independence, no other document has had a greater impact on American society than the Louisiana Purchase.

The purchase meant that the lower Mississippi Valley and the German Coast would be dramatically affected. The more democratic form of government would require unwanted change for many. Since 1793, thousands of black and white refugees had come to Louisiana from St. Domingue (Haiti), settling in New Orleans and along the German Coast. This assimilation helped to enhance the unique culture. Many German Coast settlers feared the U.S. government, wanted France to remain in control, and did not want unknown changes to disturb the established way of life, which they had struggled to achieve and maintain. There were religious and social differences. Private schools protected the French language and the Catholic religion.

However, when some wanted immediate statehood President Jefferson informed Congress that the people of Louisiana were "as incapable of self-government as children." Jefferson's statement was probably based on a letter received from William C. C. Clairborne, new governor of Orleans Territory which read—"I fear that if education be left entirely to the patronage of the inhabitants, it will continue to be neglected; for they are not sufficiently informed to appreciate its value." A majority of Congress declared that a people who had long been accustomed to the rule of Spain must serve an apprenticeship before they could be regarded as ready to adopt the government of the United States. **The Territory of Orleans and the German Coast remained a territory for nine years after the purchase. Residents of the German Coast would play a major role in Louisiana's quest for statehood.** ⚜ ⚜ ⚜

The following toast was offered by the St. Charles Historical Foundation at an "Evening with the Notables" gala, the opening event of the Louisiana Purchase Bicentennial Celebration held at Destrehan Plantation on January 18, 2003: "To our ancestors who settled this great land of Louisiana and to those brought in bondage for their perseverance, courage and ingenuity in carving out our unique cultural heritage within this great Louisiana Territory, embodying the spirit of all who came to this United States of America."

"The Cote des Allemands was pictured at the time of the Louisiana Purchase as the best cultivated part of Louisiana....The French colonial prefect, Laussat, made the suggestion to increase the population of Louisiana primarily by bringing in Germans....He supported this recommendation in the following words: 'This class of peasants, especially of this nationality (German), is just the kind we need and the only one which has always done well in this area, which is called the German Coast. It is the most industrious, the most populous, the most prosperous, the most upright, the most valuable population segment of this colony. I deem it essential that the French government adopt the policy of bringing to this area every year 1000 to 1200 families from the border states of Switzerland, the Rhine and Bavaria; the emigrants from our southern provinces are worth nothing here.'"
—Helmut Blume, The German Coast During the Colonial Era (1722–1803)
⚜ ⚜ ⚜

For as far back as these early residents could remember, they and their ancestors had been ruled by kings, princes and warlords… From the beginnings of their history, the residents…were subjects, not citizens. And subjects, as we know, do not make the laws under which they live; subjects follow them. Subjects do not choose their rulers; subjects obey them. Before 1807, the King's word was law and those men that the King appointed, enforced his law. The people were told that the King ruled over them because it was the Will of God … The King and the Catholic Church appointed all local officials in Louisiana … But in March 1807, a radically different system of government was about to take shape and dramatically change the lives of everyone living here.—Letter from Norman Marmillion, *News Examiner*, April 5, 2007

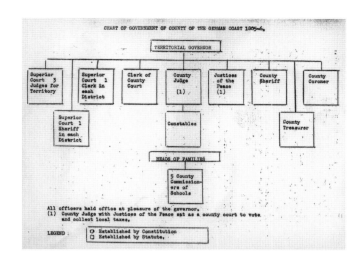

Government of the Territory of Orleans

President Jefferson signed a bill on March 26, 1804, which made the portion of the Louisiana Purchase south of the thirty-third parallel the Territory of Orleans. The portion remaining would become the District of Louisiana and was placed under the jurisdiction of the Indiana Territory. In August of 1804, the president established the new government of the Territory of Orleans by appointing William C. C. Claiborne as governor. At the legislative council's first meeting in 1804, the unorganized Territory of Orleans was divided into twelve counties, one being the County of the German Coast. Louisiana was made an organized territory in 1805. The president then added a legislative council. This structure remained in place until Louisiana became a state in 1812.

A map compiled by Gertrude C. Taylor and Glenn R. Conrad entitled *St. Charles Parish, 1804-1812* has been inserted in this publication showing detailed graphics of landowners of the German Coast during the territorial period.

Chart of Government of County of the German Coast, 1805–06. (From the Inventory of the Parish Archives of Louisiana, No. 45. St. Charles Parish (Hahnville). Prepared by the Historical Records Survey Division of Women's and Professional Projects, Works Progress Administration, the Department of Archives, Louisiana State University.)

The Little Red Church

Tradition holds that the 1740 St. Charles log chapel was destroyed by fire in 1806 and rebuilt the same year. It was replaced by a wood-framed structure and painted red. The "Little Red Church" became a famous landmark for river travelers. Passengers going downriver were relieved to see the Red Church because it meant New Orleans was only twenty-five miles away. The crews and roustabouts would be excited because they would be paid off at this point to shouts of, "Voila! L'Eglise Rouge!" or "Oh, look, there it is – the Little Red Church." In 1806, the Trépagnier family donated a statue of St. Charles Borromeo that stood on the premises for over one hundred years. This statue is the only tangible link to the name St. Charles Borromeo. The "Church of the Germans" stood for over one hundred years and was still in place when the present stucco mission style church was built in 1921. (Photo courtesy of Fay Walker Louque)

The Birth of St. Charles Parish

St. Charles Civil Parish was fourth on the list of the nineteen original parishes that were simultaneously created out of the Territory of Orleans by Act I of 1807. Act I made no attempt to do more than merely list parishes, except, perhaps in a very limited venue, to convey some semblance of their general locality. Prior to 1807, the so-called "parishes" were neither political nor legal subdivisions of the state, but mere ecclesiastic vicinities. Act I lifted St. Charles and the other parishes it created out of the status of ecclesiastic vicinities to the category of legal and official political subdivisions of the Territory of Orleans. Initially, the eastern boundary (the city of New Orleans) was purported to be fixed as the eastern boundary of St. Charles until 1825 when Jefferson Parish was created out of the western portion of the Parish of Orleans. (Information extracted from a report on the boundaries of St. Charles Parish by Research Engineer Gervais Lombard, December 5, 1939, prepared for the Louisiana Department of Public Works.)

Pierre B. St. Martin, b. 1761, d.1830; married to Marianne Perret; appointed first judge of St. Charles Parish from 1807 to 1811; judge during the 1811 slave revolt; syndic for St. Charles Parish; speaker at the first state legislative assembly; interred in Edgard, Louisiana. ⚜ ⚜ ⚜

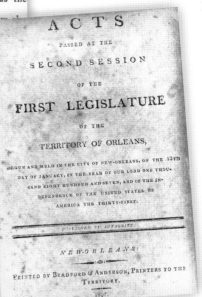

Act I of 1807 created St. Charles Parish as a civil parish. (Courtesy of the Law Library of Louisiana)

Cover of ACTS, which documents proceedings of the second session of the first legislature of the Territory of Orleans. (Photo courtesy of Law Library of Louisiana)

Extract of Official Police Jury Minutes, June 11, 1811. (From inventory of Parish Archives of Louisiana No 45, St. Charles Parish (Hahnville), Series l, Police Jury Minutes – Vol. 1811-1817. Prepared by the Historical Records Survey Division of Women's and Professional Projects, Works Progress Administration.)

According to Cecil Morgan, dean emeritus of the Tulane University School of Law, in his narrative The First Constitution of the State of Louisiana, *published by the Historic New Orleans Collection, the governing body of the parish was not set up in the first constitution, but the term police jury evolved by custom and the enactment of a series of territorial acts involving a novel use of the newly formed jury. Dean Morgan said a "jury" would be empanelled, often to do a specific job for the county or community, such as building a courthouse, bridge, or jail. Other duties followed, such as establishing a gendarmerie (police force) first to retrieve fugitive slaves, then as a regular parish police force, and later as a group to do things for the parish or county under the jury. Eventually, the "police jury" emerged as the parochial governing body.* ⚜ ⚜ ⚜

Largest Slave Uprising in Nation's History

The slave Charles Deslondes is thought to have been brought from St. Domingue (present-day Haiti) to the Deslondes Plantation in present-day LaPlace. Some slaves assumed their owners surnames.

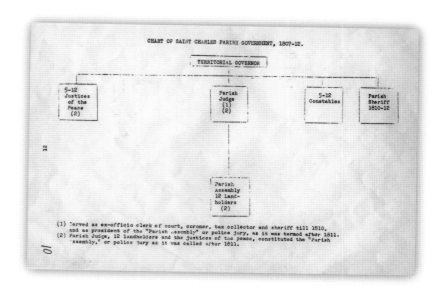

> It is noteworthy that the 1811 uprising in Orleans Territory was in a sense a direct continuation, on the American mainland, of the uprising in St. Domingue. This is because refugee slave owners and imported slaves from St. Domingue took an active part on opposite sides in the 1811 revolt. Charles Deslondes and many of his lieutenants had been brought here from St. Domingue during and after the slave revolt on the island. Runaway advertisements show that many slaves from St. Domingue who were brought to Louisiana with their masters lived in the city and on the German Coast prior to the revolt. On the other side, many of the principal Louisiana slave owners from New Orleans and the German Coast had economic, political and family connections in St. Domingue.— Albert Thrasher, *On to New Orleans, Louisiana's Heroic 1811 Slave Revolt,* Second Edition, June 1996.

Chart of the St. Charles Parish Government, 1807–12. The term "police jury" evolved by custom as well as the enactment of a series of territorial acts involving a novel use of the newly formed "jury." (From the Inventory of the Parish Archives of Louisiana. No. 45. St. Charles Parish (Hahnville). Prepared by the Historical Records Survey Division of Women's and Professional Projects, Works Progress Administration, the Department of Archives, Louisiana State University.)

Charles was temporarily employed by nearby plantation owner Manuel Andry as a wagon driver, which enabled him to move about. He began recruiting slaves from Andry's and other plantations along the German Coast to plan a revolt with the objective of reaching New Orleans to take over the city and free the slaves. Slaves were often loaned out or rented, which allowed for greater freedom to communicate. Also enlisted were Maroons, who had escaped from slavery and were living off the land in isolation in surrounding swamps and woodlands. Secret meetings were held, officers were appointed, and techniques Charles learned during the Haitian revolt were applied to train the insurgents. Armed with agricultural tools and confiscated weapons, Charles and his assembly took control of the Andry Plantation after midnight on January 8, 1811, wounding the owner and several family members and killing his son, Gilbert. Manuel Andry and Charles Perret, top militia officers for St. John and St. Charles parishes, notified Governor Claiborne of the attack as soon as possible. They then attempted to organize a cavalry and were reportedly able to raise about eighty troops. The insurgents headed downriver on foot, on horseback, and in wagons, plundering plantations and growing in number. It is reported that female slaves also participated.

Onto New Orleans. Revolt begins at Andry Plantation in LaPlace with slaves marching along Mississippi River Road toward New Orleans. (Courtesy of folk artist Lorraine Gendron of Hahnville. An exhibit of the 1811 slave revolt created by Lorraine Gendron is on display at Destrehan Plantation.)

The dreaded news spread quickly. The memory of the 1793 Santo Domingan insurrection still caused great fear and anxiety. Some St. Charles Parish plantation owners gathered their families and fled. Others stayed behind to protect their property. Owners were told to guard their slaves. It was reported that ahead of the marchers, carriages lined the River Road heading for New Orleans and beyond. Governor Claiborne, who constantly had to be on guard against a

The Tribunal at Destrehan Plantation. *The members composing the tribunal are Messrs. Jean-Nöel Destrehan, Alexandre LaBranche, Cabaret (Pierre-Marie Cabaret de Trépy), Adélard Fortier, and Edmond Fortier, all of whom had taken the oath prescribed in section four of the same act. (Courtesy of folk artist Lorraine Gendron of Hahnville)*

This grave marker of Francois Trépagnier, killed in the 1811 slave rebellion, is located in the St. Charles Borromeo Cemetery. It is also the gravesite of Elizabeth Dubord, who died in 1777, and is the earliest remaining burial plot in the cemetery. (Photo courtesy of Marilyn Mayhall Richoux)

possible coup by either the French or Spanish, notified the federal government. General Wade Hampton of Fort St. Charles placed troops on order and the territory militia on guard. Major corridors in and out of the city were secured. Upriver from LaPlace, a small troop of U.S. Army soldiers commanded by Major Milton was ordered to assist.

The marchers passed through present-day Montz to the Francois Trépagnier Plantation in present-day Norco, where Francois was killed. More slaves joined in as they continued moving downriver along River Road, and the crowd reached as many as five hundred after reaching Ormond Plantation in Destrehan. Quickly moving east into the Cannes Brulees (present-day Kenner) area, the exhausted and hungry army had covered nearly twenty-five miles through terrible, cold weather and decided to encamp near the Jacques Fortier Plantation. They planned to eat, rest the night, and attack New Orleans the next day. Around 4:00 a.m. on January 10, Hampton's infantry reached the area and encircled the group. Realizing the danger, the insurgents began to fire, retreating into the swamps and heading back upriver. Hoping to rally, they encamped near the levee at present-day Good Hope. Ammunition nearly depleted, they were overcome by heavy artillery from the assembled forces of Major Milton, Manuel Andry, and Charles Perret when attacked about mid-morning on January 11. Many insurgents died on the spot. The slaves refused to surrender and again retreated, many heading north into the swamps. Charles Deslondes was reportedly captured sometime on January 11 or 12.

St. Charles Parish Judge Pierre Bauchet St. Martin summoned a court comprised of five local property owners to hear testimony and to render a decision. The depositions revealed that some slaves had warned their owners of the uprising. The tribunal started at Destrehan Plantation on January 13, 1811, at 4:00 p.m. and continued through January 15, 1811. For their acts of insurrection, twenty-one of the accused were found guilty. Death warrants were issued, each to be shot in front of the plantation to which he belonged. The corpses were decapitated and their heads were placed on fence poles along the River Road to serve as a warning to others. A survey taken afterward indicated approximately sixty-six were killed in the revolt with others missing or captured and held for trial. Investigations were carried out for many years following the revolt. The historical accounts are based on the reports of U.S. and militia officers, St. Charles Parish Original Acts, plantation owners, oral histories, and statements of slaves. From depositions requested by the Louisiana Legislative Council and the House of Representatives, it was revealed that some slaves warned their owners of the impending revolt. By virtue of a resolution passed by the legislative council and the House of Representatives of the territory to the effect that "the parish judges of St. Charles and St. John Parishes initiate an inquisition to determine the number and names of the slaves who distinguished themselves in the face of the recent insurrectionaries, the resolution being signed by Jean Vasseau, secretary, and dates February 7 …" (Abstracts of Civil Records of St. Charles Parish, Entry No. 18, 2-20-11, Glenn Conrad) This was the last slave revolt in Louisiana.

Abstracts of Civil Records of St. Charles Parish and St. John the Baptist Parishes, 1804–1812, by Glenn R. Conrad, Book 41, entry #2, January 1811, verify that the tribunal met: "In order to satisfy the common wish of the citizens of the Country, and to contribute as much as we can to the public welfare, I the Judge, have constituted a tribunal composed of five property owners and myself, conforming to the first section of the act stating which punishments shall be imposed for CRIMES AND MISDEMEANORS committed by slaves. The said Tribunal must proceed at once to examine, interrogate, and pass sentence upon the rebels detained on Mr. Destréhan's plantation."

Investigations were carried out for many years following the revolt.

Louisiana Sets the Stage to Enter Statehood
The Constitution of 1812

In January 1811, Julian Poydras, delegate to Congress representing the Territory of Orleans, petitioned Congress for Louisiana's statehood. On February 18, 1811, President James Madison signed the "Enabling Act and Admission to Union" to form a constitution and state government. The last condition for statehood, drafting a state constitution, was still to be fulfilled. Although Jean-Nöel Destrehan was originally opposed to statehood because he felt the "common people" were not educated in the principles of freedom and the move toward statehood was premature, he went on to serve several times as president of the legislative council during the Territorial Period. It was not surprising that he was elected in 1812 to serve in the constitutional convention for statehood. Others with ties to the German Coast who participated in the constitutional convention were Stephen Henderson, Alexandre LaBranche, and Pierre B. St. Martin. All chosen were men of property and standing, whose education and attainments surpassed those of the voters that chose them. President Jefferson informed Congress that the people of Louisiana were "as incapable of self-government as children." Governor Claiborne wrote a letter to President Jefferson and stated, "I fear if education be left entirely to the patronage of the inhabitants, it will continue to be neglected; for they are not sufficiently informed to appreciate its value." A new state constitution was drawn and adopted and subsequently approved by Congress on April 8, 1812. On April 30, the new state would be admitted.

St. Charles Parish's most prominent resident, Jean-Nöel Destrehan, a vigorous supporter of the Creole position on statehood and one of the drafters of Louisiana's first constitution, was privileged to receive Louisiana's statehood documents from President James Madison in Washington, D.C. Destrehan then ran unsuccessfully to become Louisiana's first governor. He was, however, chosen by the voters to serve as Louisiana's first elected United States Senator but did not qualify to serve. It is unknown whether Jean-Nöel spoke English. A language barrier could have been the reason he was unable to qualify for his seat. He was subsequently elected to the office of state senator, serving from 1812 until 1817.

Stephen Henderson decreed upon his death that his slaves would have freedom of choice. The estate remained in litigation for over twenty-five years. Most of his will was nullified. Henderson stated, "My greatest object is to do the greatest quality of good, and to the greatest number of persons and to the poorest people." (A Dictionary of Louisiana Biography. Vol. I, A to M, Glenn R. Conrad, Editor. Published by Louisiana Historical Association, 1988)

State Constitution Delegates Gravesite. Gravesite of Jean-Nöel Destrehan deBeaupre and Stephen and Zelia Henderson. Stephen was Jean-Nöel's son-in-law. Jean-Nöel Destrehan deBeaupre, b. 1759, d. 1823; son of Jean Baptist Honore Destrehan deBeaupre, royal treasurer of the French Colony, and Jeanne Catherine Gauvry; married Marie Celeste Robin deLongy in 1786; in 1802 purchased the deLongy family plantation; devoted husband and father of fourteen children; sugar planter and statesman. In 1803 was appointed first deputy mayor of the city of New Orleans; 1806 was named president of the legislative council, Territory of Orleans, and served as a state convention delegate; 1810 became president of the board of trustees of the Red Church; served as a delegate in the 1812 Constitutional Convention, chosen to accept statehood papers from President James Madison, and was elected to the U.S. Senate but failed to qualify; became a Louisiana State Senator from 1812 to 1817. Retired captain in the Spanish Army and in 1814 helped to direct defense of the city in Battle of New Orleans. Interred in St. Charles Borromeo Cemetery.

Stephen Henderson, b. 1775, Scotland, d. 1838; immigrated to New Orleans ca. 1800; married Zelia Destrehan in 1825 after purchasing her parents' home (Destrehan Plantation). Extensive landowner, merchant, planter, businessman, philanthropist, and humanitarian. Served as a delegate in the 1812 Constitutional Convention; chosen as delegate to accept statehood papers; willed funds to churches, asylums, orphanages, charity hospital, and the poor of New Orleans; left land to the firemen of New Orleans. Interred next to wife in St. Charles Borromeo Cemetery. (Photo courtesy of Marilyn Mayhall Richoux.)

Battle of New Orleans

The German Coast was well represented in the Battle of New Orleans. Colonel Alexandre LaBranche led the 568 men of the Fifth Regiment of the County of the German Coast, St. Charles and St. John the Baptist. To help strengthen forces, a group named "St. Charles Troop of Horse" led by Captain Rene Trudeau, a former lieutenant colonel in the 44th United States Regiment, was organized. Forty-one men were in service from December 14, 1814 until March 16, 1815. Corporal Nicholas Destrehan, Michel Fortier, Samuel McCutcheon, Jean Sarpy, and Francis and Pierre Trépagnier are some that assisted in the battle to keep the British from taking control of the Port of New Orleans and the mouth of the Mississippi River.

More than two weeks earlier the Treaty of Ghent had been signed, but had not yet been ratified by the United States. This, in effect, ended the war and confirmed American independence, but the news had not yet reached the southern front. This was the second and last time that America waged war against Great Britain.

Prior to and during the Battle of New Orleans, pirates Jean Lafitte (ca.1776–1823) and his brother Pierre were involved in smuggling goods and slaves in southeastern Louisiana. They were based on the Gulf of Mexico at Grand Terre and traveled by waterways to Lake Salvador into St. Charles Parish. The Lafittes established friendships along the German Coast. In 1815, seeking a pardon for past unlawful acts and preferring to side with America over Britain, the brothers reportedly took refuge at the east bank Alexandre LaBranche plantation in the St. Rose area, told those gathered of the impending British attack, and offered their services to assist. Jean and Pierre Lafitte honored their offer to help defend the city and were granted pardons. The Lafitte brothers played a major role in helping to save New Orleans.

Re-enactment of the Battle of New Orleans. (Photo courtesy of Fay Walker Louque)

"Everywhere sluices in the levees were used to irrigate the rice fields. With high water the saw mills on the banks of the river were also put to work... the rich fruit and vegetable gardens on the Cote des Allemands were impressive ... believed that the Germans still supplied the capital (New Orleans) ... Goods were transported mainly on the river, just as always. Cuming reported in 1810 that, above New Orleans, the river was 'covered with multitudes of market boats rowing' ... On May 6, 1813 a complaint was registered in St. Charles Parish about the large number of cattle found daily on the road. The levees, especially the new ones, were being damaged by these [cattle], particularly when the river was high."— Helmut Blume, excerpts from The German Coast During the Colonial Era (1722-1803) ⚜ ⚜ ⚜

In 1824, John McDonogh, wealthy philanthropist of New Orleans, noted that Bonnet Carré would be an ideal site for an outlet into Lake Pontchartrain to prevent the flooding of New Orleans. McDonogh considered it ideal because it provided the closest approach from the river to the lake. The 1871–82 crevasse provided proof that it was an excellent corridor and proved McDonogh's theory correct. (Following the devastating flood of 1927, the Congressional Flood Control Act of 1928 provided the impetus for construction of the Bonnet Carré Spillway to begin in 1929. The Bonnet Carré Spillway gates have been opened several times since then to protect those downriver from flooding, just as McDonogh envisioned could happen in 1824. ⚜ ⚜ ⚜

Roster of Alexandre LaBranche's Fifth Regiment. Alexandre LaBranche, b. 1751; married Marie Jeanne Piseros; owner of large tracts of land in St. Charles Parish and several plantations; officer in the American Revolution; served in the Spanish Army; drafter, first state constitution; second lieutenant in the militia of German Coast; fought with Galvez against English in American Revolution; colonel, Fifth Regiment, County of German Coast Militia in Battle of New Orleans.

5th Regiment (Col. Alexandre LaBranche) County of German Coast - St. Charles and St. John the Baptist	
F. & S.	-
Capt. Zenon Boudousquie	64
Capt. Michel Caratin	63
Capt. Alexandre Chenet	44
Capt. N'los Chauvin Delery	64
Capt. Pre. Dumaine	58
Capt. Edmond Fortier	60
Capt. J. J. Haydel	72
Capt. Ursin Jacob	79
Capt. Francois Rillieux	37
Sgt. Louis Dolhonde	27
Total	**568**

7th Regiment (Col. - LeBeuf) Assumption and Lafourche Interior	
F. & S.	-
Capt. Burrel Aycock	71
Capt. Jean Guillot	73
Capt. Francois Mollere	67
Capt. Pierre Richards(?)	53
Total	**264**

St. Charles Parish Courthouse, 1826

The parish seat of government has probably been at its same location in Hahnville since the establishment of the first courthouse in the early 1800s, although no written or pictorial information on that first location has yet been discovered or translated. An 1826 picture of what is believed to be the second courthouse does exist. Early maps and records only refer to the area as Saint Charles or Courthouse.

The German Coast Influence Spreads

The Destrehan family provides the unique connection between the German Coast and the west bank of Jefferson Parish. The descendants of Jean Baptist Destrehan were instrumental in spreading the German influence to Gretna, Harvey, and other Jefferson Parish towns.

Knowing and appreciating the work ethic of the German people, Nicholas Noel Destrehan, a German Coast native and son of Jean-Nöel, actively recruited many German immigrants to assist in the construction of the Destrehan Canal, now known as the Harvey Canal. ❖ ❖ ❖

Louise Marie Destrehan was educated at Sacred Heart Academy in St. Louis, Missouri, and returned home to the family plantation (now Harvey) at sixteen years of age in 1843 to assist her father, Nicholas Noel, in managing his many business enterprises and the construction and completion of the Destrehan Canal. She was also informed at that time that she was to marry Sea Captain Joseph Hale Harvey, who had been carefully selected by her father. After Nicholas Noel's death in 1848, Louise and Captain Harvey purchased the canal, the house, and surrounding property from the estate. Captain Harvey went on to change the name of the canal from Destrehan to Harvey. In 1870, using her

The courthouse in 1826.

Portrait of Nicholas Noel Theodule Destrehan, b. 1793, d. 1848; fourth son of Jean-Nöel Destrehan; married Victoire Fortier (m.1), Henrietta Navarre (m.2); father of four children from second marriage; lived in Gretna; active in sugar cane industry; scholar, inventor, astronomer; reportedly drew blueprints for the lock system for the Harvey Canal. Served as Corporal in Battle of New Orleans; reputed to be an original developer of New Marigny (New Orleans) and Mechankham (Gretna) suburbs. Interred in St. Charles Borromeo Cemetery.

CITY OF GRETNA

Incorporated 20 August 1913. John Ehret, First Mayor. Seat of Jefferson Parish Government since 1884. German settlement laid out in 1836 by Benjamin Buisson for Nicolas Noel Destrehan as VILLAGE OF MECHANIKHAM.

Gretna Historical Marker.

Louise Marie Destrehan, a woman ahead of her time, b. 1827, d. 1903; daughter of Nicholas Noel Theodule Destrehan and Henrietta Navarre Destrehan; granddaughter of Jean-Nöel Destrehan; married Captain Joseph Hale Harvey in 1845. Interred in Metairie Cemetery.

Didier Sidney Zeringue (nephew of Charles Troxler, who was the great, great-grandson of Johann Georg Troxler) and his wife, Amelie Troxclair. (Photo courtesy of descendent Anne Petit Hymel)

father's conceptual plan, Louise and the captain had a canal lock system designed and constructed which initially ended in failure because of a deep bed of quicksand. Captain Harvey died in 1888.

Nearly forty years after the first failure of the lock system, and at seventy-five years of age, Louise Destrehan Harvey again undertook the construction of the lock system that would open a narrow barrier separating the canal from the Mississippi River. Louise would climb down the ladders to closely observe and inspect all aspects of the engineering project. Dying in 1903, she was unable to enjoy its successful end. Her son, Horace, persevered. After laborious testing in February of 1907, the system was finally approved and formally dedicated on March 29, 1907. It was sold to the United States government in the 1930s and became the Intracoastal Waterway System.

Descendants of the Early Settlers

Almost one hundred years had passed since those first German settlers survived horrific conditions at homeland ports waiting to sail and at sea, many dying enroute by starvation, illness, or later succumbing to the difficult climate after arrival in Louisiana. The new *engagés* (indentured agricultural workers) were considered *habitants* (concessionaires) of the company. They arrived debilitated and penniless, received small land grants, and were forced to sell their products to the *Compagnie des Indes*. In return and at fixed prices, they were allowed only necessities such as food and tools. Upon dissolution of the company in 1731, the German settlers were freed from all imposed obligations and were then able to become farmers in their own right.

J. Hanno Deiler in *The Settlement of the German Coast of Louisiana and the Creoles of German Descent* states, "The official census taken in November, 1724, must always be the principal source of information concerning the founders of the German Coast of Louisiana." Listed in this census is an entry of a now familiar family name (Oubre). Members of this family married into the Zeringue, Schexnaydre, Lorio, and Hymel families, whose many descendants still live along the German Coast.

"Jacob Huber, with six arpents. Native of Suevia, Germany. Catholic; 45 years old. His wife, son of 16 years. One engage'. One cow, one heifer, a pig. Made no crop on account of inundation. Good worker." (Census of 1724)

Celestine Schexnaydre. (Photo courtesy of descendent Anne Petit Hymel)

The Scheckschneider (Schexnaydre) and Zeringue families standing in front of Ormond Plantation in Destrehan. (Photo courtesy of Larry and Sharon Schexnaydre)

"Jacob Huber's son Christoph married Marie Josephine St. Ives. Descendants now write the name as 'Oubre,' 'Ouvre,' 'Hoover.'" (Census of 1724)

"Johann Georg Troxler, of Lichtenberg in Alsace. Catholic; 26 years old. A mason. His wife. 'Fort bon travailleur'. Two and one-half arpents cleared, on which he has been only since the beginning of the year having left the village in the rear. Exposed to inundation. Absent because of bad health. His wife is also sick. Lost his crop and his house. A neighbor, who cooked in a shed attached to Troxler's house, accidentally set fire to it. 1731: Two children. Two negroes; one cow. Johann Georg Troxler was the progenitor of all the 'Troxler' and 'Trosclair' families in Louisiana." (Census of 1724)

"The first priest of St. John the Baptist, the German Capuchin Father Bernhard von Limbach (1772), who wrote even the most difficult German names phonetically correct, entered the name as 'Scheckschneider', which is an old German name. The progenitor of this family, Hans Reinhard Scheckschneider, is mentioned on the passenger list of one of the four pest ships which sailed from L'Orient on the twenty-fourth of January 1721…Yet he was already called 'Chezneider', even on board ship…At present almost every branch of this very numerous family writes the name differently…."—J. Hanno Deiler, *The Settlement of the German Coast of Louisiana and the Creoles of German Descent*

Charles J. Oubre, Jr., descendant of Jacob Huber.

Charles Troxler (b. 1862) and brother-in-law Donation Lorio (son of Andre Lorio and Elmire Toups). (Photo courtesy of descendant Anne Petit Hymel)

Descendant of Jacques Perilloux, Felix and wife, Louisa Madere Perilloux. (Photo courtesy of Coleen Perilloux Landry)

Showboat's a-comin! The showboats began in 1831 and brought much excitement to all living along the Mississippi River. They were traveling theatres with stages lit by candles or oil-burning lamps; hand-painted scenery; and curtains, which were lowered and raised. Some were very lavish and some very crude. The actors and actresses lived onboard. At night torches burned brightly on the levee to guide people to the showboat. Tickets were usually about twenty-five cents. Most had to save their pennies and some paid with sacks of potatoes, sides of bacon, honey, and the like. Most farming families had precious little money to spare. By the 1850s many showboats were present up and down the river. They would stop at each town going downstream, doing the same on the opposite bank when returning upstream. Showboats continued to entertain those living along the river for one hundred years into the twentieth century.

Jacques Perilloux was the first Perilloux to come to Louisiana from France in the 1740s and was married at St. Charles Church in 1753. His descendants owned plantations in St. Charles and St. John parishes. At the Montz Plantation, there was a dance pavilion that was also used for theatrical productions. Perilloux Landing was one of the popular stops for steamboats and showboats. Like many other houses along the River Road, the Perilloux Plantation was destroyed in 1973 for a levee setback.

Montz was becoming more established by the 1860s and included enclaves named Coffee and Keller Towns. With the assistance of the Sons of Levi Benevolent Association, many black families located here when the Civil War came to an end.

Dufrein (Dufrene) Family. Pictured are Jean Gregoire Francois Dufrene (descendant of Julian Dufrene, ca. 1641?) and Emilina Dufreney (Dufrene). Originally from Nantes, France, descendants moved from Canada to Louisiana arriving at Bois Choctaw around the late 1850s. This family and others lived there until moving further inland to Down the Bayou Village Des Allemands, and Bayou Gauche. The Dufrenes became master boat builders, constructing cypress lugger-type boats first used and built in Louisiana during earliest colonial times. (Photo courtesy of Mrs. Donald (Annabel Matherne) Hogan, Sr.)

Life on the Bayou

"Johann Adam Matern, of Rosenheim, in Upper Alsace. Catholic; 26 years old. Weaver. His wife with a child at the breast; two sister-in-laws, 18 and 20 years of age. One and a half year on the place. Two and a half arpents cleared. 'A good worker', who deserves some Negroes. Three pigs. 1731: Three children. Three Negroes; seven cows."—Census of 1724; J. Hanno Deiler, *The Settlement of the German Coast of Louisiana and the Creoles of German Descent*

There were several settlements along the German Coast that are no longer in existence. A small community was settled in the late 1850s on the east side of Lake Salvador in St. Charles Parish. Early Choctaw Indians and settlers named the village Bois Choctaw which means "Oaks of the Choctaw." Trapping, hunting, and fishing provided food and livelihoods for all of the families. Some had permanent homes ashore while others lived in chalands (houseboats) to move about for seasonal hunts. Bois Choctaw fell victim to time and tide.

Bois Choctaw - gone but not forgotten. Left to right, home of Jean and Mary Corrindon Dufrene, Dufrene Store, and the home of Willie E. and Agnes Trauth Dufrene. Lake Salvador is in the foreground. (Photo courtesy of Mrs. Donald (Annabel Matherne) Hogan, Sr.)

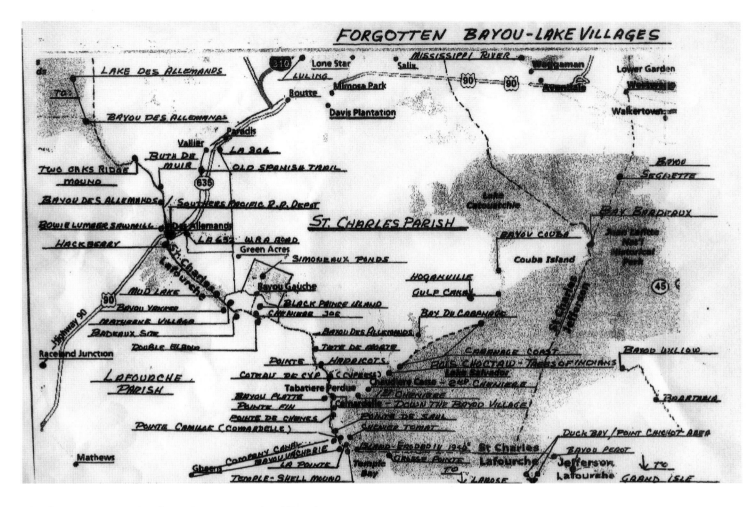

The "forgotten" Bayou-Lake Villages. (Map courtesy of Paul Hogan)

Descendants of those early settlers courageously faced many of the same overwhelming odds as their ancestors but continued to persevere and thrive in the nineteenth century.

Hogan Family. Jeremiah (Jeremie) Hogan, standing at left, departed Ireland and arrived in New Orleans in the 1860s. The family lived in Bois Choctaw. As time passed, family members moved further inland to Comardelle Village before settling in Bayou Gauche and Des Allemands. (Photo courtesy of Mrs. Donald (Annabel Matherne) Hogan, Sr.)

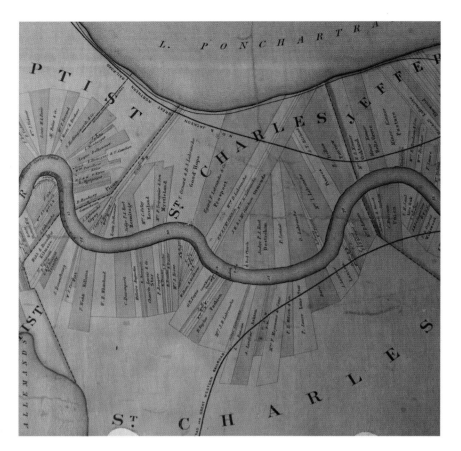

Extraction of St. Charles Parish - Persac Map (Courtesy of The Historic New Orleans Collection, Detail from Norman's Chart of the Lower Mississippi River by Marie Adrien Persac—Accession #1974.1)

The Antebellum Period, 1803–61

In the eighteenth century, many early colonists were afforded land grants and established plantations and businesses. After the Louisiana Purchase in 1803, many Americans navigated down the Mississippi River in all manner of craft to settle in the Louisiana Territory. By 1804, more than eighty years had passed since the German Coast had been established and the floodgates opened to newcomers in 1809 when Governor William C. C. Claiborne decreed that emigrants would be allowed to enter Louisiana with their slaves. It was a time of great prosperity. Sugar, cotton, rice, indigo, and tobacco accounted for the vast fortunes established in "plantation country," which became known as the Golden Coast. Etienne de Borés successful achievement of sugar granulation revolutionized the industry and enabled planters to focus on the more reliable crop of sugar cane.

Norbert Rillieux (1806–94) of New Orleans was a free person of color. He was a student of thermodynamics and a scientific genius who invented the vacuum pan process, which helped to revolutionize and streamline the sugar industry. This process was used at the Destrehan Plantation when Judge Pierre Adolphe Rost was owner. Information can be found in the Champonier's report of crops, which was published more than ten years before the Civil War began and provides additional information about other plantations along the German Coast. "A vacuum apparatus" is listed as being used for the crop year of 1855–56, with the same description the following year. Rillieux's process is still being used to manufacture condensed milk, soap, gelatin, and glue, in the recovery of waste liquors in distilleries, and in paper mills and other processes. ❧ ❧ ❧

"St. Charles Parish was graced with many plantations owing to the strategic location on the Mississippi River. Without this water highway, shipping of agricultural produce would be a long, tedious, time consuming and unprofitable enterprise. The river was essential to a plantation economy. It has for centuries spread its contents over the farm lands…Annual floods deluged the area with tons of fertile topsoil."—Henry Eugene Yoes III, A History of St. Charles Parish ❧ ❧ ❧

Comparing the map by Gertrude C. Taylor and Glenn R. Conrad entitled *St. Charles Parish, 1804-1812, Some Landowners of the Era* (inserted in this book) with the well-known Persac map of 1858, gives one a clear picture of the growth and prosperity of the German Coast during this period. As time passed, many changes in ownership took place because of normal factors of inheritances, crop successes and failures, and the normal course of free enterprise. The Mississippi River reclaimed many of the once-splendid plantations and the Civil War forever changed the physical and cultural landscape of this era. Only three of the original plantations remain in place today—Destrehan, Ormond, and Home Place. None of the descendants of the original owners are known to remain in possession.

Grave marker of Thomas Loughan, located in St. Charles Borromeo Cemetery. In Memory of THOMAS LOUGHAN; a native of Co. Galway, Parish of Kilbegnett, IRELAND; Died Oct. 20, 1853, aged 27 years. (Photo courtesy of Marilyn Mayhall Richoux)

The 1853 Yellow Fever Epidemic—Over one hundred burials took place at St. Charles Borromeo Cemetery alone in 1853. It is assumed that most of these deaths were caused by the yellow fever epidemic. General Richard Taylor of Fashion Plantation lost two sons during the epidemic. German Coast residents later learned that screening and oiling of cisterns deterred the breeding of mosquitoes and helped to prevent the dreaded disease. The last yellow fever epidemic was in 1909.

❧ ❧ ❧

Hicks Lewis Youngs was the Boutte postmaster for sixteen years; police jury president for fifteen years; school board member for twenty-five years; first railroad engineer through German Coast for the New Orleans and Opelousas Railroad; and delegate to 1898 State Constitutional Convention. Youngs School in Paradis was named after him.

Mozella Plantation—Hicks Lewis Youngs and brother Elias moved to the German Coast from New York City in 1851. The Youngs brothers acquired Joseph Marioneau's property through a series of buyouts and established a sugar and cotton plantation, which they named Mozella after Elias's wife. Hicks and his wife, Frances Culpepper Youngs, established their plantation close to Boutte, which follows the Old Spanish Trail, where cotton, sugar cane, and timber were grown. A rail line linked Mozella to Ashton Plantation. The plantation ultimately became a victim of the Great Depression.

Frances Culpepper Youngs, wife of Hicks Youngs.

Prospect Plantation was built circa 1815 by Edgar LaBranche who later expanded the plantation from the Mississippi River to Lake Pontchartrain.

Leon Sarpy was born in Tennessee and fought in the Civil War. He purchased Prospect Plantation in addition to two neighboring plantations after the war. The Prospect, Good Hope, and Sarpy Plantations became the towns of New Sarpy, Good Hope, and Sellers, which became Norco.

Ellington Plantation was also called Witherspoon. Francis Mayronne commissioned Charles Gallier to design the Classical Revival house, which was built in the late 1850s in present-day Luling at the River Road Monsanto Park site. Florenz Albrect Luling, for whom the town of Luling was named, (formerly known as St. Denis, named by a Civil War railroad owner; when the Acadians arrived in the area it became popularly known as "Cajun Town"), purchased the plantation on August 6, 1868. Luling sold Ellington Plantation on May 1, 1882, and a succession of owners followed. It was purchased in 1952 by the Lion Oil Company, which later became Monsanto. The main house was demolished in the early 1960s. Some of the smaller houses from the plantation were moved from the site to Sugarhouse Road and remain in place today. Top photo shows the front elevation with the bottom photo showing the back of the plantation house. (Photo courtesy of JoAnn and Kearney Mongrue)

Early Railroads in St. Charles Parish

The first railroads were built in the 1830s. Early railroad travel was dangerous as construction was unbelievably crude. Poorly installed rails worked loose and were forced through floors of coaches and cars. The boilers of locomotives would sometimes explode, animals strolled onto the tracks, flying cinders caused fires, heavy rains and floods washed out bridges, and railroad cars would jump the rails. At times, passengers were asked or forced to help get the train going again. To add insult to injury, the railroad crews would occasionally stop the train enroute to enjoy a bit of hunting or fishing. Travel improved for German Coast residents when the first railroad lines were opened through St. Charles Parish probably in the early 1850s. Railroad spur lines were of great benefit to plantation and business owners because they connected those sites to the main line.

New Orleans, Jackson & Great Northern Railroad Company currency. (Courtesy of Phyllis Mayhall Barraco)

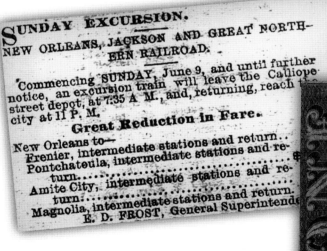

Sunday Excursion. (Courtesy of Phyllis Mayhall Barraco)

58

Cuisine

"How much pepper! What highly seasoned food! But especially how much pepper! Real fire, this food of Louisiana."—Pierre Clement de Laussat, French Colonial Prefect, 1803 ⚜ ⚜ ⚜

Gumbo

Gumbo is one of the best examples of creolization or cultural blending in Louisiana. It embodies the true essence and flavor of Louisiana's unique Creole heritage. The imprint of many cultures made possible this favorite and renowned Louisiana dish.

The word gumbo, a roux-based soup, derived its name from the Bantu word, nkombo (okra). Some cooks enjoy using it as a thickening agent, along with filé made from sassafras leaves. The German Coast families enjoyed an abundance of wildlife and seafood in addition to the standard chicken so often used. To the roux-based "soup" some added rabbit, squirrel, alligator, duck, and other indigenous animal meats, as well as shrimp, crabmeat, oysters, and fish. As if this weren't enough, they also added smoked meats, sausage, and a locally created pork sausage named andouille, in addition to generous measurements of red pepper.

The culinary evolution also produced dishes such as jambalaya, crawfish bisque, courtbuillon, etouffé, beans and rice, pain perdue, galettes, pralines, and more. The meals were usually followed by lots of coffee. The mild climate offered German Coast residents a great advantage in producing crops and helped to provide a broader range of vegetables and fruit than most Americans were able to enjoy. Other supplies were brought in from other states and finer products were imported from Europe. Cistern water was used for cooking. Yes, Prefect Laussat was correct. This assimilation of the many ethnic groups resulted in a fascinating cultural landscape and the cuisine was one of the most interesting outcomes.

The first cold spell of autumn to hit the river parishes was quickly followed by the culinary ritual of a boucherie. The slaughtering of a pig and serving it, as a local delicacy, was a favorite event for many. Entire families and their friends would gather for the three-day ritual, which included the process of slaughtering and slow-roasting the animal; cleaning the intestines for sausage casing and making the "gratons" or crackling (rendering the fat); making sausage, preparing the organs, and other meats; and making hogshead cheese. The food prepared was usually shared by many and in early days used up gradually to provide as many meals as possible. (Sketch courtesy of Lorraine Gendron)

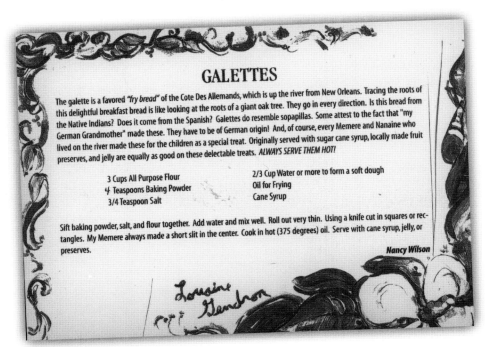

GALETTES

The galette is a favored *"fry bread"* of the Cote Des Allemands, which is up the river from New Orleans. Tracing the roots of this delightful breakfast bread is like looking at the roots of a giant oak tree. They go in every direction. Is this bread from the Native Indians? Does it come from the Spanish? Galettes do resemble sopapillas. Some attest to the fact that "my German Grandmother" made these. They have to be of German origin! And, of course, every Memere and Nanaine who lived on the river made these for the children as a special treat. Originally served with sugar cane syrup, locally made fruit preserves, and jelly are equally as good on these delectable treats. *ALWAYS SERVE THEM HOT!*

3 Cups All Purpose Flour
4 Teaspoons Baking Powder
3/4 Teaspoon Salt

2/3 Cup Water or more to form a soft dough
Oil for Frying
Cane Syrup

Sift baking powder, salt, and flour together. Add water and mix well. Roll out very thin. Using a knife cut in squares or rectangles. My Memere always made a short slit in the center. Cook in hot (375 degrees) oil. Serve with cane syrup, jelly, or preserves.

Nancy Wilson

German Coast *Train Depots*

Left: Luling Depot.
Below left: Goodhope Depot.
Below right: Hahnville Depot.
(Courtesy of Herald Guide profiles)

Above: Des Allemands Depot. (Courtesy of Opal Dufrene)

Left: Norco Depot. (Courtesy of Herald Guide *profiles)*

Left: Train Crossing over Bayou des Allemands. (Courtesy of Opal Dufrene)

Below left: Destrehan Depot. (Courtesy of Herald Guide *profiles)*

Below right: St. Rose Depot. (Courtesy of Herald Guide *profiles)*

Church Timeline
Emergence of Protestant Churches

After almost 150 years of Catholic dominance, the emergence of Protestant churches on the German Coast began. New Catholic and Protestant churches continued to be established in the twentieth century. ❧ ❧ ❧

1806—Original St. Charles Log Church in Destrehan burns and is replaced by wood-framed church painted red (Little Red Church).

1859—First Protestant church is organized on Old Spanish Trail.

1862—St. James Methodist Church is established in Hahnville.

1865—Bethlehem Baptist Church in Hahnville is founded by African American missionaries.

1866—L'Eglise Notre Dame du Rosaire (Our Lady of the Rosary) Chapel is established in Taft.

1866—Baptist Church, Killona, is established.

1895—Mount Airy Baptist Church of Boutte is established.

1897—St. Matthew Baptist Church, New Sarpy, is established.

In 1887, forty arpents were added to the 1770 land grant donated to St. Charles Borromeo Church for religious purposes. The Church now held 617.68 acres. After the Louisiana Purchase in 1821, these lands were registered with the United States government. In 1890, the "Little Red Church," built in 1806 on this land grant, entered a period of interdiction, losing pastoral support of the archbishop due to conflicts with the church charter and wardens. During this period, the parishioners worshipped at St. Charles Parish west bank and Kenner churches.

St. Matthew Baptist Church, New Sarpy, 1897. Used as school for colored children. (Courtesy of Joseph Schexnayder)

Old church on Rost (Destrehan) Plantation. Used as colored church and school.

Bethlehem Baptist Church in Hahnville, 1865. Founded by African American missionaries.

L'Englise Notre Dame du Rosaire Catholic Chapel (Our Lady of the Holy Rosary) in Taft, 1866–1964. Only the cemetery remains.

St. Gertrude the Great Catholic Mission Chapel in Des Allemands, 1901.

St. James Methodist Church in Hahnville. Land was donated by Governor Hahn to build a church. Church was also used as a school.

St. Anthony of Padua Catholic Mission Chapel in Luling, 1902.

Paradis Presbyterian Church, 1914. Became St. Andrew Episcopal Church in 1967.

St. Mark Catholic Mission Chapel in Ama, built circa 1912.

St. John the Baptist Church in Paradis.

St. Isidore "The Farmer" Catholic Chapel in Montz, 1924. Destroyed by Hurricane Betsy in 1964.

First Communion processional to St. Anthony of Padua Catholic Church in Luling.

St. Anthony of Padua Catholic Church in Luling, 1926. Currently owned by the St. Charles Parish School System.

New Red Church Pastor—Father Paret Reveals Early Life on the Mississippi River

Approaching the middle of the nineteenth century, life was good and prosperous for most people in St. Charles Parish. St. Charles was a wealthy sugar parish. At that time, Louisiana supplied the nation with over half of all sugar in American markets—the second most important agricultural crop of the nation. St. Charles had an abundance of sugar plantations lining the Mississippi River—over fifty. For most St. Charles citizens, it was a leisurely lifestyle, where gentlemen of the German Coast wore top hats and waistcoats and rode with wives and daughters in their buggies along River Road surveying their own and other plantation estates or visiting neighbors. Often they might travel alone on horseback. Young people spent their days hunting, fishing, boating, swimming, or racing their horses on River Road. Many of the women were aristocrats appearing in public in hoop skirts, shawls, bonnets, and sometimes using parasols—all in keeping with their wealthy southern lifestyle.

It was at this time in parish history that the Little Red Church welcomed a new pastor, Fr. Joseph Michel Paret. Fr. Paret was born in 1807 in the small village of Pélussin, France, and was sent to the Louisiana missions in 1847 by the Catholic Church. In 1848, he arrived at Little Red Church to serve the spiritual needs of his parishioners in the midst of an agricultural economy that was thriving. Fr. Paret would serve at Red Church twenty-one years, leaving in 1869. He would witness firsthand an exceptional period in the parish history, when great sugar plantations were prospering and later the profound consequences of the Civil War were occurring. In 1853, in the midst of the state's worst yellow fever epidemic, Fr. Paret wrote long and detailed letters to his family back home in France, titling the collection of correspondence, *My American Journal* (*Mon Journal d'Amerique*). About 1858 or thereabout, Fr. Paret traveled by steamboat to New Orleans where he purchased a sketchbook in a Chartres Street stationery store near the St. Louis Cathedral. In the coming months and years he began painting watercolors of Red Church, the presbytery, and plantations across the parish, all showing daily life in St.

Father Joseph Paret.

Charles. In all, Fr. Paret painted fifty-three watercolors. It is easy to determine from these watercolors that St. Charles Parish was indeed very prosperous. In 1869, the watercolors went back to France with Fr. Paret when he returned home. The watercolors and journal eventually became the property of his brother August Paret and his descendants. Over one hundred years later, the sketchbook and journal were found in an old trunk in Pélussin, France.

Thanks to Fr. Paret, one is able to travel back in time, to glimpse the history, to view life as it was in St. Charles. The following is only a small part of the series of fifty-three watercolors painted on the pages of an ordinary sketchpad so many years ago.

Eglese Rouge. St. Charles
20 Mars. 1859.

Watercolors
from St. Charles Parish, Louisiana, 1859

Painted by Father Joseph M. Paret

At the time of discovery of the Paret watercolors, in a proposal to publish the 1859 paintings, Louisiana State University (LSU) Art Museum Director Pat Bacot said the Paret paintings were "the most important single group of landscape paintings done before the Civil War in Louisiana. Nothing is comparable to them. Yet, these paintings have never been displayed in Louisiana."

His paintings were subsequently published by LSU Press. His journal, *Mon Journal d'Amerique*, a collection of correspondence with his family in 1853, was published in France by Marcel Boyer 140 years later, in 1993. More information regarding Fr. Paret's watercolors and journal can be found in *Plantations by the River* by Marcel Boyer, edited by Jay D. Edwards and published by LSU Press. (Photos courtesy of Fred B. Kniffen Cultural Resources Laboratory, Department of Geography and Anthropology, Louisiana State University)

Red Church, March 20, 1859. The Little Red Church on a Sunday afternoon. The German cemetery is one of the oldest in the South, with tombs dating back to 1770. Many earlier gravesites fell victim to the Mississippi River. Deceased west bank residents were transported across the Mississippi River in boats to be buried at the Red Church cemetery. A replica of the Red Church is on display on the grounds of St. Charles Borromeo in Destrehan at the entrance to the cemetery.

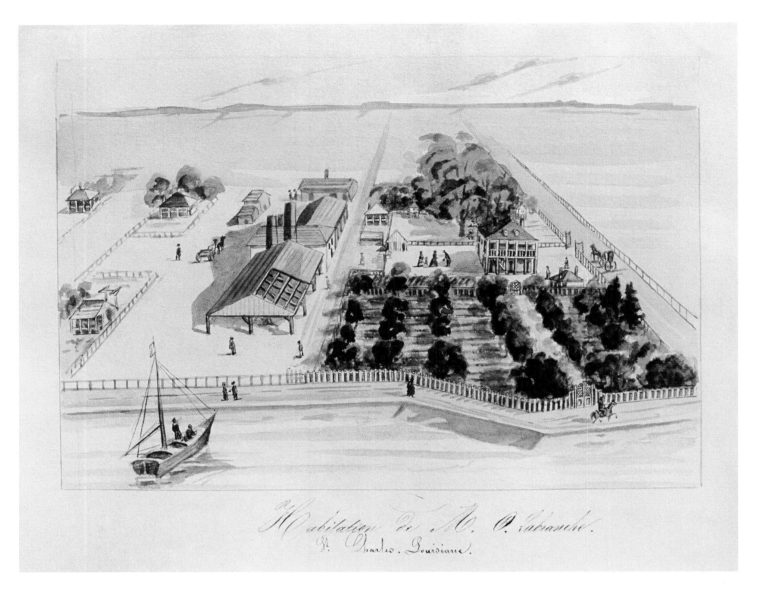

Home of the M. O. LaBranche. La Branche Plantation. The German Zweig family surname was Gallicized to LaBranche. Octave was the son of Alexandre LaBranche. He was a member of Captain Trudeau's Troop of Horse and a veteran of the Battle of New Orleans. Octave served as speaker of the Louisiana House of Representatives from 1827 to 1829. The LaBranche family and Fr. Paret enjoyed a warm relationship. The LaBranche's owned several plantations. The house pictured was located in the present St. Rose area.

Bird's eyeview. 1859—Father Paret's beautiful watercolor painting depicts the Little Red Church and its surroundings in the heart of St. Charles Parish. The area displays present-day locations of Dufresne (Esperanza) and Hahnville on the west bank, across the river from Destrehan and New Sarpy on the east bank. The east bank Little Red Church, its old cemetery, and the presbytery are surrounded by several dependency buildings. The birds-eye view provides a fascinating visual of pre-Civil War St. Charles Parish.

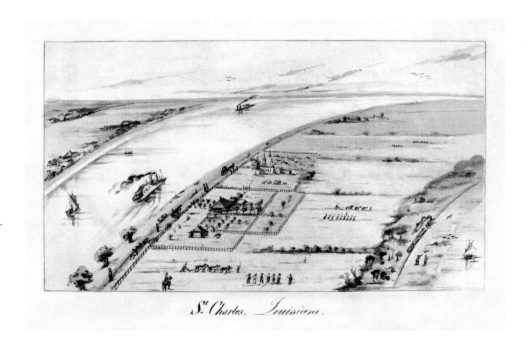

Oxley Plantation. *The residence of Charles and Martha Kenner Oxley, daughter of William Kenner (Roseland), was located in the present-day Bonnet Carré Spillway. Charles Oxley was a native of Liverpool, England, and became a New Orleans cotton broker. The Greek revival architectural style became popular in Louisiana as early as 1830. However, the Creoles continued to favor the West Indies style. Located at this site is an African American cemetery named Kenner Cemetery. Fr. Paret displays his sense of humor by including himself in this painting.*

Good Hope Plantation was the home of brothers Thomas and Edouard Oxnard and brother-in-law, Brice Similien LaBranche. Brice LaBranche served in the militia, was a member of Captain Trudeau's Troop of Horse in the Battle of New Orleans, and served as a churchwarden and member of the Louisiana State Legislature. The Oxnard family remained involved in the sugar industry throughout the twentieth century. Good Hope was bought by Leon Sarpy after the Civil War. This site is now the town of Norco and home to Shell/Motiva. Note the many dwellings and support buildings ("dependencies"). Each plantation was designed to be as self-contained as possible.

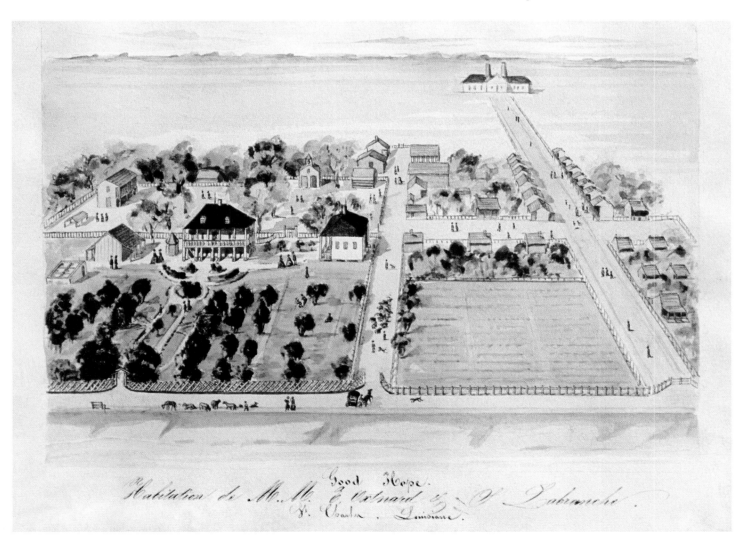

The Hermitage Plantation was owned by Judge Pierre Adolphe Rost and was located at the center of the present Bonnet Carré Spillway. Judge Rost was married to Louise Odile Destrehan and also owned the former Destrehan Plantation. He was considered one of the most significant and wealthy plantation owners along the German Coast. The Hermitage was seized by the federal government after the Civil War and later returned to Judge Rost. George Frederick Kugler served as overseer for Judge Rost and later acquired Hermitage Plantation. The property was subsequently sold to the United States government to be used as the site for the spillway project. Lumber from demolition of the Hermitage Plantation was used to build houses on Apple Street in Norco. Another African American cemetery known as the Kugler Cemetery is located at this site. Legend lends an interesting story that George Kugler planted many of the oak trees along the River Road.

Fr. Paret's paintings provide so many aspects of life in St. Charles just two years before the Civil War, giving firsthand views of plantation layouts, fence and building materials, gardens, and so much more. Many plantations in St. Charles appear to be small villages, which included amenities such as a family cemetery, chapel, and schoolhouse.

Prominently featured in almost all of Father Paret's paintings are the Mississippi River and its many diverse modes of transportation. Using canoes to transport goods and to travel, American Indians traversed the river long before Europeans arrived. Samuel Clemens's Mark Twain was fascinated with and came to love and respect the Mississippi River and all surrounding it. It was the backbone of the German Coast. The most coveted and valuable land was that fronting the river. Many styles of boats were designed for different uses. Flatboats were popular and even had living quarters. When a destination was reached, most were taken apart and lumber was used for construction or firewood. As with limestone used for ballasts in sea-going vessels and eventually used as masonry for New Orleans homes, many houses from this era include salvaged flatboat wood. Many early sidewalks (banquettes) were constructed of flatboat wood. Those settling downriver in St. Charles Parish also reused all salvageable materials onboard. Bargeboard houses are located throughout St. Charles Parish.

Buggies appear to be the main mode of travel in the parish. Those traveling by water are seen in luggers, bateaux, pirogues, flatboats, paddle wheelers, and steamboats. Creole architecture dominated the landscape. Except for Ormond, all of the Paret plantations, including all of the accessory buildings, have disappeared from the landscape, perhaps destroyed by the Civil War, Mother Nature, or progress.

The presbytery of the Red Church, now called a rectory, was Fr. Paret's residence and is so vividly portrayed in his watercolors. But it lasted not even a quarter-century, burning in 1877. During his tenure at Red Church, Fr. Paret convinced his brothers to visit the financially stable civil parish and his home at Red Church. One brother became a permanent resident of the parish, leaving descendants in Louisiana today.

But not all of the people in St. Charles were wealthy, affluent plantation owners as depicted in Paret's watercolors. The small farmers of the German Coast continued to exist with the larger plantations. Many "Americans" immigrated to the parish in search of riches they often did not find. The plantation economy depended on slaves and census reports at the time show St. Charles had five slaves to every white person. Only about one-third of the white population did not have slaves at this time. Of the fifty-two plantations in the parish, the largest were on the west bank. Since it has been documented that there were more doctors than schoolteachers in the parish, plantation laborers may have been very well cared for by their owners as reported.

Interestingly, at that time, many of the Catholic churches had either slaves or free blacks living at the rectory address. Apparently the slaves living at Red Church

The Ormond Plantation is one of the few houses that escaped fires, floods, and the Civil War. It was originally built in 1790 by Pierre Trépagnier on land granted to him by Spanish Governor Bernardo deGalvez for his service during the time of the American Revolution. In 1805, the property was acquired by Richard Butler, who named the plantation Ormond after an Irish ancestor, the Duke d'Ormonde. Upon his death, Ormond was deeded to Butler's sister whose husband was naval officer Samuel McCutchon (Fr. Paret spelled it McCutcheon). Ormond Plantation adjoined the Little Red Church property, housed a post office, and had a large boat landing. Ormond is the only plantation included in Fr. Paret's series of watercolors that survives into the twenty-first century.

Ormond Plantation
H. M. McCutchon

Habitation de J. B. Labranche frères.
Paroisse St. Charles.

Estate of Jean Baptist LaBranche. *After Widow J. B. LaBranche (nee Marie Trépagnier) died in 1868, her three sons, Judge Jean-Louis, Euphemond, and Cyprien, inherited the Jean Baptist LaBranche Plantation. By 1850, it was one of the German Coast's most prominent and successful. Note the Spanish style dependency building. This is the site of the present-day Esperanza Plantation owned by Judge Edward A. Dufresne, Jr.*

Habitation J. L. Labranche
Rive D. Paroisse St. Charles.

Judge Jean-Louis LaBranche Plantation. *Judge Jean-Louis LaBranche was born in 1805 in St. Charles Parish. A major crevasse occurred on May 8, 1858, at this site, followed a few days later by another levee break in the same area. On February 13, 1869, the* L'Avant Courseur *reported, "The hard times, the family losses, the brutalities of subordinate officers who acted like military police in St. Charles during and after the war, and finally the recent death of his aged mother all took their toll on Judge LaBranche's fragile constitution." He died on February 7, 1869.*

Ranson Plantation. *Louis Ranson was a member of a very prominent and influential New Orleans family that were formerly involved in Spanish government. He was the son of Zenon Ranson, one of the wealthiest planters in the parish, and married Flavie Troxler, a descendant of early German Coast settlers. The Ranson Plantation was located across the Mississippi River from present-day Destrehan. In 1866, as head churchwarden, he was asked by Father Paret to find a site for a west bank chapel. He served briefly in 1866 as sheriff of St. Charles and served as a captain in the Confederate Army. During the Civil War his property was seized and not returned until 1867.*

were not listed as belonging to Fr. Paret, but to his French housekeepers, a couple he recruited from France.

One could assume that Fr. Paret's appetite for sketching the beautiful plantation estates of St. Charles was completely tempered by the destruction he witnessed during the Civil War—to the point that his sketchbook is silent on the subject. But perhaps not—perhaps he gave some of his watercolors to friends in St. Charles. The discovery in France only emphasizes the possibility that other such treasures could be hidden in family closets, albums, or attics in St. Charles or elsewhere.

Fr. Paret's watercolors and journal are presently owned by the Choretier family in the Forez-Viennois region of the Department of Loire, France.

"Although travel accounts, diaries, and collections of correspondence exist from this same period, the importance of these colorful visuals (by Fr. Paret) survives not only as a chronicle of social history, but as documentation of properties that, for the most part, no longer exist...The ability to compile records that mean little as individual items and much as a group is central to the recording and understanding of the history of any region. Seen in conjunction with the array of materials for the study of the plantation culture of south Louisiana, the watercolors stand out as a unique body of work...As former colonies search for validation and connection with their parent countries, a bond through observed realities reaffirms their mutual influences."—Mary Louise Christovich, President, Kemper and Leila Williams Foundation ⚜ ⚜ ⚜

Information on Fr. Paret and his paintings has been extracted from *Plantations by the River* by Marcel Boyer published by LSU Press.

The citizens of Louisiana, in particular the citizens of St. Charles Parish, are grateful to Fr. Paret's family for agreeing to share the journal and watercolors.

Fashion Plantation was located in Hahnville and was owned by former U.S. President Zachary Taylor, although he never resided there. It was inherited by his son Lieutenant General Richard Taylor in 1851. General Taylor served with distinction in St. Charles Parish and throughout the south in the Confederate Army. Fashion Plantation was plundered and destroyed by Union troops. Personal accounts attest that it had been one of the most splendid in the area. The Mississippi River claimed the original site. Fashion Plantation residential developments are now located on the remaining portions of the plantation.

Old Spanish Trail

Legend holds that the "Old Spanish Trail," which runs through St. Charles Parish, was used by the Spanish and Indians enroute to Florida and Civil War troops bringing supplies and food to encampments during the war. It was also probably used by German Coast residents to traverse to and from the bayou area. According to local historical researcher Gerald Zeringue, "From the west, the Old Spanish Trail crossed south Louisiana, passing through Boutte Station, following the Boutte railroad. It continued to what is now known as Sugarhouse Road in Old Town (Luling) to the River Road, passing Ellington Plantation and its large sugarhouse then in place." According to police jury minutes of 1866, "the President is hereby authorized and empowered to issue Warrants for the amount allowed to Mr. P. Maillard's and Mayronne's Lands selected and purchased by the Parish, to lay out the New Public Road from the River to Magnolia Ridge, and that they should be first paid, out of the special funds appropriated for that

purpose." This new public road replaced the Sugarhouse route and became part of the Old Spanish Trail. Eventually the new route was named Paul Maillard Road. A ferry at Paul Maillard connected Luling to the east bank of the river. Many new businesses developed along the new corridor and Luling became a "boom town." The Klondike Store and other businesses on or near this corridor were built from barge lumber. Many of these businesses closed as a result of a Luling levee setback and when later constructed, Highway 90 connected the German Coast to the new Huey P. Long Bridge.

Early Roadways

In 1860, the German Coast residents still had dirt roadways that remained well into the twentieth century. Road construction was left to the respective parishes. The most used roads on both banks were those running along the Mississippi River. Those riding on horseback or in horse-drawn buggies were faced with many obstacles, depending on the weather. Planks were sometimes laid to reinforce the dirt roads. Crude ferries carried travelers across the larger bayous, but the Mississippi River continued to be the major corridor for travelers and interstate commerce and continued to benefit the German Coast. ❖ ❖ ❖

The Busalacchi family owned a dance hall, an ice business, and a farm before opening Busalacchi's Restaurant and Pool Hall in 1948. Under new ownership today, the original structure is in commerce and remains on Paul Maillard Road. (Sketch courtesy of Janis Blair)

Nick Gendusa and his bride Annie Catanzaro Gendusa are shown with their wedding party. The Gendusa/Catanzaro wedding was a traditional, formal Italian wedding. Nick Gendusa was a truck farmer living on River Road in St. Rose bringing his produce to the New Orleans market for decades. (Photo courtesy of RoseMarie Gendusa Palmisano)

Lussan Store, Luling, was built in the late 1800s and moved three times for levee setbacks.

John Busalacchi moved from St. Gabriel to Luling in 1899 and began managing his father's general merchandise store in 1917. John and Miss Jennie were married in 1920. (Photo courtesy of the St. Charles Herald)

Layous Gassen, b. August 20, 1870, d. April 6, 1904. Son of Antoine and Florestine (Kinler) Gassen. Antoine Gassen was born in 1830 and began his business career as a planter and in mercantile pursuits. He served in the Confederate Army during Civil War, was on the school board for over thirty years, and was warden of the Red Church for many years after his father's death. Layous was educated in the public schools, and at sixteen years of age became his father's partner in planting and merchandising. His brothers were included in the partnership when they came of age. At twenty-two years of age, Layous was elected treasurer of St. Charles Parish and by repeated re-elections remained in that office. Layous Gassen worked at the courthouse for fifty-two years. On June 22, 1892, Layous and Miss Louisa Tureaud were united in marriage. (Photo courtesy of Edith Gassen Donnaud, granddaughter)

Louise Theresa Tureaud Gassen, wife of Layous Gassen (b. June 25, 1862—d. February 21, 1943). (Photos courtesy of Edith Gassen Donnaud, granddaughter)

George Lorio and family, later owners of Star Plantation.

Louis Bourbon, one of the owners of Star Plantation.

St. Charles Parish in the Spotlight

Star Plantation on the River Road in Taft was recognized in *Grandeur of the South*, a publication of the National Historical Society, as an architectural treasure of early America. Star Plantation was owned by J. Levois of Paris, France. Thomas Clark Porteous was born in Edinburgh, Scotland, and managed the plantation of the Levois family. Porteous lived in New Orleans, but frequently visited the parish to make sure that all was well at the Star Plantation. It was located near the present intersection of La. 3142, which is now occupied by the Dow Chemical Company. The George Lorio family later acquired the plantation. It fell victim to the Hymelia Crevasse in 1912.

Star Plantation.

Tourist View of St. Charles Parish, 1860

    While St. Charles Parish was growing and developing, individuals frequently described the area from an "outside" point of view. J. W. Door, a gentleman connected with the editorial department of the *New Orleans Crescent*, was one of those detailing parish activities and geography in the mid-nineteenth century. He made a horse-and-buggy tour of a considerable portion of the state of Louisiana during the spring and summer of 1860, publishing letters in the *Crescent* between April 30 and September 10, 1860. Each letter was signed "Tourist." – *The Louisiana Historical Quarterly*, Volume 21, No. 4, October 1938

"Louisiana In Slices
Number I:
Parish of St. Charles
Up the Coast—The Scenery—Statistics—Parish Seat—The Large Planters—
The Crops, Levee, etc., etc.
(From our Special Traveling Correspondent.)
St. Charles Court-house, April 26, 1860

Dear Crescent—I thus begin serving up to you the first slice of Louisiana, intending to keep on doing so, if horse-flesh and your correspondent hold out, until I have cooked up in style, which I hope will suit the taste of your readers, the whole of the State. Since Wednesday morning, when I left the city and the Crescent office behind me, crossed the river at the Stock Landing and started with all the State before me, I have been buggying along the levee "up the coast", amid the charming and peculiar scenery of that region.

There are many in New Orleans who have lived there many more years than your correspondent, who have a very poor idea as to what the "coast" is. They fancy they have seen it from the deck of steamers plying on the river, but they are mistaken. They have only had glimpses of the country and dissolving views of the tops of the houses behind the high levee as they dashed past. To see and appreciate this Acadian land they should be behind a good horse and rattle along the levee road, which is now as smooth as the new Canal shell road. A constant succession of wealthy estates keep the interest alive, for there are few of them that will not repay pausing to admire. Splendid old homesteads dot the road at the distance of a quarter of a mile apart, the out-buildings, negro quarters, etc., forming at each a considerable village, so that the road up the coast is almost like a street of a vast, thinly built city. The plantations having a narrow front on the river and running far back, the houses are thus brought close together, and render the levee road a suburban avenue unequaled in the world, bordered on one side, as it is, by the unequaled river of the world, the clustering steamers and other crafts on which give an animated variety to the changeful scenery.

It is no sort of use for me to attempt to describe any of the splendid residences of the princely planters, for during yesterday's journey I passed dozens, each worthy more than a passing notice. All that tasteful architecture, ornamental shrubbery and magnificent moss-hung trees can do towards the beautifying of the sugar planters' residences in Jefferson and St. Charles parishes, as far as I have been, is effected. The farther I go from the city the more costly, elaborate and extensive the planters' houses seem to be. Seven or eight miles above the city the estates begin to show the most striking evidences of wealthy and refined occupancy, though there are a few fine places in the lower part of Jefferson parish.

Since I have been traveling up this "coast" it has occurred to me that people who take the trouble to travel thousands or hundreds of miles from New Orleans to find some pleasant and healthful locality to sojourn or settle, are taking a great deal of unnecessary and unremunerative trouble, for they can certainly find nowhere else a more delightful country than they have right at their doors. Along the pathway of the wide river a constant current of cool air pours above its rolling tide below, and thus the temperature is kept comfortable in the warmest season. A continual draft is created by the cool air of the river rushing across the banks to supply the heated interior."

"St. Charles Parish

I write you, vide date, from St. Charles Court House, where is located one of the three post-offices which the parish boasts. This "village" contains the court-house building and jail, which are of recent construction, and well and quite handsomely built of brick, and some five or six houses, one of which is occupied as a store. The settlement is twenty-nine miles from New Orleans. The other post-offices are McCutcheon's Landing, on the left bank, opposite this place, and Taylor's on the right bank, thirty-six miles from New Orleans.

The value of real estate held by residents of the parish of St. Charles is $1,646,900, and of non-residents $56,366. These figures are legally correct, and are one year later returns than have been published by the Auditor of the State. The value of slaves $2,053,300; of cattle, $25,200; of carriages and vehicles $8450; of capital invested in trade, $15,000. This last item is very small, for New Orleans is too near to give country dealers much chance. The few stores in the parish are nearly all scattered along the levee four or five miles apart, and are small affairs. The largest and best stocked concern that I have yet seen is that of J. B. Gassen, at Gassen's Landing and Ferry, twenty-six miles above the city. The other stores in the parish are Levet's, Bistouls, Vial's and Labat's, all on the right bank of the river, and Boutte's back on the Opelousas Railroad. Thus, you perceive, "merchandising" is a very inferior interest in these parts.

The area of the Parish of St. Charles is 8-1,4-13 acres, of which 45,884 acres is under cultivation, and 35,529 uncultivated. About 38,000 acres are in cane; about 6000 in corn, and three or four hundred in rice. These are very nearly accurate, their deviation from actual fact being so trifling as to be of no general consequence. The total population of the parish is about 5000, of whom about 900 are whites, 37-19 slaves and about 200 free colored. The Parish pays about $12,000 taxes, of which the mill tax, for the support of public schools, amounts to about $3800. There are three public school districts in the Parish, and one school in each, and the number of educable children is about three hundred.

The Parish officers of St. Charles are—Samuel McCutcheon, President of the Police Jury, whose post-office is at McCutcheon's Landing, and Messrs. Noel St. Martin, Sheriff; C. St. Martin, Clerk District Court, and Parish Treasurer also, and Emile Tastet, Recorder, whose post-office address is St. Charles Court-House. Among the "solid men" of the parish, are the following, some of whom are very "solid" in the matters of money, lands and negroes: Messrs. George Wailes, Sosthene Deneufbourg, Webb & Broaddus, Francis Webb, W. B. Whitehead, Charles Davenport, Chauvin, Levois & Co., Francis Bougere, Troxler Brothers, George E. Payne, Richard Taylor, Louis Ranson, A. Lanfear, Meyronne Brothers, Gautier & Ory, P. Sauvé, Ezra Davis, Nosin Zeringue, Montegut & Lagrove, P. A. Rost, George Pincard, E. F. Labranche & Co., J. W. & S. McCutcheon, Pierre Soniat, Octave LaBranche, Lestang Sarpy, A. Duplantier, George R. Price and Henry Frellson. There are quite a number of rich widows in the parish, I am told, so rich that they deserve to be ranked among the "solid men", but I will not give their names, lest they and the other good people of the parish should be afflicted with an invasion of fortune-hunting bachelors."

"The Crops, Levees, Etc.

The planters are complaining very much of the backwardness of the rattoon cane in coming up, and the scattering and imperfect manner in which it does come. The plant cane, however, is very promising, and the general prospect of the crop, at this early date, is accounted good. Corn is looking very finely.

The levee all along, so far, is in splendid condition. The fracture made by the Labranche Crevasse is most thoroughly healed, and like the whole of the levee from the city up to this point, will defy all that any flood can do against it.

My next letter will be from the parish of St. John the Baptist fourteen miles from here."

[6.] From Daily Crescent, *April 30, 1860.*

These letters depicted a beautiful, peaceful picturesque setting of the German Coast at that time prior to the Civil War. However, that would all soon change. ⚜ ⚜ ⚜

The Ordinance of Secession

St. Charles was one of twenty-nine parishes that supported secession on January 26, 1861. General Richard Taylor of Fashion Plantation was elected to represent the German Coast. His signature is included among those signing the document with the notation "of St. Charles" directly below. The German Coast was then no longer a part of the United States. For two months the German Coast was part of a new nation named the Republic of Louisiana. Then, on March 21, 1861, Louisiana became a part of the Confederate States of America.

As chairman of the Committee on Military and Naval Affairs, General Richard Taylor warned at the state convention that the lower Mississippi River should be reinforced because New Orleans was open to attack. His warning was not heeded, as many thought the Union would not attack New Orleans. Governor Moore stated that the Baton Rouge Arsenal held all that was needed to hold off Union troops. General Taylor was aware of the inevitable destruction and with profound sadness returned home. He decided not to serve the South, unless asked, because he considered this a futile cause. He was called in April of 1861 and, being loyal to his state and to the German Coast, joined in the battle.

When New Orleans fell without a shot in 1862, the German Coast fell to occupation by Union troops. Life was difficult for the people at home. The war department forced the local militias to participate and offered $50.00 for enlistees. The German Coast wanted to cooperate and offered an additional $40.00 to insure a full complement. The Mississippi

Lieutenant General Richard Taylor, b. 1826, d. 1879, was the owner of Fashion Plantation. He was the son of President Zachary Taylor and the brother-in-law of Confederate President Jefferson Davis. Taylor was a U.S. Senator, 1856–1860; a colonel in the Louisiana Ninth Infantry (appointed by Governor Moore); was appointed brigadier general in 1861; fought with distinction under Generals "Stonewall" Jackson and Robert E. Lee; was a member of Louisiana Secession Committee and chairman of the Committee on Military and Naval Affairs; and enacted the Conscription Act to enlist aid to fight Union troops. He is interred with his wife at Metairie Cemetery.

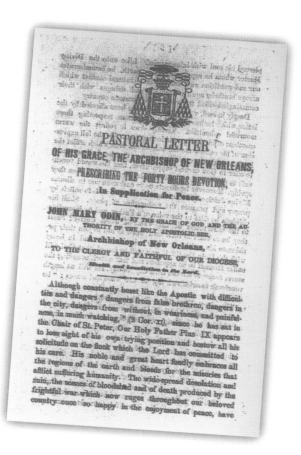

A pastoral letter from A History of the Archdiocese of New Orleans *by Charles E. Nolan.*

To dissolve the Union between the State of Louisiana and other States united with her, under the compact entitled:

"The Constitution of the United States of America"

We, the people of the State of Louisiana, in convention assembled, do declare and ordain and it is hereby declared and ordained, That the Ordinance passed by us in Convention on the 22nd day of November in the year Eighteen hundred & Eleven, whereby the Constitution of the United States of America and the amendments of the said Constitution were adopted, and all laws and ordinances by which the State of Louisiana became a member of the Federal Union, be and the same are hereby repealed and abrogated; and that the union now subsisting between Louisiana and other States under the name of "The United States of America" is hereby dissolved.

We do further declare and ordain, That the State of Louisiana hereby resumes all rights & powers heretofore delegated to the Government of the United States of America; that her citizens are absolved from all allegiance to said Government; and that she is in full possession and exercise of all those rights of sovereignty which appertain to a free and independent State.

We do further declare and ordain, That all rights acquired and vested under the Constitution of the United States, or any act of Congress, or treaty, or under any law of this State, and not incompatible with this Ordinance, shall remain in force and have the same effect as if this Ordinance had not been passed.

Adopted in Convention at Baton Rouge the 26th of January 1861.

Pour dissoudre l'Union de l'État de la Louisiane et des autres États faisant partie avec lui de cette Union, en vertu du pacte intitulé:

"La Constitution des États Unis d'Amérique."

Nous, le peuple de l'État de la Louisiane, réunis en Convention, déclarons et ordonnons [illegible] Mil huit cent Onze [illegible]

Nous déclarons et ordonnons de plus Que [illegible]

Nous déclarons et ordonnons de plus Que [illegible]

Adopté en Convention à Baton Rouge le 26 Janvier 1861.

A True Copy from the Original

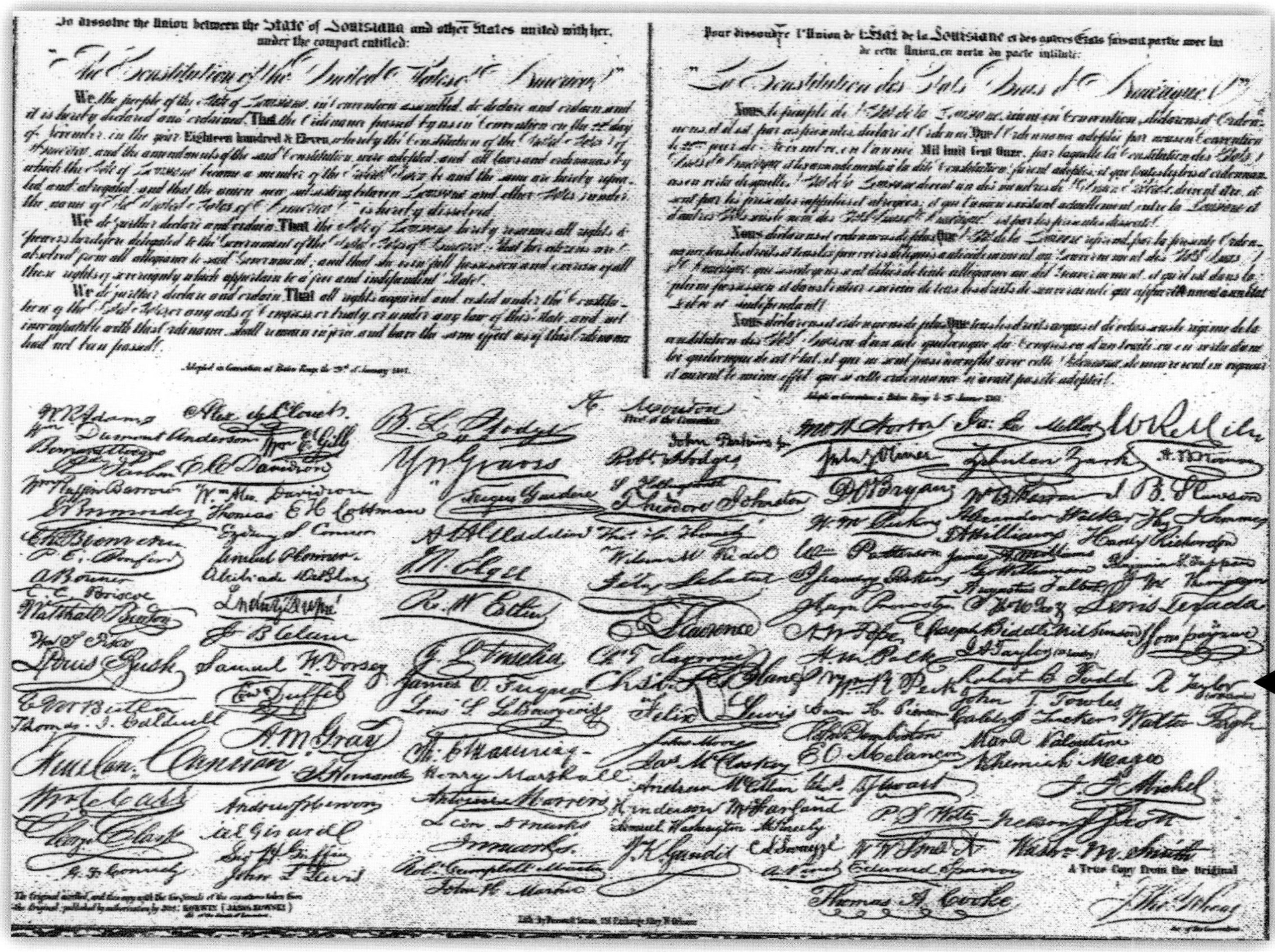

Arrow indicates General Taylor's signature.

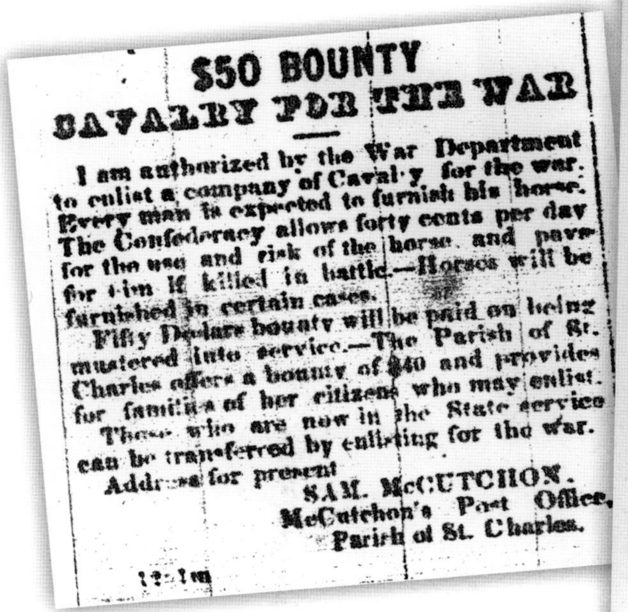

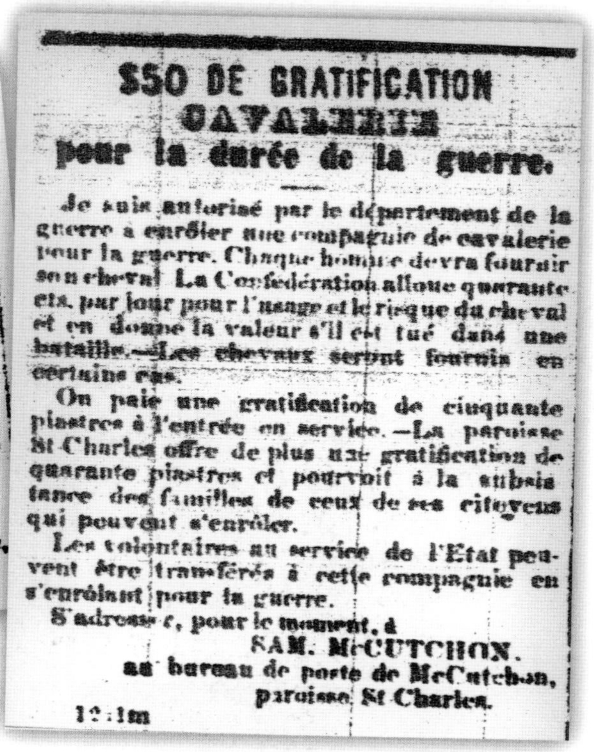

$50 BOUNTY

CAVALRY FOR THE WAR

I am authorized by the War Department to enlist a company of Cavalry for the war. Every man is expected to furnish his horse. The Confederacy allows forty cents per day for the use and risk of the horse, and pays for him if killed in battle.—Horses will be furnished in certain cases.

Fifty Dollars bounty will be paid on being mustered into service.—The Parish of St. Charles offers a bounty of $40 and provides for families of her citizens who may enlist.

Those who are now in the State service can be transferred by enlisting for the war. Address for present

SAM. McCUTCHON,
McCutchon's Post Office,
Parish of St. Charles.

12-1m

A Call for Calverymen, L'Avant Coureur, *April 19, 1862.*

$50 DE GRATIFICATION

CAVALERIE

pour la durée de la guerre.

Je suis autorisé par le département de la guerre à enrôler une compagnie de cavalerie pour la guerre. Chaque homme devra fournir son cheval. La Confédération alloue quarante cts. par jour pour l'usage et le risque du cheval et en donne la valeur s'il est tué dans une bataille.—Les chevaux seront fournis en certains cas.

On paie une gratification de cinquante piastres à l'entrée en service.—La paroisse St Charles offre de plus une gratification de quarante piastres et pourvoit à la subsistance des familles de ceux de ses citoyens qui peuvent s'enrôler.

Les volontaires au service de l'Etat peuvent être transférés à cette compagnie en s'enrôlant pour la guerre.

S'adresser, pour le moment, à

SAM. McCUTCHON,
au bureau de poste de McCutchon,
paroisse St Charles.

12-1m

A Call for Cavalrymen—Advertisement in the April 19, 1862, edition of L'Avant Coureur – Journal Officiel de Saint-Charles.

Georg Michael Hahn
Steady Patriot

Georg Michael Hahn, 1830–86.
Louisiana's Constitution of 1864"..."drawn under Georg Michael Hahn's active direction ...Not only abolished slavery and provided for the eventual enfranchisement of blacks ... opened the public schools to every child, black and white between the ages of six and eighteen; provided for a progressive income tax; established a minimum wage and a nine hour workday ... Louisiana has not had so many honest, highly principled Governors that we can afford to forget the ones we have had... Michael Hahn was such a man...yet his memory has been all but totally obliterated...it is time to recognize this man." Amos F. Simpson and Vaughan Burdin Baker.
"It is said the community was draped in black when he died." (Original picture in possession of Mrs. Raymond Schoonmaker, New Orleans, Louisiana.)

A press clipping from one of Michael Hahn's newspapers. (Courtesy of Phyllis Mayhall Barraco)

New Orleans Republican.

OFFICIAL JOURNAL OF THE UNITED STATES
OFFICIAL JOURNAL OF NEW ORLEANS

NEW ORLEANS, JULY 4, 1872.

NO PAPER TO-MORROW.

In order to give the attaches of the REPUBLICAN an opportunity to enjoy the national holiday in such a manner as they shall deem proper, no paper will be issued from this office to-morrow. The counting-room will, however, remain open until eleven o'clock this morning.

The whole policy of the *Picayune*—"Anything to beat Warmoth."

Vigilance committees, for the eradication of lightning rod men are forming in Indiana.

A deposit of a few more hundred million tons of guano has been discovered in Peru.

Southern Illinois is now in the middle of its wheat harvest. The crop is good, but laborers are scarce.

An Irish editor says he can see no earthly reason why women should not be allowed to become medical men.

It requires fully one-half of all the American iron produced to build our railroads and keep them in repair.

"Mamma," said a little boy who had been sent to dry a towel before the fire, "is done when it's brown?"

A Michigan divorcee met a man of like experience, went for him with a will, and realized $500 on a breach of promise suit.

The Postoffice will close to day at twelve o'clock, for the better observance by the various employees of the national holiday.

Lobby
St. Charles Parish Courthouse
River Road • Hahnville
A blend of history and art using the works of historians Amos Simpson and Vaughan Baker, and folk artist Lorraine Gendron
Sponsored by
St. Charles Historical Foundation
St. Charles Parish Government

Georg Michael Hahn
1830 - 1886
(Founder, Village of Hahnville)

- Born in Klingenmnunster, Bavaria, 1830
- Immigrated to United States as a child
- Grew up in the German community, New Orleans
- Admitted to the Bar in 1851 at age 21
- Bitter opponent of secession and slavery
- Member, New Orleans School Board at age 22
- Representative, U.S. Congress, 1862-63
- Established lifelong friendship with Abraham Lincoln
- Owned/Edited several newspapers in New Orleans
- Served as Governor of Louisiana 1864-1865
- Elected to U.S. Senate in 1865
- Moved to St. Charles Parish in 1872
- Began publication of St. Charles Herald, 1872
- Speaker, LA House of Representatives, 1872-76
- State Registrar of Voters, 1876
- **Founded the Village of Hahnville, 1877**
- Superintendent, U.S. Mint, New Orleans, 1878-79
- Served as Federal District Judge, 1879-85
- Elected again to U.S. Congress, 1884
- Died in Washington, D.C., 1886
- Died a pauper

Georg Michael Hahn
on the German Coast

Born in Bavaria, Germany, raised in the German community of New Orleans, Governor Hahn was probably most comfortable spending the last years of his life living among his German countrymen on the German Coast in St. Charles Parish. In 1872, Michael Hahn retired to his plantation in St. Charles Parish, established the Village of Hahnville and began publication of the St. Charles Herald. Hahn became a Public School Director, Police Juror, Representative to the Louisiana House of Representatives and a District Judge. "In his quiet country home, Hahn was looked up to with the confidence of a father. His advice was sought by all, and his decisions settled difficulties, smoothed asperities, and preserved order."*
Hahn's old home still stands today at 141 Elm Street, moved years ago from his property on River Road.

*Memorials in the U.S. House of Representatives in 1886 on the Life & Character of Georg Michael Hahn.

Georg Michael Hahn Exhibit, St. Charles Parish Courthouse in Hahnville, by St. Charles Historical Foundation.

HAHNVILLE. DAILY STAGE!

Notice to Travelers.

A Daily Stage leaves Hahnville every morning and evening, connecting with the New Orleans and Donaldsonville Railroad.
Leaves Hahnville from the Postoffice, next door to the St. Charles Herald office, at 9½ a. and 3 p. m., daily, and returns to the same point immediately after the arrival of the train.
Fare, only 50c per passenger, each way.

During this time the Hahnville Daily Stage continued to follow its schedule and made stops between railroad depots and towns away from railroad lines. (Photo courtesy of St. Charles Herald)

Home of Governor Michael Hahn, River Road, Hahnville, and later became the estate of Louis Albert Keller. (Photo courtesy of Emily Bourgeois)

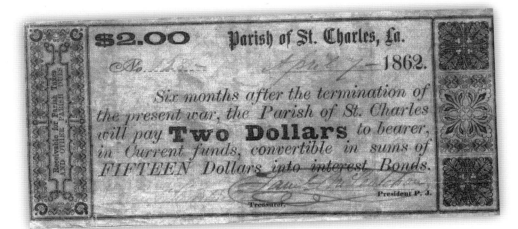

River was patrolled by Union ships, some of which fired shells over the levees. Reportedly, cannon shells hit Ormond Plantation. General Butler authorized Union troops to appropriate anything at will, which resulted in plantations and smaller farms being wantonly looted and destroyed. Some property owners fled, leaving everything behind. The state and local governments were unstable and often powerless to enforce the laws. Some slaves fled and joined the Union army, while some decided to remain in place; crops could not be sold, banks did not have money to lend, and merchants could not afford to give credit. All markets were cut off for the German Coast. Had General Richard Taylor's warning been heeded that New Orleans was vulnerable, the outcome might have been very different.

Three Major Skirmishes Took Place in St. Charles Parish

HAHNVILLE COURTHOUSE: On August 29, 1862, Union troops marched from Boutte to the courthouse to camp for the night. The next day they encountered troops delivering cattle to feed Confederate soldiers. A battle ensued and the Union forces prevailed.

BOUTTE STATION: A Union train with sixty men was ambushed by Confederate forces of Louisiana militia and volunteers on September 4, 1862. The train escaped to New Orleans after twenty-two Union soldiers were wounded and fourteen killed.

DES ALLEMANDS: Numerous skirmishes occurred at this location. The final outcome resulted in the capture of an entire detachment of Union soldiers led by General Richard Taylor on September 4, 1862.

The German Coast was to remain under federal occupation until 1877.

Lionel Joseph Cambre (son of Olidé Thomassin and Marie Perilloux Cambre). (Photo courtesy of Ronald Cambre)

The LaBranche Dependency House. From all accounts LaBranche Plantation in St. Rose was one of the grandest on the German Coast. Along with Fashion Plantation, it was destroyed during the Civil War. All that remained was the Dependency House, also called a garconniere (French for bachelor quarters). Olidé and Marie Perilloux Cambre purchased the Dependency House and property in 1902. Pictured here in 1910 from right to left are Olidé Thomassin Cambre (father) (1872–1923), Marie Perilloux Cambre (mother), Lionel (son), Thomas Olidé (son), Marie Cambre Williams (daughter), Bernadette Millet (niece), Elvetia Cambre Gilbert (daughter), and Gretta Cambre Jacob (daughter). The Lentini family of Kenner purchased and restored the property in 1983. The Dependency House is significant because of its exceptional Federal woodwork and rarity as a dependency. It is listed on the National Registry of Historic Places. (Photo courtesy of Ronald Cambre)

The Emancipation Proclamation

On January l, 1863, President Lincoln issued the final Emancipation Proclamation, which freed all slaves in those areas of the Confederate States of America that had not yet returned to Union control. Due to early control by the North, thirteen parishes were exempt from the proclamation as they were considered to be "Union parishes." St. Charles was one of the thirteen. Congress then passed the Fourteenth Amendment to the United States Constitution, which helped to ensure the rights of freed slaves by granting citizenship, due process of law, and the right to vote. Louisiana refused to ratify this amendment. Congress passed the Reconstruction Act in 1867 and southern states were placed under military control. Louisiana was removed only when it agreed to ratify the amendment and had written a new constitution.

A former slave, Polidore came to Louisiana from Virginia during the Civil War and fought on the Union side. After the war he settled in the area and changed his name to John Smith. He married Margurite Thomas and had six children. He was listed in the 1880 census as a laborer. He is buried in the Kenner Cemetery located in the Bonnet Carré Spillway. His descendants operated the Smith's Grocery Store in Hahnville for over eighty years. (Photo courtesy of descendant Carolyn Smith Boyd)

Former slave George Essex served in the Union Army and as sheriff and president of the police jury of St. Charles Parish from 1872 to 1878. ❖ ❖ ❖

"The Heritage of Slavery – The slaves made enormously valuable contributions to the wealth of their owners, of the southern economy, and of the nation. They also made valuable contributions to the culture of the South. However, these contributions were made at enormous costs to the slaves… An important legacy of the slavery system of the American South was the addition of spirituals to the nation's musical culture. Spirituals were religious folk songs, usually based on stories from the Bible…The slaves sang spirituals not only in church but also while they worked. Spirituals kept alive the musical traditions the slaves had brought with them from Africa…After the Civil War the singing of spirituals spread throughout the nation. Today spirituals remain one of the most popular and best-known forms of music in this country…"—Lewis Paul Todd and Merle Curti, Triumph of the American Nation ❖ ❖ ❖

Reconstruction

The period from 1865 to 1877 has been called the "Reconstruction Period." This term implies that building and reconstructing should have taken place. However, little of that occurred or was even addressed by the federal government. In reality, it marked a period of non-violent military occupation. Slaves were freed, the economy was in chaos, and poverty was widespread. Many of the slaves chose to remain on the plantations, residing in the same living quarters working for the owners. Wages were paid in the form of tokens, which could be used only at the plantation store. Levees were in very poor condition and laborers were scarce to perform necessary reinforcements and repairs. Great numbers of "carpetbaggers" flocked to the plantations. In order to move forward, it was necessary to restore local government, reestablish the devastated local economy, and develop industries, which would provide basic necessities and define a place in society for the newly freed Negro. There was much to be done before Louisiana and the German Coast would be readmitted to the United States. The Louisiana legislators ratified the Fourteenth Amendment on July 9, 1868, and Louisiana was once again a part of the United States.

The former slave quarters of Destrehan Plantation became freed Negroes' homes after the Civil War.

Freedman's Bureau—Rost Home Colony

In March of 1865, Congress created the Federal Bureau of Refugees, Freedmen, and Abandoned Lands, most often referred to as Freedmen's Bureau, a quasi-military organization charged with aiding the newly freed slaves with financial, educational, social, and political matters, tasking them to help those freed to adjust to their new lives. In Louisiana, four "home colonies" were created as self-sustaining agricultural collectives that also provided schools, commercial stores, and a hospital. These colonies were planned to provide safe havens, training, and preparation for post-Civil War transition. One of these was established on the government-expropriated property of Judge Rost (Destrehan Plantation) who was married to Jean-Nöel Destrehan's daughter and was in exile in Europe. It became the Rost Home Colony, which was established by Order #29. It is a lasting tribute to the administration of the bureau and the freedman laborers that in 1866 they produced 31,500 pounds of ginned cotton, 10,500 additional pounds of unpicked cotton, and 350 acres of sugar cane that produced 420,000 pounds of sugar and 6,000 gallons of molasses.

Under the leadership of retired Assistant Commissioner Major General Absalom Baird, the Rost Home Colony on the German Coast was the most successful of the four Louisiana colonies. Although it existed for only two years, the meticulous colony records, the "Registers of Arrivals and Departures," have left genealogists with an invaluable resource and the potential for tracing family histories for the more than one thousand residents. As an example, the register reveals Fountain Johnson and his twenty-one family members who were former slaves from St. Charles Parish, arrived at Rost Home Colony on March 20, 1865. These valuable records are housed in the National Archives in Washington, D.C. Judge Rost returned from Europe and requested the return of his properties. Rost's other properties were returned, but it was determined the Rost Home Colony would continue to exist until the end of 1866 at which time the colony would end. Judge Rost received rental payments from the Freedmen's Bureau until that time. The last colonists left the Rost Plantation in early December 1866. Judge Rost continued to practice law until his death in 1868.

Judge Pierre Adolphe Rost, b. 1797 in France, d. 1868, married Louise Odile Destrehan. He was a plantation owner, state senator, Louisiana Supreme Court Justice, and Confederate ambassador to Spain. He is interred at St. Charles Cemetery. (Photo courtesy of Destrehan Plantation)

The Rost Plantation House in 1893 with Judge Emile Rost, son of Judge Pierre Rost, standing on the right and Mr. Destours on left. Photo taken by Mrs. George Don Luce in 1893. (Photo courtesy of Destrehan Plantation)

At the turn of the century, German Coast Italian farmers grew "truck" crops and took them to packing sheds. Shown is the Christina Packing Shed in Kenner with several St. Rose farmers and their wagons. Crops were shipped by rail across the entire country. In later years a packing facility was opened in St. Rose—the Vitrano Packing Shed. (St. Charles Herald Profile, August 15, 1991)

Italians are Invited to Come to Louisiana

The Breadbasket continues…

During the 1870s, many blacks left Louisiana for more desirable opportunities in the North, which caused a major labor shortage. The sugar producing parishes were particularly affected. Remaining laborers took advantage and threatened to strike for better wages. The planters organized to resolve this situation and a plan was formulated to enhance the labor pool and control the cost of labor.

During the mid-1880s, the Louisiana Sugar Planters Association distributed information throughout Sicily and southern Italy. It sent agents to encourage the Italians to immigrate and established an office in New Orleans, which would provide aid on arrival. The Louisiana Agriculture and Immigration Association also extended "An Invitation to Louisiana for Italian Tenant Farmers and Agriculturalists." It is reported that between 1870 and 1920 at least 300,000 Italians (primarily Sicilians) immigrated to the New Orleans area.

Many of the Italians settled on the German Coast and made a significant impact. Like the Germans who came before them, they were hard working and productive farmers and craftsmen. However, they were faced with profound prejudice and the realization that they were placed very low on the social ladder. Salvadore Portera, a typical Italian immigrant, arrived on the German Coast in 1880. He and his wife, Mary Grace Pizzuto, were from Sicily. They lived in Hahnville and were forced to live behind the levee, not being allowed to live "on the other side." The Italians introduced new fruit and vegetables and expanded the truck farming industry, which added a new dimension to the wholesale and retail trade. Packinghouses lined the railroad tracks to ship their produce across the country. Many Italians

These passports were issued to Italian immigrants. Note the physical description at left. (Courtesy of American Italian Museum and Library, New Orleans)

Pietro Vitrano became a bona fide citizen of the United States of America. (Courtesy of American Italian Museum and Library, New Orleans)

An 1891 advertisement to lure Italian laborers to Louisiana states, "All persons who work laborers in great numbers find the Italian immigrant a valuable acquisition because of his willingness and his peculiar adaptability to hard work." There were differing scales of pay. Whites received the highest, African Americans less, and the Italians were at the bottom of the scale. (Courtesy of American Italian Museum and Library, New Orleans)

Josephine and Samuel Bosco in Confirmation and First Communion attire. (Photo courtesy of Kathy Tamburello Woulfe)

The Bosco family, immigrants of Sicily, are shown left to right: Ester (mother), Guisseppi (son), Lena Nelli Bosco (wife), and two-year-old daughter Ester. The Bosco family lived on River Road in St. Rose and owned a large farm, a grocery store, an oyster house, and participated in the New Orleans French Market. Bosco descendants now own many successful businesses in the parish. (Photo courtesy of Kathy Tamburello Woulfe)

Using the skiff they named the Virgin Mary, *the Portera family sold produce up and down the Mississippi River. The family later entered into the retail business. (Photo courtesy of Cynthia Portera)*

were also proficient in masonry, carpentry, stonecutting, tailoring, and advanced horticulture. Italian immigrants formed social and benevolent organizations and carried on their beloved customs and traditions. The St. Joseph Altar Societies and other Italian organizations continue to nurture and hand down these traditions along the German Coast. Other familiar family names were Gilardi, Giangroso, Giardina, Palmisano, Giglio, Gendusa, Vitrano, Barraco, Pizzolato, Bosco, Migliorie, and Marino.

With the help of the Italian immigrants, farmers of the German Coast continued to be major food suppliers to the markets of New Orleans. The German Coast packinghouses shipped by rail vegetables and produce to major United States cities.

Thomas J. Sellers
Diamond Plantation

While he was still a young man working on the Mississippi River, Thomas Sellers met Samuel B. Clemens, who later became the famous writer Mark Twain. Sellers and Clemens shared a warm, long-lasting friendship. Sellers adopted the title "Colonel" from one of Twain's fictitious characters, Colonel Mulberry. Clemens was a frequent visitor at the Sellers plantation.

The Trépagnier Plantation, which later became Myrtleland, was built by Francois Trépagnier. Myrtleland Plantation was sold to Thomas Sellers in 1876 and the area (present-day Norco) became known as Sellers. The Bonnet Carré Crevasse of 1882 brought about the end of the flourishing plantation but the house remained intact. Sellers and neighboring upriver Roseland Plantations were consolidated to form Diamond Plantation, which was later sold to Leon Godchaux in 1897. (Sketch courtesy of William E. Riecke, Jr., 1973)

In 1862, Thomas J. Sellers (middle, back row) joined the Confederacy to serve with Ogden's Calvary Regiment and returned to the German Coast after the war. The Sellers family moved to New Orleans around 1882 and returned to the west bank of the German Coast to the Lone Star Plantation in 1889. The Davis Crevasse forced another move to Alice Plantation (named after his daughter) in Ama in 1893. "Colonel" Sellers died in 1915 and was buried in the family plot at St. Charles Borromeo Cemetery in Destrehan. (Photo courtesy of St. Charles Herald)

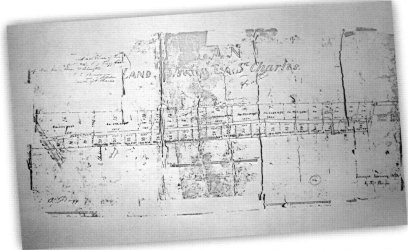

Settlement of Flaggville, drawn by Othello J. Flagg.

	Jesse	9	M	B	At school
"	Eliza	12	F	B	"
"	Lee	6	M	B	"
Fortier	Norbert	49	M	B	Laborer
"	Genevieve	40	F	B	Keeps house
"	Pierre	16	M	B	Laborer
"	Gabriel	11	M	B	At school
"	Felicity	1	F	B	
Pierre	Gilbert	52	M	B	Laborer
"	Frances	25	F	B	Keeps house
"	Marie	12	F	B	At school
"	Adeline	10	F	B	"
"	Francois	8	M	B	"
"	Baptiste	4	M	B	
"	Delphine	1	F	B	
Baptiste	Lizzie	55	F	B	Keeps house
Robertson	Darling	63	F	B	Keeps house
Flagg	O. J.	45	M	W	Parish judge
"	Mary	45	F	W	Keeps house

1870 St. Charles Parish Federal Census Extract. This census entry contradicts a long-standing belief regarding Flagg's race.

Flaggville and Hahnville

In 1870, Judicial District Judge Othello Jerome Flagg, a Union soldier formally affiliated with the Freedmen's Bureau, purchased five arpents of land adjacent to the area called the courthouse site. In 1872, Civil Engineer Thomas Sharpe surveyed and with Flagg developed the Village of Flaggville. The Flaggville Colored School, which continued until the end of the nineteenth century, was the last remnant of the town's name.

In 1872, former Louisiana Governor Georg Michael Hahn retired to his sugar plantation in St. Charles Parish and established the Village of Hahnville less than three miles upriver of the courthouse area. The village included a street layout and upgraded levee. Hahn built a concert hall, started a parish newspaper, and built stores of every variety. The Village of Hahnville soon became a bustling country town. The following are some of the businesses: Kraemer Furniture Manufacturing, Gordon's Saddle and Harness Maker, Peperkorn's Boat Building, Attorney-At-Law F. B. Earhart, Hunzleman's Grocery, Schneider's Cisterns, Fox the Village Blacksmith, Moffit Groceries and Dry Goods, Boot and Shoemaker Joseph Stein, Henry Aichel Tin Gutters, Manade Cigar Manufacturing, Jacob Banzhaf Hahnville Golden Star Store, Chapsky's "Red" Store, Almstedt Cabinet and Furniture Making, and Antz Creole Store.

Records in years thereafter indicate that Fortier Plantation (now Home Place), the courthouse area (the parish seat), the United States Post Office, and the Village of Flaggville were apparently "annexed" into the Village of Hahnville.

Perhaps the influential Governor Hahn, reportedly "in control of the Parish," was able to cement his name and legacy in Louisiana history by giving the parish seat his name.

Flaggville Historical Marker.

Plot map of Hahnville in 1877 showing some original street names. (Courtesy of Henry E. Yoes III)

Numa Zeringue's Mamzelle Store in Destrehan was built in 1875. Pictured are owners Numa and MiMi Zeringue in front seat, Numa Jr. in center, and sister in back. (Photo courtesy of Bryan Zeringue)

The employees of Mamzelle. Note the barrels and ice box at the back.

On the east bank, a unique new business was established in Destrehan. Numa Zeringue from Ama operated his original business from a little flatboat near the batture in front of the Red Church in Destrehan for three years beginning in 1872. Business continued from his boat until 1875 when he constructed and opened Mamzelle Store on the River Road a short distance west of Red Church. The store served the east bank as a popular shopping stop for over fifty years. Numa grew rice on his property from the River Road to the railroad tracks. Some of the rice was sold in his store and the rest was shipped downriver to be sold in New Orleans. Numa later was a warden/trustee of the Little Red Church congregation. His name is listed on the cornerstone of the church.

Spanish Influence on the Parish

Joaquin Crespo arrived in New Orleans from Spain via Ellis Island in 1872. He worked at odd jobs and saved his money. On his travels along the muddy River Road on the east bank he was taken with a parcel of land in the present day St. Rose area. Joaquin purchased the parcel and built his home, which became Crespo Plantation. He married Elmire Becnel and they had a son and daughter. Joaquin was unable to speak English well and consequently, his son Sidney assisted in ordering lumber from the Lutcher Moore Lumber Company. After Elmire's death, Joaquin married Malvina Songy and they had eight children. A devout Catholic, Joaquin constructed a chapel on his property and asked a priest from Kenner to conduct services. He donated a flock of sheep to the St. Charles Church (Little Red Church) to help control the growth of grass and weeds. Joaquin also donated land for the first St. Rose School for whites and the first colored school in Free Town (St. Rose). St. Charles Parish named the street alongside of the St. Rose School Crespo Avenue in honor of Joaquin Crespo. He overcame very modest beginnings to become a successful sugar cane planter on the Mississippi River.

Crespo Plantation once occupied the present site of IMTT on River Road in St. Rose. Owner Joaquin Joseph Crespo (hand on hip) is pictured with family and friends. (Photo courtesy of Billy and Sidney Crespo)

Joaquin Joseph Crespo, b. 1854—d.1916, and Malvina Songy Crespo, b. 1868—d.1914, are interred in the St. Charles Borromeo Cemetery. (Photos courtesy of Billy and Sidney Crespo)

International Matex Tank Terminals (IMTT) now owns the property where Crespo Plantation once stood. Two rows of pecan trees are still visible and considered by some family members to be those that once lined the road leading to the main house.

Other Spanish names in St. Charles Parish included Lopez, Acosta, Gonzales, Rodrigue, Truxillo, Morales, Medina, Cortez, Sanchez, Torres, and Perez. ⚜ ⚜ ⚜

FENCES: Every owner of a plantation or of land fronting on the public road shall be bound to have on the whole front thereof a well-conditioned and lawful fence, kept in good repair and shut up at all times of the year; and whenever gates are placed on such front, to keep such gates closed when not in use.

All neat cattle, horses, mules, asses and jennets shall be allowed to rove at large on the levees and batture of the parish during the low water season. When the height of the water renders such roaming dangerous or injurious to the levees, the Syndics shall give public notice for one week in the official journal that all cattle must be kept up until further notice.

Every peddler, hawker or trader, doing business or trading in this parish shall, on demand of any inhabitant or Parish Officer, produce his license, and on refusing to do so, through malice or otherwise, shall be considered as having none, arrested and brought before a Justice of the Peace for trial ...

Any person convicted of throwing any dead animal into the river shall be fined not less than ten nor more than fifty dollars for each offense. Excerpts from Policy Jury Regulations, Parish of St. Charles, 1876 ⚜ ⚜ ⚜

Joaquin Crespo, having "behaved as a man of good moral character, attached to the constitution of the United States, and well disposed to the good order and happiness of the same..." is sworn in as a citizen of the United States. The document was signed in 1896 by Crespo; Judge Rost, owner of Rost Plantation; and Clerk of Court John B. Martin. (Photo courtesy of Billy and Sidney Crespo)

The St. Charles-Herald *was published at the Triche House in Hahnville from 1888 to 1954. The addition to the right of the house was added to prepare and publish the newspaper.*

Rear elevation of the Triche House with members of the Triche family in the foreground. Note attached kitchen to left and wooden cistern to right.

Left to right top: Josepha Triche, Denise Triche, Philip, Middle: Josie, Beatrice Triche, Inez Vial, Sybille, J. C., Triche Sr., Bottom: Polymnia, Judith, Taft Triche, and Spot the dog. Missing - Clem Triche, Jr.

First Parish Newspaper

The first issue of the *St. Charles Herald* was dated February 15, 1873. It is understood that this newspaper was started and owned by ex-Governor Georg Michael Hahn. With a friend, Marsellus Vallas, Hahn opened an office on the corner of Hahn and Front streets in Hahnville. *The Herald* was considered Hahn's "mouthpiece" and was quick to include and defend his views during Reconstruction when he was constantly being criticized as a vocal Union activist. During the early years several people managed the newspaper and ownership changed several times after Hahn's death in 1886. *The Herald* was purchased in 1888 by J. C. Triche and Company from T. T. Boudouin for $75.00. Triche served as secretary of the St. Charles Police Jury, as deputy clerk of court, and was appointed clerk of registration for St. Charles Parish for Governor Nicholls in 1890. Triche's nephew, J. B. Martin, Jr., later ran *The Herald* for the family out of a small office in front of his home in Hahnville before he became superintendent of schools of St. Charles Parish. He was never officially listed as editor. J. C. Triche, Jr., then took over but soon enlisted in the armed forces when World War I began. W. A. Brady then assumed temporary editorship. J. C. Triche, Sr., died while the younger Triche was at war in Europe. Immediately upon his return he took over management of *The Herald*, also working for Shell Oil Company in Norco. When Triche, Jr., married, his sister Polly assumed the role of editing but retained her brother's name as official editor. When Polly married, sister Beatrice took over managing the paper. Lucien T. Triche, J. C. Triche, Sr.'s, other son, was listed as editor but was never active in that role. Beatrice kept *The Herald* alive for as long as possible. On August 19, 1954, sixty-five years after her father purchased *The Herald*, Beatrice Triche Troxler sold the newspaper to the Henry E. "Gene" Yoes, Jr., family. Gene's journalism studies had been interrupted when he left LSU to enlist in the armed forces for four years during World War II. When discharged in 1946, he reentered LSU and received his bachelor of arts degree in journalism. *The Herald* was run as a family business with Iola Yoes serving as office manager, H. E. Yoes III as associate editor, Cynthia Yoes as graphic designer, and the remaining six Yoes children serving in one capacity or another. Thirty-five years later son, Patrick, and his wife Gail purchased the newspaper. It continued in operation until 1993 when a merger with the Louisiana Publishing Company's *St. Charles Guide*, owned by the Lottinger family of Luling, took place to become the *St. Charles Herald-Guide*. Louisiana Publishing Company bought out the Yoes's portion of the publication in 2006. The *St. Charles Herald-Guide* serves as the official journal of St. Charles Parish.

ST. CHARLES HERALD.

A Local and Family Newspaper, Published Weekly at Three Dollars per Annum.

OFFICIAL JOURNAL OF THE PARISH OF ST. CHARLES. 1877.

LOCAL NEWS.

This is the time of year for croquet and love making.

Crops in good condition, though a little rain would benefit them.

The bridges across our public roads are sadly in need of repairing.

There are to be ten public schools opened during the next school term.

Beautiful nights; moonlight drives and sweet, soft nonsense in order.

Capt. Ranson will bring out a new boat in the coast trade, next week.

"The grove of willow trees on the batture at the Home place has been chopped down."

The cane on Mr. Emile Rost's "Destrahan" plantation is reported to be in excellent condition.

The Ashton plantation recently purchased by Mr. Charles Howard, of New Orleans, is undergoing a repairing.

A baker's dozen of rice hands left our village on Monday to work in St. John. They are paid better prices there, so they say.

It is a sorrowful thing to see our Courthouse officials lazily drooping around in spots, waiting for some individual to plank down a fee.

We have on hand and ready for delivery, in quantities to suit, a blank form to be used by Syndics in notifying landed proprietors to repair their roads and bridges.

J. STEIN,
PRACTICAL BOOT
—AND—
SHOE MAKER,

Informs his friends and the public generally that he is now ready, at his shop, No. 3 Morgan Avenue, Hahnville, to receive orders for BOOTS and SHOES of every description and style, such as Fancy Dress, Riding and Mud Boots.

Gaiters, Malakoffs, Oxford Ties Low-Quarters, Balmorals, Brogans, Spring Shoes, Prince Alberts; etc Ladies' and Children's Shoes a specialty

OFFICIAL DIRECTORY.

STATE GOVERNMENT.
Governor—F. T. Nicholls.
Lieutenant Governor—L. A. Wiltz.
Secretary of State—W. A. Strong.
Auditor of Public Accounts—Allen Jumel.
Superintendent of Public Education—P. M. Lusher.
Adjutant General—D. B. Penn.
JUDICIARY.
Supreme Court—T. C. Manning, Chief Justice; R. H. Marr, Alcibiade DeBlanc, W. B. Egan, W. B. Spencer, Associate Justices. Alfred Roman, Clerk.
SIXTH SENATORIAL DISTRICT.
Comprising the parishes of St. John the Baptist, St. Charles, Jefferson, and sixth district parish of Orleans.
State Senators—Henry Demas,
—T. B. Stamps.
FOURTH JUDICIAL DISTRICT.
Comprising the parishes of St. Charles, St. St. John the Baptist, St. James and Ascension.
District Judge—Morris Marks.
District Attorney—F. B. Earhart.
PARISH GOVERNMENT.
Representative—Michael Hahn.
Parish Judge—Peter Harper.
Sheriff—George Essex.
Deputy Sheriff—J. L. Martin.
Parish Attorney—Noel St. Martin.
Clerk of Court—J. B. Martin.
Parish Assessor—Theodule T. Baudouin.
Recorder—Lewis Ory.
Tax Collector—B. S. Labranche.
Deputy Tax Collector— Thibaut.
Parish Treasurer—Arthur Robbins.
Coroner—Clement Colly.
Official Journal—St. Charles Herald.
Police Jury—J. L. Boutte, President; A. D. Bougere, P. M. Kenner, Emile Rost, N. Longue, R. Troxler, Coy Clinton, M. Bennett, George Scott. H. C. McCutcheon. C. A. Bourgeois, Secretary.
School Board—Emile Rost, President; Leon Sarpy, P. M. Kenner, A. D. Bougere. H. L. Youngs, T. T. Baudouin, P. Darensbourg, H. C. McCutcheon; Geo. Essex. T. T. Baudouin, Secretary; , Treasurer.

CREOLE STORE,
HAHNVILLE,
St. Charles Parish, Louisiana.

THE UNDERSIGNED has just opened a magnificent store, the largest and most eligible in the parish; and intends to keep a splendid stock of goods and sell at low prices —not excelled by any New Orleans House. He invites the custom of planters, farmers and laborers of this and St. John parish and promises to give entire satisfaction in all his dealings.
GEO. J. ANTZ.

FOR SALE. SPLENDID CHANCE
For a Carriage Maker at
Hahnville, St. Charles Parish La.

A lot of ground, measuring 200 feet in depth and fifty feet front, with good dwelling house and shop thereon, and a good run of custom, will be sold cheap on easy terms. The present owner's reason for selling is on account of departure. Address M. P.. Carriage Shop.

ST. CHARLES HERALD,

Independent of Politicians, Rings or Cliques!

Devoted to the material development of the State of Louisiana, and the spreading of light and toleration among her people, it stands in the front ranks for

REFORM!

It makes war on all monopolies and corruption, and untrammeled by fear or favor; does not hesitate to mention names on all proper occasions, and yet it always assumes high ground, and is conducted with the dignity and

INDEPENDENCE

which command confidence and respect. Its articles are distinguished by decency of language, candor of statement and moderation in debate. It eschews the coarse invective and vulgar insolence which have so often marred the political controversies of the past; it avoids slanders and personal quarrels; it is

A Paper for Gentlemen and Ladies,

fit for the parlor, the study and the home fireside, rather than the bar-room. Not only the common events of the day, but the tendencies of popular thought and the currents of political, social, intellectual and religious discussion are faithfully reproduced in its columns.

The success, the trials and the wants of the productive classes are studied with particular care. The progress of invention and of labor saving contrivances, the development and utilization of our vast material resources, the extension of facilities for bringing producer and consumer together, receive from this paper the fullest attention and encouragement.

THE ST. CHARLES HERALD

Is published in a parish noted for its large SUGAR, RICE, ORANGE and PECAN Crops, and for the Education, Refinement and Liberality of its Citizens. It is the Official Journal and ONLY PAPER IN THE PARISH. It already has a LARGE CIRCULATION, is read by every class of people, and is powerful in creating a healthy and tolerant public sentiment. The HERALD is issued every Saturday morning, at HAHNVILLE, St. Charles parish, La., by

H. VALLAS,
Editor and Publisher,
at only THREE DOLLARS per annum.

Chas. Hubschman, M D,
Resident Physician and Surgeon,
Hahnville, Louisiana.

Always keeps a sufficient assortment of good, fresh medicines with which to put up his own prescriptions

Pottery to Rent.

THE HAHNVILLE POTTERY, supplied with all the appliances of a first-class Louisiana pottery, is for rent. To a good, industrious, sober man, having a family, and understanding the pottery business, extra inducements will be offered. The native clay, found at Hahnville, will make well the usual articles in the red ware line, such as flower pots, pitchers, bowls, jars, jugs, etc. Apply to
EDITOR ST. CHARLES HERALD.

Full page graphic of old St. Charles Herald *press clips.*

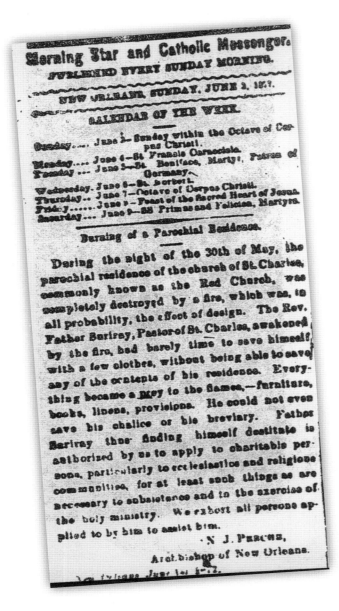

Red Church Rectory Fire

Press release of the Morning Star and Catholic Messenger, *June 1877 regarding the Little Red Church Rectory Fire:*

"In 1877, an arsonist set fire to the Presbytery (rectory) of the Little Red Church. It burned to the ground and 150 years of church records were destroyed. The original register from 1739 to 1755 is the only book that survived the fire. Churchwardens continued to collect revenues from farm acreage and to manage the property. Over 40 years would pass before a new rectory would be built. After the fire, the Red Church pastor resided on the west bank in Taft and continued to serve his parishioners from that location." Clippings presented are from the Morning Star and Catholic Messenger.

In 1880, former slaves demanding better wages launched the first labor strike in Louisiana. After the strike was over, an interesting article appeared in the March 27, 1880, issue of the St. Charles Herald which read, "One of the most pleasing incidents of the late strike troubles was the presentation by the ladies of our modest town of Hahnville to Col. LeGardeur, Major William A. Strong and Major Bourg, of the Louisiana Field Artillery, while on duty here, of magnificent bouquets, gathered by their own fair hands. This signified peace, plenty and the spanning of the firmament with the rainbow of Flora ..."

Front Elevation. Father Paret enjoyed gardening and breeding of animals. He wrote to his brother, "I would like for you to see this big garden and how pleasant and inviting it is. Without false modesty, I think the inhabitants of St. Charles will be jealous of it." At that time Fr. Paret had planted 488 trees consisting of orange, pomegranate, persimmon, peach, plum, mulberry, crepe myrtle, and magnolia along with althea and rose bushes. (Photo courtesy of LSU Press)

Red Church Presbytery rear elevation. Father J. M. Paret lived in this presbytery from December of 1848 until October 1869, which spanned the golden age of the antebellum years to the era of Reconstruction. This included the Civil War and its profound social changes. The levee was raised only five to seven feet during this time. Wood was gathered from the Mississippi River twice a year during December and March, which the residents considered a Godsend. (Photo courtesy of LSU Press)

The Bethlehem Benevolent Society

The Bethlehem Benevolent Society was incorporated in 1881. It was an example of one of the many benevolent societies for St. Charles Parish Negroes. These fraternal organizations provided medicine, paid doctor bills, purchased food and apparel for those in need, and helped to bury their dead. Each society purchased enough property to accommodate a hall and a cemetery. The property for the Bethlehem Society was purchased in 1900 from O. J. Flagg in Hahnville (formerly Flaggville).

Other groups were St. Mary Society of Luling, the Swampers of Boutte, and the Elizabeth Tabernacle Society of St. Rose. The halls were used for schools, meetings, church gatherings, suppers, weddings, and receptions.

In 1996, the Bethlehem Benevolent Society Hall is shown on its journey to the West Bank Bridge Park on River Road in Luling to be used as the St. Charles Parish Tourist Information Center. (Photo courtesy of St. Charles Department of Economic Development and Tourism)

Conveyance Records, St. Charles Parish.

In a September 1883 edition of the St. Charles Herald, *an article read, "On Tuesday last, while in the city, Manager Huck, of the Telephone Co., informed us that he would, if possible, have a switch-board located in Hahnville, next week, at the Herald Office, in order to enable our merchants and the community to speak with friends above or below us. The charge will be for five minutes or less between here and New Orleans, twenty-five cents." This notice appeared frequently in the* St. Charles Herald *during the late 1800s.*

Bethlehem Benevolent Society Hall now serves as the St. Charles Parish Tourist Information Center. (Photo courtesy of St. Charles Department of Economic Development and Tourism)

Mail Service

Mail service along the German Coast was improving. Special delivery service to villages began in 1885 and rural delivery in the 1890s. Louisiana was a bit ahead of other states in that it was one of the very first to have free rural delivery mail routes. Imagine how excited German Coast residents were when they saw the mailman coming.

Major Crevasses Continue to Plague the German Coast

By the turn of the nineteenth century, crude levees were in place along the Mississippi River and provided a measure of protection. Individual landowners were responsible for construction and maintenance of the levee system. By the 1830s, states began to be involved with flood control by receiving direct funding and creating levee boards. The boards were then responsible for levee construction and maintenance funded by taxes paid by landowners. However, in spite of all efforts,

Reportedly, this is the last hanging in St. Charles Parish. Generally traced to Charles Lynch, an eighteenth-century Virginia farmer who appointed himself a hanging judge in the revolutionary interest, lynching was a prescribed method of punishing criminals for various crimes until the Lynch Law was repealed. At that time in history, lynching and other forms of punishment were social pastimes.

Levees became major public projects in the late 1800s.

Recorded German Coast Crevasses

Bonnet Caree (St. John - Eastbank)	Anchor (Montz - Eastbank)	Davis (Westbank - Luling)
1849	1892	1884
1857		
1867		
1871		
1874		
1882		

Louisa (Luling - Westbank)	Lone Star (Luling - Westbank)	Prospect (Goodhope - Eastbank)
1871	1889 or 1890	1892

Sarpy (Eastbank)	LaBranche (Westbank)	Fortier (Westbank)
1892	1858	1849

there was still major flooding, primarily from crevasses. These floods and Civil War devastation caused the levee system to be perilously endangered by the 1870s. Appeals to the federal government intensified. Congress established the Mississippi River Commission in 1879. Federal involvement improved matters but floods and crevasses continued to occur.

The Davis Plantation was the site of the 1884 west bank crevasse in Luling. The plantation was first settled during the Spanish Colonial period. The Davis Crevasse began at 1:00 a.m. on March 8. A rice-flume cut in the old levee was not refilled properly and loose dirt began to wash away. It quickly grew to one thousand feet in width. The residential Davis Drive area and the Davis Fresh Water Diversion now occupy part of this site. ⚜ ⚜ ⚜

"The crevasses at Davis and Fashion have caused our back country to be submerged to a considerable extent. Surely the railroad companies will not allow these crevasses to remain open."—St. Charles Herald, *March 1884* ⚜ ⚜ ⚜

"Because of Louisiana's beginnings as a French agrarian colony, it is unique within the Southern experience. It was in South Louisiana that Creole, Anglo, and African traditions blended to create a distinctive New World culture. The River Road is not merely a random slice of the antebellum South, but a rare subculture embedded within it."—"Louisiana Cultural Vistas," Richard Sexton, River Road ⚜ ⚜ ⚜

German Coast Dwellings

There was a broad spectrum of architectural styles ranging from the crude and rustic cabins of early settlers, farmers, and slaves, to business people and the mansions of wealthy planters. Some plantation owners held large tracts of land but lived in simple houses. Some built with whatever could be scraped together. Others chose to build on a grand scale. The French Colonial cottage and West Indies influence remained the favorite of the Creoles.

"Driftwood is running freely in the Mississippi River owing to the recent rise. Now is the time to secure your firewood."—St. Charles Herald, *January 1884* ⚜ ⚜ ⚜

Most Louisiana towns still depended on ice supplies from New Orleans during the 1880s. The ice was placed in barrels packed with sawdust. By the 1890s, ice factories began appearing. ⚜ ⚜ ⚜

Creole houses once spanned the River Roads on the east and west banks of St. Charles Parish. Local artist Janis Blair illustrates the graceful architecture of that period.

The Luke Troxler family house in Hahnville, circa 1870, is one of the very few French Colonial cottages still in existence in the parish. It has bousillage in the walls, square nails, a hip-gabled roof with tin covering, clapboarding on the exterior walls, a triple front door with a central hall, transoms and sidelights, decorative porch posts, a rear screened-in porch, and French doors with shutters on several of the front doors. The interior chimney and real lean-to addition have been removed.

Pictured is the home of Dr. Victor Lehman, who served as coroner from 1890 to 1920, one of the longest tenures in parish history. The French and Spanish Creole houses changed very little from the colonial period. The "Acadian Cottage," as popularly known, had a steep roof which enclosed a front gallery (porch) and attic bedrooms. The stairway leading to the upstairs bedrooms was on the outside at one end of the gallery. Many of the yards were enclosed by picket fences. (Photo courtesy of the St. Charles Herald)

Originally built as slave cabins, these dwellings became housing for freed slaves, Italians, and other immigrants after the Civil War.

Alice Plantation in Ama was purchased in 1893 by Thomas J. "Colonel Mulberry" Sellers and named for his daughter, Alice Augusta Sellers. Alice Plantation had a massive front gallery, sixty feet in length with roll-down canvas shades to create an additional room in inclement weather. With forethought, and past experiences with plantation disasters, Sellers and his sons built Sellers Canal as a shortcut through the marsh to Grand Isle. The canal was particularly useful when the Hymelia Crevasse struck in 1912. Sellers and his family rode to safety via the canal. Alice Plantation was relocated once to avoid the encroaching river, but in 1938 a mysterious fire razed the old place. St. Charles Airport now occupies the Alice Plantation site. Many family members served in office in such positions as superintendent of public schools, assessor, and sheriff. The "Colonel" died at Alice Plantation in 1915 and is buried in the Red Church Cemetery in Destrehan. (Photo courtesy of the St. Charles Herald)

"Rosedon" (the Dorvin House), circa 1820s, is a beautiful Creole house, rescued, restored, and named "Rosedon" by Don and Darlene (nee Mollere) Ellis and the Mollere family. The restoration began in 1979. The house is constructed of cypress with briquette entre poteaux (brick between posts). Located in Taft, the one-and one-half story residence built by Antoine Dorvin exemplifies the late transition to Anglo-American architecture on the German Coast. It retains many Creole elements while including more of an English floor plan (wide central hallway), Greek revival motifs, and a symmetrical facade. This house is also one of only three remaining Creole structures which exemplify the emerging American influence during the fast evolving 1840s and is listed on the National Register of Historic Places. (Photo courtesy of Don and Darlene Ellis)

Parish officials, circa 1890, are standing in front of old courthouse. Back row, left to right: Anthony Madere, a later sheriff; Mr. Bestoso, court crier; Mr. Terregrossa, a deputy sheriff, and Frank Friloux. Mr. Charles Elfer, assessor, stands in the middle. Lower row, left to right stand: Judge Gauthier; Hicks Lewis Youngs, police juror; Sheriff Lewis Ory, who was later murdered; William Lussan, who later served as president of the police jury and its treasurer for twenty-eight years; and J. C. Triche, Sr., clerk of court, whose family owned the the St. Charles Herald *for over sixty years.*

Public School System in St. Charles Parish

The LeMoyne brothers, Iberville and Bienville, were timeless advocates of schools to educate the colonial children. "He [Bienville] proposed the establishment of a school in New Orleans where the boys could be taught geometry, geography, and other subjects. He wrote, 'young men brought up in luxury and idleness are of little use.'" (E. Davis, *Louisiana: The Pelican State*) During the colonial period and before the establishment of public education, schooling was predominantly carried out in church buildings. Some students were sent abroad to be educated, some had private tutors, and others went to private schools in New Orleans. Classes were also held in other buildings and residences. The area being primarily agricultural, many children were needed to help their parents plant, maintain, and harvest crops and were unable to attend school. After the Territory of Orleans was established, the first higher education system put in place was the College of Orleans created by a legislative act in 1805. According to Josepha Breaux, the college was a pattern for other schools and the first institution of higher education under state control in this country *(Louisiana Historical Quarterly*, Vol VII, 1913–1914). Its regents were given authority to establish academies in each county, with appropriations from the state treasury. In 1819, a law was passed which superseded all previous legislation regarding public schools and required administrators of county schools to answer to the police juries of the parishes in which they were located. This was done to coordinate schools into one parish system.

To coordinate public education throughout the state, the secretary of state was made superintendent in 1833. All school administrators were then required to report to him. The period of public education began with the Constitution of 1845, which created the office of state superintendent. Alexander Dimitry, who has been called the "Father of Louisiana Elementary Education," held this office from 1847 to 1851, during which he organized and put into operation a statewide public school system. The office of superintendent of public schools was abolished in 1852 and the president of the police jury was given the authority to fill vacancies in any school's board of directors. The first superintendent of the German Coast was J. M. Dieudonne who began his term in 1852.

The Constitution of 1868 decreed that there be at least one free public school in each parish for children from ages six to twenty-one "without distinction of race, color, or previous condition." Schoolhouses in rural areas were very rustic and were built of logs. Holes were left to serve as windows. The students walked on earthen floors and "desks" and seats were constructed of split logs with wooden peg legs. One half of the proceeds from poll tax collections were used to support the schools. However, each school was expected to raise its own funds for textbooks. A state board of education was established to oversee all public schools and the state was divided into six school districts. Boards of school directors for each parish were appointed in 1871 with terms of two years, superceding ward boards and boards of cities and towns having a population of less than one thousand. The scope of authority and duties of parish boards relative to improvement and extension of schools was defined. The town and city boards, which were determined unnecessary, were abolished. During Reconstruction, many blacks served on school boards. The first St. Charles Parish School Board included blacks and whites.

In 1877, a parish school board, appointed for a four-year term, was constituted a body corporate with the power to make contracts, including written contracts with teachers.

The 1879 Constitution provided parish school boards the power to appoint parish superintendents, who were to be ex-officio secretaries of the boards. All proceeds of poll tax collections were dedicated to support parish schools in which collected, but none of the raised funds could be used to support any private or sectarian school.

In 1879, the St. Charles Parish Public School System was established and placed under the jurisdiction of the police jury. At the first recorded school board meeting were President Emile Rost, P. M. Kenner, Leon Sarpy, W. C. Certerian, H. L. Youngs, George Essex, Pierre Darensbourg, and Theodule Telesphore Baudouin, who served as the board secretary and superintendent. A. Robens served as parish

School Board Proceedings, October 11, 1879.

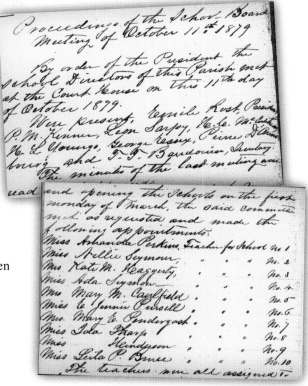

Teacher Appointments, April 3, 1880.

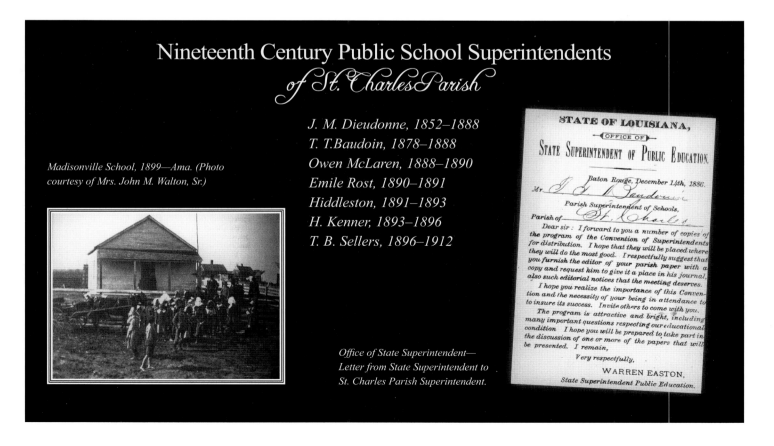

Nineteenth Century Public School Superintendents
of St. Charles Parish

Madisonville School, 1899—Ama. (Photo courtesy of Mrs. John M. Walton, Sr.)

J. M. Dieudonne, 1852–1888
T. T. Baudoin, 1878–1888
Owen McLaren, 1888–1890
Emile Rost, 1890–1891
Hiddleston, 1891–1893
H. Kenner, 1893–1896
T. B. Sellers, 1896–1912

Office of State Superintendent—Letter from State Superintendent to St. Charles Parish Superintendent.

STATE OF LOUISIANA,
OFFICE OF
STATE SUPERINTENDENT OF PUBLIC EDUCATION.

Baton Rouge, December 14th, 1886.

Mr. _T. T. Baudouin_
Parish Superintendent of Schools.
Parish of _St. Charles_

Dear sir: I forward to you a number of copies of the program of the Convention of Superintendents for distribution. I hope that they will be placed where they will do the most good. I respectfully suggest that you furnish the editor of your parish paper with a copy and request him to give it a place in his journal, also such editorial notices that the meeting deserves.

I hope you realize the importance of this Convention and the necessity of your being in attendance to to insure its success. Invite others to come with you.

The program is attractive and bright, including many important questions respecting our educational condition. I hope you will be prepared to take part in the discussion of one or more of the papers that will be presented. I remain,

Very respectfully,

WARREN EASTON,
State Superintendent Public Education.

THE SCHOOL FUND.

The State's Apportionments.

The following letter explains itself:

STATE OF LOUISIANA,
Treasurer's Office,
Baton Rouge, Nov. 17, 1884.

Hon. Warren Easton, State Superintendent of Education:

Sir—I have the honor to submit to you a statement of the condition of the current school fund of 1883, and the amount in the treasury subject to apportionment up to Nov. 1, 1884:

Amount collected to Dec. 31, 1883..	$20,938 24	
Amount collected to Oct. 31, 1884...	136,976 34	
		$157,914 58

Unexpended or surplus balances to the credit of the current school funds of 1880-81-82, transferred to the current school fund of 1883, to wit:

From the current school fund of 1880............	$5,386 83	
From the current school fund of 1881...........	2,254 50	
From the current school fund of 1882............	7,405 82—	15,047 15
		$172,961 73

Less amount reserved for various other appropriations, act 63 of '82, detailed statement previously reported...	$87,049 51	
Feb. 9, 1884, apportionment No. 1, made by Hon. E. H. Fay, late Superintendent......	21,752 56	
June 5, 1884, apportionment No. 2, made by Hon. Warren Easton, Superintendent.......	42,025 08—	150,857 15
Leaving a balance in treasury subject to apportionment to No. 1, 1884......................		$22,104 58

I am, respectfully, yours,
E. A. BURKE, State Treasurer.
Per JAMES CAMPBELL.

Under this notification the following apportionment has been made of the balance of $22,104 58:

ENUMERATION OF YOUTHS AND SCHEDULE OF APPORTIONMENT, 1884.

Number

School Board Proceedings.

AUGUST 18, 1877.

The members of the Board of School Directors in and for the parish of St. Charles, pursuant to previous adjournment, met this day at the Courthouse.

Present—Messrs. Kenner, Davisbourg, McCutcheon, Essex and Baudouin. Absent—Messrs. Rost, Sarpy, Youngs and Bougere.

On motion of Mr. McCutcheon, Mr. Kenner was appointed President pro tem., and the minutes of the previous meeting were then read and approved.

The reports of the committee on school houses were read, and after due deliberation, it was resolved that the public schools of this parish shall be opened on the first Monday of September next at the following named places, to-wit:

First Ward—In the school house located on the property of Pete Campbell and others.

Second Ward—In the Hahnville School House, Hahnville Concert Hall, and in the Bethlehem Church just below the Courthouse.

Third Ward—In the school house located on the property of Au Zeringue.

Fourth Ward—In the school house located on the Louis Labranche plantation.

Fifth Ward—In the school house located on the Red Church property.

Sixth Ward—In the house formerly rented from Mrs. Mary Duncan on the Hermitage plantation.

Seventh Ward—In a church and the house known as the Scott's Store at Boutte Station.

Being ten _____ of which viz: _____ of schools two or _____ in the Hahnville Concert Hall

School Board Proceedings, August 18, 1877, St. Charles Herald.

---

treasurer. In the beginning, ten schools were located throughout the parish and were identified by number. The "schools" were churches, private homes, and other buildings. Enrollment in 1882 was recorded as 393 black students out of a potential of 1,595 and 113 white children out of a parish population of 356. It is assumed that other children were educated in their homes by tutors or parents. There were ten teachers and each received four hundred dollars per year. White schools were at Gassenville (Luling) and Hahnville. Schools for black children were at Boutte Station, Bethlehem Baptist Church in Hahnville, and other black churches and benevolent societies throughout the parish. The initial school program went only to fourth grade. Children living over two miles from schools were provided transportation. In 1884, nine out of ten existing schools opened. Two schools had to close that year due to the Davis Crevasse. In 1888, the General School Act decreed that having police juries assess no less than one and one-half mil on owned land in respective parishes would fund public schools. In 1891 there were seventeen public and four private schools on the German Coast. In 1896 seventeen schools were in existence with ten attended by white students and seven by blacks. Using private buildings was still popular, and only six school buildings were owned by the parish. In 1895, T. B. Sellers, son of Colonel Sellers, was made superintendent.

The 1898 Constitution and all those following provided free but separate public schools for white and colored children. In 1898, parish school boards were again created to elect parish superintendents. After 1898, the tax assessor made an enumeration of educable children every four years.

(Extracted from the WPA Project Inventory of Parish Archives of Louisiana, #45 Saint Charles Parish (Hahnville), November 1937.)

"The St. Charles Parish school board members would continue to be appointed by the police jury into the twentieth century. The first elected parish school board members began their terms January 4, 1912."—From the diary of J. B. Martin, School Superintendent ❖ ❖ ❖

List of Parish Ferry Landings Linking East and West Banks

Foot ferries were also a popular mode of travel on the river and bayous. In 1887 parish officials decided the ferry system landing fees should be studied. In the past, travelers were at the mercy of having to pay fair and "not so fair" fees to whomever provided landings. Competition at other landings was irrelevant as traveling up or down the River Road to get to the next landing was, at times, very difficult. After several years of allowing ferry service without parish jurisdiction, it was determined that ferry privileges throughout the parish would be implemented with parish oversight.

The Nineteenth Century Draws to a Close

Throughout this period the home was the center and focus of life. A young man wishing "to call" on a young lady would send a friend to ask permission of her father. Couples were chaperoned and rarely left alone.

When a person died, it was customary for all the clocks in the house to be stopped, mirrors were covered, and black crepe hung on the front door. Black coffins were used for the elderly, gray or lavender preferred for the middle-aged, and the children were laid to rest in white. All wore black mourning clothes. As there were no funeral parlors at that time, the deceased were mourned and buried from their homes.

Superstitious cures such as aching joints being treated with ointments made of mashed lightning bugs, babies being given mud-dauber-nest tea to promote good health, and sassafras tea sipped in the spring to thin blood which had become thick over the winter were still being used. It was thought that having a haircut on Fridays would certainly cause an illness and that a person should burn onion peelings or carry a snip of verbena to prevent losing money.

Those in the city gave balls. The settlers in the country gave dances. Negro dances mostly continued as during slavery when some plantations had dance halls. Home and community singing was very popular. Song festivals were held. Some of the early Creole, work, and riverfront songs, and Negro spirituals became interwoven and a part of the German Coast heritage.

Throughout the nineteenth century, the German Coast residents resisted change in order to preserve and protect their beloved culture and way of life. The floodgates opened after the Louisiana Purchase and Americans poured into the lower Mississippi Valley resulting in the beginning of a major assimilation of many diverse cultures. The German Coast struggled through establishing statehood, the War of 1812, the Civil War, and Reconstruction, continuing to hold fast to its traditions. The great "assimilation" resulted in a unique heritage as the different cultures blended into a rich melting pot. Italian farmers of the German Coast joined German farmers in bringing their surplus food to New Orleans markets continuing to feed the region. The exclusive influence of the Catholic Church was diluted as other denominations emerged. Most were not prepared for the major change and prosperity which would follow in the twentieth century. Some historians have called this period, "Old Louisiana."

LIST OF PARISH FERRY LANDINGS

St. Charles Herald
October 13, 1883

First - From estate of C. Bourgeois to Widow Trepagnier's Place.

Second - Start Store to Mary Duncan's Store.

Third - Hahnville to Leon Sarpy's Plantation.

Fourth - Fashion Store to Deynoodt Plantation.

Fifth - J.B. Gassen's Store to Rost's Lower Plantation.

Sixth - Peter Harper's Place to Grim's School House.

Seventh - Brousgnet & Apleunute Plantation to H. Frellsen's Plantation.

There were seven German Coast ferry landings in 1883 as this October 13 St. Charles Herald indicates. Similar notices appeared frequently in The Herald. *The Mississippi River remained a major corridor for travelers during the eighteenth century. During the nineteenth century, the dirt roadways were still, at times, impassable due to rainstorms and crevasses, and the river remained a primary "highway."*

Taft to Norco foot ferry. (Photo courtesy of Bryan Zeringue)

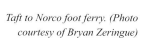

Bayou Des Allemands foot ferry. (Photo courtesy of Pat Yoes)

Twentieth Century

1901—Oil is discovered in Louisiana.

1904—St. Rose Plantation, located near St. Rose Avenue, is demolished.

1911—George Cousin's Lumber Camp is established behind Lakewood West Subdivision.

1912—The Hymelia Crevasse begins on May 14 at 6:30 p.m. near the St. Charles/St. John parish line.

1912—On November 11, a massive train wreck occurs in Montz.

1914—World War I begins.

1914—Destrehan Plantation property is sold to Mexican Petroleum Company for the establishment of an oil refinery.

1915—The "Great West Indian Hurricane" ravages south Louisiana on September 28.

1916—The New Orleans Refining Company acquires Good Hope Plantation property to establish a marine petroleum supply terminal.

1917—First Flood Control Act enacted as a result of Bonnet Carré, Hymelia, and other crevasses.

1917—Congress declares war against Germany.

1917—After twenty-seven years of interdiction, St. Charles Borromeo Church Parish is reinstated to the diocese.

1918—After forty-one years of closure due to fire and interdiction, Red Church is assigned Father John Basty as pastor.

1918—Louisiana Legislative Act 114 bans use of the German language in churches, schools, and newspapers.

1918—Cousin's Lumber Camp closes.

1919—Carson Petroleum begins operating on the site of old Cedar Grove Plantation, St. Rose.

1921—Present-day St. Charles Borromeo Church is built; old Red Church is torn down in the later twenties.

1921—The courthouse is renovated and expanded.

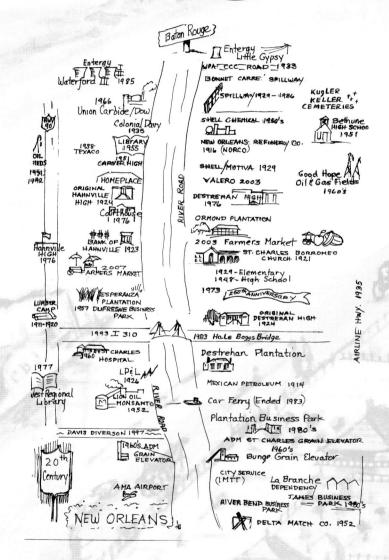

(Sketch by Janis Blair and authors)

1922—Cities Service Oil Company begins operating in St. Rose at Carson site.

1923—Bank of Hahnville is established.

1924—Destrehan and Hahnville Public High Schools are established for white students.

1925—General American Tank Storage Terminal and General American Transportation Company begin operation in Good Hope.

1927—The Great Mississippi River Flood affects the nation and initiates planning for construction of the Bonnet Carré Spillway.

1927—Prospect Plantation (Good Hope) is torn down in a levee setback project.

1928—Flood Control Act of 1928 marks the beginning of the end to serious flooding in the Lower Mississippi Valley.

1929—Bank of Good Hope is established.

1929—Bonnet Carré Spillway construction begins in July.

1929—The Great Depression begins in October.

1929—St. Charles Borromeo Elementary School opens in Destrehan as the first private, parochial school in the parish.

1929—Shell Petroleum Corporation, forerunner of Shell Oil Company, acquires the New Orleans Refining Company facility and it becomes Shell Norco Refinery.

1933—The federal government establishes the Civilian Conservation Corps (CCC).

1935—Colonial Dairy opens in Taft and becomes one of the largest dairies in Louisiana.

1935—Dr. John Earle Clayton builds Claytonia, a large and stately residence north of Airline Highway in Norco.

1935—The federal government establishes the Works Progress Administration (WPA).

1936—Bonnet Carré Spillway is completed.

1937—President Franklin Roosevelt visits the spillway project in Norco.

1938—Fire destroys Alice Plantation in Ama.

1938—The Mississippi River levee setback claims riverfront properties in Luling.

1938—Texaco drilling operations in Paradis Field begins.

1938—Bayou Des Allemands Oil Field is discovered.

1939—Paradis Oil Field is discovered.

1939—World War II begins.

1941—The United States enters World War II as Pearl Harbor is bombed by Japan.

1948—St. Charles Borromeo High School opens in Destrehan.

1949—St. Charles Parish Waterworks District I is created by the police jury.

1950—Korean War begins in June.

1951—Bethune High School in Norco and Carver High School in Hahnville are established for black students.

1952—Lion Oil Company begins construction of its facility in Luling and merges with Monsanto in 1955.

1955—Shell Chemical Company opens in Norco.

1955—First parish library opens in Hahnville as a "demonstration library." Charlotte Gaylord serves as the first librarian.

1957—Edward A. Dufresne, Sr., builds Esperanza Plantation House in Luling. It remains a working plantation (2010) on which sugar cane has been grown since circa 1763.

1958—American Oil Company closes its refinery in Destrehan.

1959—Earl K. Long visits the parish.

1960—Bunge Grain Elevator opens.

1960—The Louisiana legislature establishes the South Louisiana Port Commission authorizing management of a public deep-draft port on the Mississippi River for the three river parishes: St. Charles, St. James, and St. John the Baptist.

1961—United States special military force build-up begins in Vietnam.

1962—Local independent union at Shell Oil Company strikes and later joins the Oil, Chemical and Atomic Workers (OCAW), a national union.

1964—President Lyndon Baines Johnson signs the Civil Rights Act of 1964.

1965—First United States combat troops arrive in Vietnam.

1965—Hurricane Betsy devastates south Louisiana. St. Charles Parish is ravaged and a tragic fire destroys Claytonia in Norco during the storm.

1965—Our Lady of the Holy Rosary Church moves from Taft to Hahnville.

1966—Union Carbide Company, now Dow–St. Charles Operations, opens in Taft on the site of the old Providence and Star Plantations.

1966—Hooker Chemical, now Occidental Chemical, purchases the old Colonial Dairy site.

1968—The River Road Historical Society is organized with the purpose of preserving and restoring Destrehan Plantation. Foundress Wayne Gaupp serves as the first president of the historical society.

1969—Parish public schools are integrated.

1970—Bunge Grain Elevator in Destrehan explodes, killing one and severely injuring two others.

1971—American Oil Refinery donates the deteriorating Destrehan Plantation house to the River Road Historical Society.

1973—All bays of the Bonnet Carré Spillway are opened to avoid major flooding downriver.

1973—Perriloux Plantation in Montz is torn down in a levee setback project.

1973—St. Charles Borromeo Parish celebrates its 250th anniversary.

1974—Luling/Destrehan Bridge construction begins.

1974—Waterford III Nuclear Power Plant permitted for construction on the site of the former Waterford Plantation.

1974—Voters approve a new Louisiana Constitution.

1976—The parish celebrates America's bicentennial; President Gerald Ford visits the parish.

1976—The new Destrehan and Hahnville High Schools open.

1976—On October 20, the *Frosta*, a Norwegian freighter, hits the *George Prince* ferry as it crosses the river from Destrehan to Luling.

1976—The new courthouse opens and the old courthouse is demolished.

1977—Voters approve the St. Charles Parish Home Rule Charter.

1977–78—West and east regional libraries are built.

1978—Implementation of the new Home Rule Charter government begins on January 7.

1980—The first parish president and council members assume office on June 2.

1983—Luling/Destrehan Bridge opens on October 6 as the first cable-stayed structure to cross the Mississippi River with the longest cable-stayed span in the United States.

1983—Ferry service is discontinued on November 13.

1983—Good Hope Refinery conducts a major buyout of homeowners' property in the town of Good Hope.

1984—Luling/Destrehan Bridge is officially dedicated as the Hale Boggs Bridge by Act 346 of the 1984 Louisiana legislature.

1985—Hurricane Juan causes major flooding in the parish.

1985—Waterford III Nuclear Power Plant at Taft opens on September 26.

1988—The May 5 catalytic converter ("cat cracker") explosion at Shell Oil Refinery in Norco impacts most parish communities.

1990—St. Charles Borromeo Parish celebrates the 250th anniversary of its patron saint.

1992—Hurricane Andrew causes extensive damage to southeast Louisiana.

1995—Record rainfall on May 8, referred to as a five-hundred-year flood, inundates St. Charles and surrounding parishes.

1996—St. Charles Historical Foundation is established.

1996—The Olympic Torch passes through St. Charles Parish on the way to Atlanta.

1997—Construction begins below Luling on the Davis Freshwater Diversion Structure.

1998—Shell Norco Museum opens.

1999—Denver and Champion historic luggers (cypress boats) are donated to the parish by the Victor Matherne Family of Des Allemands.

2001—On September 11, terrorist attacks on the East Coast paralyze the nation.

2001—Two Catholic pastors from St. Charles Borromeo and St. Gertrude drown in a boating accident.

2002—The Shell buyout of Diamond and other Norco properties is finalized.

2003—Valero, a Fortune 500 diversified energy corporation, opens in the parish with the purchase of the defunct Orion Refinery.

2003—The Louisiana Purchase Bicentennial is celebrated in St. Charles Parish.

2003—The German Coast Farmers Market opens on June 7.

2005—Hurricane Katrina strikes southeast Louisiana and the Mississippi Gulf Coast on August 29. Several weeks later, Hurricane Rita wrecks havoc on southwest Louisiana.

2007—The St. Charles Museum and Historical Association is established from the merger of River Road Shell Museum and St. Charles Historical Foundation.

2007—The two-hundredth anniversary of the civil parish of St. Charles Parish is celebrated on March 31.

From Plantations to Petroleum

The Breadbasket continues...

As the centuries changed, so did the landscape of St. Charles Parish. In colonial times, the German Coast was the breadbasket of the colony. The breadbasket continued through the prosperous Spanish era as it did during the plantation era, when the wealthy planters and their landholdings dominated the economy and politics. From the McCutcheons, Destrehans, Rosts, LaBranches, and Trépagniers to the Sellers and St. Amands, the power of land translated to the power to govern. As the nineteenth century ended and the twentieth century began, plantations began to fade into the past as large industrial complexes sprang up on the enormous stretches of land along the Mississippi River on the east bank. Easy access to the river, rail, and air service would become a winning combination and would set the stage for the emerging industrial age to grow and prosper.

The lure of steady jobs, paid vacations, and benefits further enhanced the desirability of working in industry as opposed to being out in the field and facing the unpredictable forces of Mother Nature. Workers came willingly and in large numbers to the new commerce of St. Charles Parish. Although the breadbasket would be filled with new "foods," the people of the German Coast would continue to "feed" the region and America.

A 1900 issue of the St. Charles Herald.

Destrehan Plantation House in the early 1900s.

Ormond Plantation in the early 1900s. (Photo courtesy of Chip Zeringue)

Wheels! Wheels! Wheels!

How life in St. Charles Parish would change in the first half of the twentieth century with the arrival of the automobile and the improvement and construction of roadways!! Sixty percent of Louisiana was rural at the turn of the century and St. Charles Parish was a rural parish! Mud roads were everywhere. Roads were so often impassable that wagons and buggies would get stuck. Farmers had difficulty bringing their produce to market and often used the river instead. Doctors struggled to reach their patients. In order to reach their students, teachers often lived on school premises or rented rooms nearby. Voters even had difficulty reaching the polls. But change was on the horizon!

PHOTOGRAPH COURTESY OF HENEDRIX "BROTHER" BOU

npagne, Fred Heurst, J.W. McClelland and A.J. "Buck" Bourgeois on bridge in 192

917: First bridge for autos buil
ver Bayou Des Allemands

1917, the first wooden
idge for automobiles was
on Highway 90 over Bayou
Allemands, which sepa-
Lafourche Parish from St.
les Parish," wrote
drix "Brother" Bourgeois
estwego.
urgeois, who submitted the
photograph, said the
hern Pacific Railroad

ground.
"On the far right is my dad,
A.J. 'Buck' Bourgeois, assistant
superintendent for Bouie Lumber Co. No. 2," he wrote. "This
lumberyard made cypress shin-
gles that were used for roofing,
cypress fences, etc. It utilized
all steam power, and mules
were used to pull the wagons."
Bourgeois said the lumber-

his father and the man nex
him, J.W. McClelland, who v
superintendent of Bouie Lu
ber. Next to McClelland is
keeper Fred Heurst. The m
next to Heurst, whose first
name Bourgeois does not
call, is identified only as "M
Champagne." He was an a
tant bookkeeper from Rac
land

Early Sheriffs

Sheriff Lewis Ory (1848–1903). One of the earliest unsettling events which took place in the beginning of the twentieth century was the untimely end to Sheriff Lewis Ory's long years of service as sheriff. Ory and other peace officers were attempting to apprehend a known criminal when they were fired upon by a fugitive from Jefferson Parish. Sheriff Ory was hit in the temple and died at the scene. The Daily Picayune's *account of the event praised the sheriff for his bravery and declared that he was a well-known and respected man who would be missed by many in the law enforcement community. His death is recorded as January 26, 1903.*

Anthony "Tony" Madere (right) replaced Ory and served as sheriff of St. Charles Parish from 1903 until 1912. Sheriff J. S. Paterson served a one-year term from 1912 to 1916. (Photo courtesy of David Pizzolato, Sr.)

Leon C. Vial, Sr. (1878–1939).

Old Spanish Trail Project

In 1908, Henry Ford began producing his Model T. In 1915 in Mobile, Alabama, a group of automobile enthusiasts, spirited by the Spanish padres and conquistadores, met and organized the "Old Spanish Trail Project." The project promoted a paved automobile highway across the southern United States connecting St. Augustine, Florida, to San Diego, California. Louisiana became a thorn in the side of the trail organization, failing to pave the road and replace ferries with bridges. In 1919, shamed by the completion and opening of the trail in all other states except Louisiana, Governor Huey Long paved the highway with asphalt all through the state and contributed more than half of the construction funds for the Huey Long Bridge. (The bridge was and still (2010) is owned by the New Orleans Public Belt Railroad, which is owned by the City of New Orleans and managed by the Public Belt Railroad Commission.) In 1935, the Huey Long Bridge replaced the Walnut Street Ferry removing the last Old Spanish Trail obstacle.

In St. Charles Parish, the new two-lane Old Spanish Trail Highway (now U.S. 90) built by Governor Long was a diversion from the original path, which lies nearby. A portion of the original historic Old Spanish Trail, probably in existence since the 1700s, remains today in St. Charles paralleling the railroad track from Paul Maillard Road in Boutte through Des Allemands to the Lafourche Parish line. (U.S. 90 was expanded in the 1960s to a four-lane highway and is proposed to become a part of the new I-49 corridor.) ⚜ ⚜ ⚜

The King of Spain sent a representative to America to participate in the dedication of the twentieth-century trail. ⚜ ⚜ ⚜

Vial Era Begins

Early in the century, a young man would emerge on the political scene as a member of the House of Representatives and then parish assessor. Finally in 1916, at the age of thirty-

The Vial House on Fashion Plantation property was built about 1900 by local luminary Leon C. Vial, Sr. The Vial House is currently owned by Leon C. Vial III and his wife, Mary Janet Vial. Following his grandfather and father into public service, "Sonny" Vial has served as assistant district attorney and parish attorney for many years. His brother, the late David Vial, served as parish coroner for years. ❧ ❧ ❧

An election handout shows Vial, Sr., running for sheriff. (Courtesy of the Suzanne Friloux collection)

The unfortunate deaths' which r moved from the River Parishes thr fine men in the persons of Sheri Leon Vial of St. Charles, Coron Gaston L. Gaudet and Lucien Ande mann of St. James may bring abo the first political skirmishing of th year 1939.

* * * * *

Who will succeed Sheriff Vial is problematical. St. Charles is now headed by Coroner Landry, whom we understand doesn't relish being Sheriff for even a short while. No doubt the good Sheriff wanted the job to remain in his family as he had held the position since 1916. But . . . his death was so sudden that he may not have had time to build the foundations for this move . . . We don't know.

A newspaper account of Sheriff Vial's death. (Courtesy of the Suzanne Friloux collection)

Past Sheriffs of
St. Charles Parish

Noel St. Martin	1854–1862
Louis Ranson	5/21/1866–6/7/1866
Victor Laurent	6/8/1866–7/13/1868
Morgan Morgans	7/14/1868–8/15/1871
J. G. Badenhouser	8/16/1871–8/24/1871
Morgan Morgans	8/25/1871–12/17/1872
George Essex	12/18/1872–9/30/1878
Owen McLeran	10/1/1878–11/4/1878
Clement Colly	11/5/1878–4/20/1880
B. Similion LaBranicke	4/21/1880–4/22/1883
Enest Lafitte	4/23/1883–9/7/1883
T. T. Baudouin	9/8/1883–4/21/1884
Lewis Ory	4/22/1884–1/27/1903
Anthony Madere	4/28/1903–4/15/1912
J. S. Paterson	4/26/1912–4/17/1916
Leon C. Vial, Sr.	4/18/1916–3/28/1939
Marie Keller Vial	3/28/1939–4/17/1940
Ralph Dubroca	4/18/1940–4/17/1944
Leon C. Vial, Jr.	4/18/1944–3/2/1964
John O. St. Amant	3/3/1964–6/30/1972
Julius B. Sellers, Jr.	7/1/1972–6/8/1976
John O. St. Amant	6/9/1976–11/29/1979
Herbert P. LeRay, Jr.	11/30/1979–6/30/1980
Charles C. Wilson	7/1/1980–6/30/1984
Johnny Marino	7/1/1984–6/30/1996
Greg Champagne	7/1/1996–present

(List courtesy of Sheriff Greg Champagne's Office)

J. Hanno Deiler (1849–1909) was born in Bavaria, Germany, was educated and taught in German schools, and emigrated to the U.S. in 1872. He settled in New Orleans, becoming principal of a German school. He later was appointed a professor of German at the University of Louisiana (Tulane). His most notable work was published in 1909, The Settlement of the German Coast of Louisiana and the Creoles of German Descent, *which uncovered historical information lost for almost two centuries. Deiler, a linguist, was able to determine that many descendants of the German Coast settlers were for the most part German and not French. He was interred in Greenwood Cemetery, New Orleans. (Photo courtesy of the Historic New Orleans Collection)*

eight, he would become sheriff for twenty-two years until his death in 1939. He was Leon C. Vial, Sr., whose ancestry could be traced back to the mid-1600s in Rhone, France. The family migrated over the centuries to Mexico and later to St. John the Baptist Parish. Sheriff Vial was succeeded in office by his widow, Marie Keller Vial, who completed her husband's term. In 1940, Ralph Dubroca was elected sheriff, serving one term in the Vial era until 1944. Dubroca was married to Shirley Tinney, granddaughter of the late Sheriff Vial. In 1944, Leon C. Vial, Jr., son of the former sheriff, was elected to the position and served five successive terms for twenty years until 1964, when the Vial era ended after nearly fifty years of public service. Many members of the Vial family continue to hold prominent local, state, and federal government positions well into the twenty-first century.

Unlocking Our Heritage

Deiler Reveals Our Past

Reading J. Hanno Deiler at Hahnville High School, Nancy Tregre Wilson told her father, "We are German, not French." "But how can that be," he remarked, "I read my prayers in French." ⚜ ⚜ ⚜

1912—Disaster Strikes Twice

Great 1912 "Crawfish" Crevasse

The yearly spring rise of the Mississippi brought fear of crevasses to those living on the riverbanks. Early in the twentieth century their worst fears were realized.

On May 14, 1912, a "crawfish hole" began to weaken the levee at Hymelia, just upriver from present-day Killona. It quickly grew to a five-hundred-foot wide gap in the levee spilling water across a huge area from Hymelia to as far as Donaldsonville and Thibodaux to behind Gretna. The Hymelia Crevasse would send water rushing for hundreds of miles. The west bank of St. Charles Parish was severely impacted. Late that night, water was three feet deep in the streets of Killona, which was three and a half miles from the break. As with all crevasses, once the water left the river,

In 1912, the Mississippi River burst through the levee at what Lena B. Lacroix remembers as the Hymelia Crevasse. The floodwaters from the river went to the "back" into the swamp near Killona and built up until it began moving back toward River Road. A photographer standing on the Luling Railroad Depot on Railroad Avenue (now called Luling Avenue) took this picture of the Bushalacchi Grocery and Bar as the muddy Mississippi reaches for the porch. A wooden plank walkway extends from the depot to the store and members of the family and customers watch the photographer. (Photo from Le Meschacebe.*)*

its force was felt for many miles. Dr. Emile Burch, son of the owner of Hymelia and Glendale Plantations, had to provide for the safety and well being of his family just as many others did. Laborers were marooned in an old, abandoned sugarhouse on Hymelia's grounds. Water rose to four and five feet in Paradis and Des Allemands, respectively, in the days following the break. Hundreds of state convicts were drafted to work on the levee repairs as ordered by the governor.

First-hand account of the Hymelia levee break from the *LeMeschacebe* **newspaper,** *Les Voyageurs*, **Vol. XX VII, No. 1, March 2006:**

Hymelia Levee Breaks Near Old Crevasse
Some of Largest Sugar Plantations Flooded

(Number of smaller farms exposed to inundation by break in levee near parish line in St. Charles, Jefferson, St. John, St. James and Lafourche will be affected) Submitted by Alton J. Terrio.

LeMeschacebe—May 1912

"The Hymelia levee, on the West Bank of the Mississippi, just below the division line of this and St. Charles parishes, gave way Tuesday night at 7 o'clock, three acres below the spot where it broke in 1903, and church and plantation bells rang out the call for help and assistance. Messengers on horseback rode up and down the break corroborating the awful nature of the alarm.

"Wednesday morning the break was over 400 feet wide, with both ends of the levee caving rapidly. Waves four feet high surged through the gap and where trees stood in its path, the water lapped up five or six feet. The noise of the rushing water can be heard for miles around and the surrounding sugar plantations are being flooded in quick succession. Acres made marvelously fertile years ago by just such overflows will again be inundated and growing crops destroyed.

"We were reliably informed, Friday, that a determined effort is being made to close the crevasse. Capt. C.O. Sherrill, of the Fourth United States levee district is in charge of the stupendous proposition and is assisted by Major Kerr, of the State Board of Engineers and assistant U.S. Engineer, W. E. Knoblock. The Texas and Pacific Company has its

The Hymelia Crevasse of 1912. (Photo courtesy of the George Lorio family)

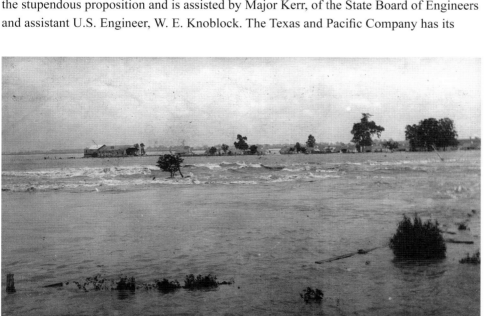

A sugar cane field is covered with water following the Hymelia Crevasse break. (Photo courtesy of the George Lorio family)

An old sugarhouse and residential quarters are surrounded by water. (Photo courtesy of the George Lorio family)

Convicts fill sand bags at the crevasse site. (Photo courtesy of the George Lorio family)

bridge gangs on the spot and 250 convicts arrived on the scene from Baton Rouge early yesterday morning. The ends of the broken levee have been secured and the crib-work is now in progress. Thousands of sacks are being filled with dirt on both sides of the crevasse and the work progresses satisfactorily with chance of ultimate success. It is estimated that ten or twelve days will be required to close the break, unless unforeseen obstacles should arise to impede the work.

"About 1,800 men are employed at Hymelia and these are divided into three shifts, thus keeping the work going night and day. During the night the place is illuminated by gasoline flare torches, set out along the levee."

Area men work trying to stop the crevasse with cribbing, which would later wash away. (Photo courtesy of the George Lorio family)

116

Work On Closing Hymelia May Be Abandoned

May 12, 1912

"The Hymelia crevasse is rapidly widening, not withstanding all efforts made to hold the ends. On Thursday 175 feet gave away on the upper end, making the gap over 1,500 feet wide. The cribbing at that point, due to the greatly increasing speed of the current, began to weaken and it was decided to abandon the work there and resume operations some 600 feet further in. This setback is most regrettable and has impaired the optimistic feeling which the engineers were imbued.

"The cribbing held better on the lower end and the work of driving piles there is progressing well. Drivers, working four abreast on a sliding platform, do the work at each end of the break."

Hymelia Crevasse Widens

LeMeschacebe—June 8, 1912

"The Hymelia levee continues to crumble away section by section until the breach, at this writing, is nearly a mile in width. Monday night over 300 feet gave way with a roar that could be heard for miles.

"There is now more water passing through the crevasse than at any time, not withstanding the fact that the pressure from the river has lowered. The additional width makes up for this. The back waters continue to rise and St. John has some of the finest plantations under water. Glendale, Gold Mine, Maxie, Church Place, Columbia, Carroll Evergreen and Whitney count but a few acres above water. A desperate fight was made to hold the back levee on these places, but to no avail. Gold Mine alone holding out against great odds.

The lower end of the Hymelia Crevasse is filled with bags of dirt to prevent breakage. (Photo courtesy of the George Lorio family)

Mrs. Patterson's store in Killona shows the first signs of flooding as the levee breaks. (Photo courtesy of the George Lorio family)

Hymelia water covers a cane field in Star Plantation. (Photo courtesy of the George Lorio family)

Crevasse water takes over a store in Taft. (Photo courtesy of the George Lorio family)

A control channel helps to handle the Hymelia Crevasse. (Photo courtesy of the George Lorio family)

"How long the Mississippi will continue to pour through Hymelia can only be conjectured, but when it does cease the planting season will be too far advanced for profitable planting. Truly, the immediate future of agricultural and other interest is not promising."

Few Plantations Escape Waters

LeMeschacebe—June 29,1912

"All the plantations near Thibodaux and Lafourche Crossing in Lafourche parish, except perhaps one or two near the Gulf that were in the path of Hymelia Crevasse waters, are reported under water."

The Hymelia Waters Stir Up Controversy

Assumption Pioneer—July 1912

"A cry of distress is being heard from the flood stricken people of lower Lafourche. It is a pitiable sight which greets one in that once prosperous section. Water on every side for miles, and no chance to recoup the loss, as the water is still covering all that section and is falling less than an inch in twenty four hours.

"This week, appeals were made to the governor to close the break so that the people can get some measure of relief from the terrible effects of the flood. The Lockport 'Lafourche Leader', in its last issue has the following to say about the highwater situation in lower Lafourche:

It is indeed deplorable when one thinks of the existing conditions of affairs in this section of the country: bounded on the north by Donaldsonville; on the South by the Gulf of Mexico, on the East by the Mississippi River and on the west by Bayou Lafourche, in which section the water is in a great number of places over seven feet deep and spread out from three to a few inches all through this territory. There are thousands of people in this stretch of country who would be glad to go to work and make crops of some description on lands that are now covered by waters of the Hymelia crevasse did it look as though this water would ever recede. It is now the 4th of July and the water in this territory has fallen but ten inches from its greatest height, while the river has fallen about 9 feet, and unless something is done to impede the flow of the water at the Hymelia break, there will be want, starvation and pestilence engendered through the lack of efforts of those who should do something to slacken the flow of water, if not entirely close the gap in the levee at Hymelia.

Should not the Lafourche Levee Board, with the amount of money they have in their Treasury do something to check the flow through the break! This matter should be taken up with all the members of the Lafourche Levee board in order to do something to alleviate the conditions of persons who have lost their all through this calamity.

Great Gap In Hymelia Levee Closed In Twenty Five Days

Times Democrat—August 1912, reprinted in *LeMeschacebe*

(Night and day struggle with the Crevasse Torrent Results in Victory for the Engineers and Contractors - First Attempt by United States Engineers Failed Because of the Terrific Water Pressure. The Method Pursued in the Engineering Work)

"Hymelia is closed. By today the last timbers of the big dam will have been driven into place and the massive structure will stand like monster canal locks ready to impede the inland rush of the waters from the Mississippi. The successful closing of the crevasse will mark one of the greatest conquests over the old Father of Waters in a decade. If one should now stand on the dame [sic] he would observe the great sheet of water."

Hymelia Crevasse was one of the last major crevasses to affect St. Charles Parish prior to construction of the Bonnet Carré Spillway.

Pile drivers move into place to fix the Hymelia break after the river waters go down. (Photo courtesy of the George Lorio family)

Workers rebuild the Hymelia levee. (Photo courtesy of the George Lorio family)

FIFTEEN DEAD, TWO DYING, AND MANY BADLY HURT, IN THE RAILROAD TRAGEDY

Midnight Excursion Train Halted at Montz, by Mishap, Run Into by Speeding Freight Which Crushes and Cremates Cars Crowded With Passengers for Woodville.

Source: Times Picayune

Montz Train Disaster

In November of the same year, a spectacular train wreck shattered the stillness of the night in the town of Montz. The headlines of the *Times Picayune* on Tuesday, November 12, 1912, stated, "Midnight Excursion Train Halted at Montz by Mishap Run into by Speeding Freight Which Crushes and Cremates Cars Crowded with Passengers for Woodville" (Mississippi). That headline spelled out in dramatic terms what had happened on Monday, November 11, 1912. The article following that headline gave very graphic information, including the names of the fifteen fatalities and the passengers who were injured, along with the names of railroad employees involved in the wreck. The wreck occurred in a remote location, slowing medical assistance from reaching the victims. The water supply was inadequate and there were few buckets to use. Injured passengers able to flee the train sought refuge in the nearby cornfields, which were illuminated by the wreckage flames. Most passengers panicked and were unable to assist the injured. Those who did not panic tore their clothes into strips for use in bandaging burned passengers. Both the dead and wounded were scattered about the cornfields of Montz. Many long hours passed before a doctor was able to reach the scene. The injured would not arrive in New Orleans by train to receive medical assistance until late the next day.

Blame shifted throughout the weeklong investigation, which included the convening of a grand jury in St. Charles Parish. Further, a joint inquiry of state and interstate commissions at Baton Rouge would be the first of its kind to be conducted in this country. The investigation results announced the culpability of many individual employees as well as the Yazoo and Mississippi Valley Railroad Company. Poor judgment, poor training, and poor equipment all contributed to the event cited as America's worst rail disaster. As quickly as the railroad tragedy burst upon the front page of the *Times Picayune*, by Monday, November 18, 1912, it was no longer headline news.

TELESCOPED CARS AFTER THE WRECK.

ONLY SLIGHT FRAMEWORK LEFT OF ONE, AND OTHERS SHOW TERRIFIC FORCE OF THE IMPACT.

A train wreck in Montz in November 1912 was termed the worst rail disaster in the United States. (© 2006 The Times Picayune Publishing Co. All rights reserved. Used with permission of The Times Picayune.*)*

The Destrehan Plantation house was used as an office building for refinery administrators of the Mexican Petroleum Company.

Improvements and Growth

Destrehan is Site of Old Jefferson Highway Dedication

Old Jefferson Highway, dedicated in 1919 as one of the first cross-country automobile highways traversing the continent from New Orleans to Winnipeg, Canada, came through St. Charles Parish in the era before U.S. highways. The original stretch through the parish was the road that is now River Road, or La. 48, and it started in New Orleans continuing into the Jefferson, St. Charles, and St. John the Baptist parishes and beyond. Nicknamed the "Palm to Pine Highway," it was built with help from associations of early motoring groups. That original route soon blended into other routes. But it apparently was front-page news in New Orleans on Friday, February 5, 1926, when the mayor of Winnipeg, Canada, arrived in Destrehan to welcome acting New Orleans Mayor Arthur J. O'Keefe at the dedication of the highway. Many locals were on hand for the party held near the tennis courts at the Mexican Petroleum plant site.

The school for African American students was located at Pan American Petroleum. Negro schools began in churches or other dwellings. This church, on the Pan American Oil Refinery at Destrehan, served as a school for black children whose parents worked at the refinery. John Smith, a member of the St. Charles Parish School Board since 1991, attended his first education classes in this building. Smith is currently a retired deputy superintendent of schools in Orleans Parish. (Photo courtesy of the Louisiana Library, Works Progress Administration Program.)

An aerial view of the Pan American/Amoco Refinery in Destrehan.

The Pan American Refinery Hospital.

Industrial Growth

In the first thirty years of the twentieth century, the culture of the east bank changed slowly but dramatically. The natural deep channel of the river allowed ocean-going vessels to safely dock at wharfs to load and unload products. Replacing the fading plantations were petroleum refineries and the employee communities, which were established to house the workers who otherwise had to be transported in daily by rail. In 1914, Destrehan Plantation was sold to the Mexican Petroleum Company, which began operating in 1918. An entire village was developed to support the needs of the workers including a hospital, schools, and a company store. Many of the five hundred employees lived at the refinery in neat, well-built "modern" homes or bungalows. They enjoyed many recreational amenities. Some African American employees were housed in the former slave quarters. The old plantation house was eventually used for offices of the new

From the cab of "Old Reliable" Bill Mongrue (left) and Ned Gauthreaux survey the refinery area. "Old Reliable" was the engine that shifted, pushed, and pulled Pan American Refinery railroad cars for decades. Bill Mongrue, head switchman, and Ned Gauthreaux, engineer, worked side by side at Pan American Refining Company in Destrehan for nearly three decades starting in 1927. Bill lived in Luling when he began working at the refinery in 1919 and rowed across the river by boat to Destrehan. When it was dark or foggy, his father would stand on the riverbank waving a lantern to guide him to the landing area. In later years, he crossed by ferry when service began. Ned lived above Lutcher and began working at Pan Am in 1921, moving later to switchman of the three-mile refinery track within which gondolas, flat and box cars were dropped off from the main line and repositioned for loading, unloading, and lineup for destination. "Old Reliable" was capable of moving from forty to fifty cars around the yard. There was never an accident or injury during their twenty-seven years of working together. (Photo courtesy of Kerney and JoAnn Mongrue)

Pan American offered homes for its employees on the Destrehan Plantation grounds.

An aerial view of New Orleans Refining Company in 1927. (Source unknown, currently part of the Suzanne Friloux collection)

refinery. In time, the refinery became Pan-American, then Amoco. Beginning in 1950, the houses moved into various subdivisions in the community. Amoco closed in 1958, but today most of the plantation property is owned by British Petroleum.

Upriver in the town of Sellers, the New Orleans Refinery Company was established in 1916 on 366 acres of Good Hope Plantation. The town of Sellers eventually lost its identity to the new industry. The postmistress of the Sellers post office and the manager of the refinery met to clear up a confusing mailing situation. Mail for the refinery was going to both Sellers and Good Hope, so they coined the name NORCO, the first letters of the company's name, and that became the place to which refinery correspondence was sent.

Several other industries sprang up in the same area. Island Refinery opened on Prospect Plantation in New Sarpy in 1918. In 1925 in Good Hope, the General American Transportation Corporation, which included a tank car repair shop, and the General American Tank Storage Terminal opened. The terminal soon became the site of the world's largest petroleum tank storage terminal. An unusual industry, the American Molasses Company (one of the largest in the world) was also located in Good Hope. Wesco Water Paints, Inc./National Gypsum occupied a site on Wesco

Construction of the Guard House at Shell Norco.

The twenties version of the pick-up truck, a Model A Ford, was often used to bring workers to the Shell Refinery as shown in this Norco Street scene in the 1920s.

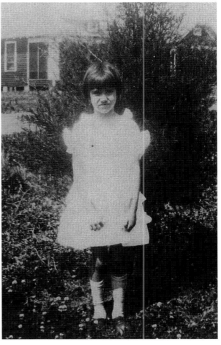

Clarissé "Sis" Vitrano stands among Norco Village houses in 1927.

Road at the border of Good Hope and Norco. These industries led to the development of the "Wonder Town" of Good Hope as it was called in a full-page story in the *Times Picayune* in March 1931. Good Hope had a school, restaurant, bank, hotel, drugstore, a post office, and its own newspaper. Two other industrial sites opened on the east bank in St. Rose on Cedar Grove Plantation: Carson Petroleum Company in 1919 and Cities Service Oil Company in 1922.

Many east bank business sites remained in place for decades, some with new names. Others disappeared over time just as the plantations they had replaced faded from the horizon.

The schoolhouse at Shell Oil in Norco.

Clubhouse of the Cities Service Oil Company at St. Rose, circa 1940s.

An aerial view of Cities Service and Export Company.

Conveyor loading drums at the General American Tank Storage Terminals in Good Hope.

Plant Day in St. Rose in 1923.

The GATX softball field in Good Hope. (Photo courtesy of Joan Weaver Becnel)

A view of Wonder Town, Good Hope.

West Bank Commerce

Major industrialization would not begin on the west bank of the river for another forty years into the second half of the twentieth century. Commerce was primarily agricultural but pockets of small businesses existed to meet the basic needs of citizens in many villages. Commercial fishing and sugar cane farming supported the economy. Another major player was the lumber industry, which had been an important part of the economy since the early days of the French colony.

Magnificent forests of oak and other hardwoods were cleared along with cypress trees, which dominated the swamps of the area. Draping the magnificent trees in the marshes was moss, a valuable commodity since colonial and antebellum days when it was used in the bousillage (entre' pateaux, mud between posts) of Creole homes. Landry's Moss Gin in Paradis bought moss for three cents a pound but according to the Reverend John Dorsey of Boutte, the backbreaking labor of picking and hauling the moss with a mule-drawn slide paid off

Good Hope News, *June 7, 1930.*

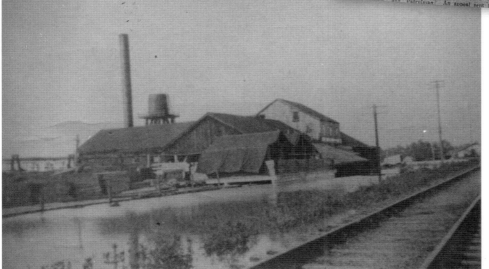

The sawmill in Des Allemands. (Photo courtesy of Opal Dufrene)

Recreation time at the George Cousin's Lumber Camp sometime between 1912 and 1918. Notice how the workers have donned their "good clothes" for the event.

The Bowie Lumber Company Boarding House.

Workers fell cypress trees at George Cousin's Camp from 1912 to 1918.

as his family thrived from the profits of the hard work. Folklorists Jon and Jocelyn Donlon once recanted the legendary story of Henry Ford purchasing Louisiana moss but requiring that all moss be shipped to him in cypress boxes, the moss to be used for stuffing seats in his Model T, the valuable cypress (free to Ford), as wood interiors in the autos.

Cypress, which has great strength and durability and resists the heat and moisture of the southern climate, was in great demand and had been used by the Germans in colonial times. Although lumber was milled at plantation sawmills during most of the nineteenth century, large commercial sawmills were established in the latter part of the century. There were several mills on the west bank including ones at Bayou Gauche and Des Allemands. The largest of these was the Louisiana Cypress Lumber Company mill established by Joseph Cornelius Rathborne in 1889. The company owned 50,000 acres of swampland from which it drew vast supplies of timber. Some of this land was in St. Charles and in June 1911, George Cousin (born in Alsace-Lorraine) signed an agreement with Rathborne and it was at this site that Cousin's Camp was established and served as home base for the workers. Each of these camps typically offered a variety of necessities including a boarding house, a general merchandise store, a machine shop, an entertainment hall, and a saloon among other things.

Harvesting cypress was a laborious task. The workers went into the swamps in the fall when the water was low and felled trees. When the waters rose in the spring, logs were made into rafts, which were towed by steamers to sawmills. The loggers, who were called "swampers," endured many hardships including malaria. Cousin's Camp, located behind the current Lakewood West Subdivision off U.S. Highway 90, was at its peak from 1912 to 1918. The lumber industry faded away as the supply of timber in the vicinity became largely exhausted.

Development Plans Abound

Paradis

Marie Martin Labry, great-granddaughter of John Baptiste LaBranche and sister of J. B. Martin, the "Father of St. Charles Parish Education," was herself an educator. One stop on her journey through the system was in 1914 at the Paradis School built by a Chicago firm called Louisiana Development Corporation. In an article in the *River Parish Focus* of January 1979, she shared some of her memories with Henry E. Yoes III. "They were going to move the Courthouse there; they were going to move everything there (Paradis). They built a big building and called it a high school but it wasn't. They were coming down here to develop this land and we were very, very glad. A bank was built and lots of cottages. Along the railroad there was a park and a big old gray hotel. There was a moss gin and a saw mill. They even had street lights. At first they were very successful." Unfortunately the settlement failed in later years. Mrs. Labry, however, was successful and flourished in the school system for forty-one years. She taught in many schools at many levels and apparently enjoyed all of it. When asked at the age of eighty-six if she had any regrets she said, "Yes, I wish I was still teaching."

Big Plans for Black Prince Bayou

During this same time period in the far reaches of the parish, near Des Allemands, a speculative land deal was taking place. The St. Charles Development Company, Inc., of Waterloo, Iowa, was soliciting individuals to move to a tract of land which encompassed "thirteen thousand acres of smooth prairie land and five hundred acres of timber, consisting of cypress, gum, hackberry, and live oak," according to a promotional brochure. The site was located on Black Prince Bayou. Already available to any newcomers was a hotel situated on a boat landing. Prospective buyers were told of the suitability of the land for planting, the availability of the bayou for fishing, the favorable climate, and the close proximity to the city of New Orleans.

Included in the brochure were letters from individuals who had already settled in and had experienced the "glowing promises" of the developers. The company offered to pay all expenses to anyone making the trip to the area. This included travel, hotel accommodations, and as an added bonus, a trip to New Orleans.

Like many other entrepreneurial projects, this one faded away over the years. However, the promotional brochure offered insight into the makeup of the parish in the early 1900s.

A Spunky Little Lady

By Henry E. Yoes III

Ferries were skiffs back then, she says. A rowboat. "I remember well, Charley the ferryman."

According to 86 year old Marie Martin Labry, the river was from levee top to levee top. The ferrymen worked for themselves; you had to pay them to cross the mighty Mississippi.

Every village had one, more or less, she says. They only took you straight across. If the boat was on the other side of the river, you could hoist a flag for them to come over, or you could just call across.

Call across the Mississippi? Was it narrower in 1900?

No, she answers. "It's about the same width as today; but in those days there weren't so many things in the river, so much noise." And the only way you could get a horse and wagon across the river was to hire a regular river boat.

That's a glimpse of St. Charles Parish at the turn of the century.

Marie Labry has lived through a St. Charles Parish that has changed greatly during her years. Great granddaughter of a prominent New Orleans doctor, daughter of a St. Charles Clerk of Court, and sister of the parish's first full time superintendent, J. B. Martin, Jr., she has seen more than most, gained more insight than most, and been involved more than most.

And talk about fiesty! Active, alert, she'll challenge anybody on any subject if it behooves her.

For instance, a young upstart editor of the local newspaper several years ago, wrote that St. Charles Parish had no culture. Mrs. Labry became aroused. Indeed, no culture!

"When the show boats would come, all the kids would go out and pick what they could sell, bones were one of the things you could

Marie Martin Labry, a veteran teacher, stands beneath a painting of her great grandfather John Baptiste LaBranche.

(Source: River Parish Focus, January 1979)

The Paradis School built by a development company. In 1914, Ms. Labry (on steps, in black dress) was one of its teachers. (Source: River Parish Focus, January 1979)

Soy Beans—a wonderful feed crop.

Boat Landing on our Property.

Scenes from Black Prince Bayou Project early 1900s

Frank Lowe. Vinton, Iowa, in his corn field on St. Charles property. July, 1917.

Sugar Cane, 40 tons to the acre. This country is called the "sugar bowl" of America.

At our boat landing. Water Melons and Cantaloupes ready for shipment. June, 1917.

Planting Sweet Potatoes—a stick and the "slips" are all that is required.

Our Hotel—The St. Charles on beautiful Black Prince Bayou.

Following is a copy of a letter written by Mr. Wm. Ritchie, Des Allemands, Louisiana. The letter was dated August 30, 1916, was addressed to Mr. Chas. T. Knapp, Chicago, Illinois, and published in *The Gulf States Farmer* in the August 1917 issue by the Louisiana Meadows Company.

(Source for photos on opposite page and above: Publication published in the early 1900s by the St. Charles Development Company, Waterloo, Iowa; currently part of the Suzanne Friloux collection)

"Dear Sir: In answer to your letter of August 22nd with reference to farming conditions, etc., down here in Louisiana.

I came here five years ago with my wife and five children from Ohio. We have not had one day's sickness. Doctor has never been in the house. Few states have a more delightful climate than Louisiana. Those who condemn it as disagreeable and unhealthful do so through ignorance. There is no need to seek mountain and sea shore resorts in summer, for the breezes from the Gulf keep the summer months pleasant. The summers are long, but the maximum temperature never exceeds, and seldom equals, that of inland cities much further north. The winters are mild and all but the most delicate plants grow through the winter.

"Oats, wheat, rye, barley, speltz, rape and all clovers, planted in September and October can be pastured all winter up to March and then left for a grain crop, which will be ready to harvest in May and the same again planted in corn. We have a long growing season, corn can be planted from February to July 1st and we grow real corn. What we need most down here is real farmers - the fellows that stick. Just get them down here and let them see for themselves, and they will find the richest of soils here. I am convinced that we can raise cattle and hogs cheaper here, than in any other state of the Union.

Yours very truly, Wm. Ritchie."

Des Allemands Lighthouse on Torres Island.

"In two hours time one can get from the St. Charles property to the city by automobile. We can also take a motor boat from our property up the beautiful Black Prince Bayou and Des Allemands Bayou to Des Allemands - a thirty minutes trip. Or one can go directly from the property to New Orleans by boat.

"Freight is delivered by boat from the city to our property. Any farmer on this tract can have this boat pick up his freight and deliver it into the harbor at New Orleans at a reasonable rate or can have freight brought out from the city and delivered on the property. Thus the people on this tract of land have three methods of transportation.

"This is primarily a country for *Cane, Corn, Cattle* and *Hogs* but if one wants to grow oranges or grape fruit or winter truck, he can do it here just as well as in Florida or California. The largest orange grove in the world is within twenty-five miles of our land 7,000 acres in one body.

"We have erected a commodious hotel on the property for the accommodation of our friends and prospective purchasers and, from the top of this hotel, one can see practically every acre of this land except that portion which is covered by timber which is in a compact body near one side of the property."

James H. Collins, in an article in *The Country Gentleman,* said:

"If the Corn Belt farmer will follow his own soil down the Mississippi River to the Delta Country below New Orleans, he can find a new farm so fertile and deep that I should not give him too many particulars because he probably would not believe the facts until he sees for himself."

"Mr. Collins is a writer on agricultural subjects who holds an enviable position among the best authorities on agriculture. What he says of the Delta Country near New Orleans is true. **For centuries the most fertile soil of some thirty-three states drained by the Mississippi River and its tributaries, has been deposited in this section."**

Early Des Allemands. (Photo courtesy of Opal Dufrene)

World War I

The United States entered World War I in April of 1917. In St. Charles Parish, lives were turned upside down. Men were called away to duty and families were fragmented. However, the country's involvement in the war was relatively short-lived. The Treaty of Versailles in 1919 was just one of the peace treaties signed to end the war. Families were then reunited, and people tried to forget about the war and put behind them the shocking fact that over 100,000 Americans lost their lives. They sought out entertainment and attempted to benefit from the flourishing economy, which would eventually take hold. Many servicemen returned home with money in their pockets and their purchasing power, limited perhaps before the war by few educational opportunities, was greatly enhanced. During the war, many blacks had been recruited by Henry Ford to work in his automobile factory. This migration was one of the most significant population shifts of that century. The war brought about profound changes in the cultural landscape. The 1918 Spanish Flu pandemic occurred in the midst of the war and not only affected the troops, but also affected the lives of German Coast residents as over one-half million U.S. citizens died from the flu, five times as many people as were killed in the war.

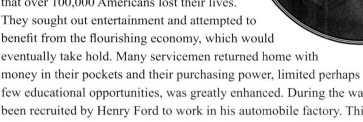

Stephen J. Friloux of Ama was typical of many who served and returned to St. Charles to continue their lives. (Photo courtesy of Suzanne Friloux)

When the United States entered the war, Germany became the enemy and in 1918 the Louisiana legislature passed Act 114 banning all expressions of the German culture and heritage, especially the spoken or printed word. Although the law was repealed three years later, the damage had already been done. On the German Coast and in other German communities in Louisiana, the German culture would remain suppressed for decades.

The American Red Cross made a significant contribution to the war by caring for the wounded and emphasizing the necessity for individuals to learn how to care for themselves and perhaps their animals, too. ⚜ ⚜ ⚜

THE COST OF WAR

"I Summon you to Comradeship in the Red Cross"
Woodrow Wilson

Posters like this one, drawn by Harrison Fisher in 1918, attracted new recruits into the Red Cross, where they were desperately needed to nurse the casualties of World War I.

The help of the American Red Cross extended beyond humans. (Photo courtesy of Patrick Yoes)

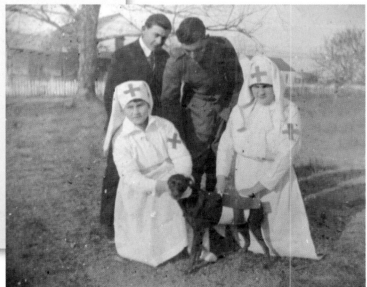

The Mississippi River was the gathering place for many church baptisms. Church members and others from the community would gather on the levee to view the moving ceremonies. The river waters were used as a major part of the ritual or tradition carried on for decades. Candidates for baptism were submerged in the water by their pastor and other members of the congregation. (Photo courtesy of Clarisse "Sis" Webb)

Historical Notes on St. Charles Borromeo: Little Red Church, 1918

The Little Red Church, built in 1806, has been standing now on the 1770 Spanish land grant for 112 years as a landmark for travelers on the Mississippi River. The church was without a pastor for forty-two years due to the 1877 fire, which destroyed the rectory, and the 1890 interdiction brought about by charter and warden conflicts with the archdiocese. But all of that would soon change with the appointment of a new pastor and lifting of the interdiction. Mr. Pat Kelly of the Mexican Petroleum Company and other church parishioners negotiated with the archdiocese to reopen the Red Church. In 1917, a parochial charter was adopted and St. Charles Borromeo Church Parish was reinstated to the diocese. The new pastor would accept the assignment without a place to live, but Mexican Petroleum offered a temporary residence at its refinery. Red Church was dilapidated from years of neglect, so it needed repairs and to be enlarged.

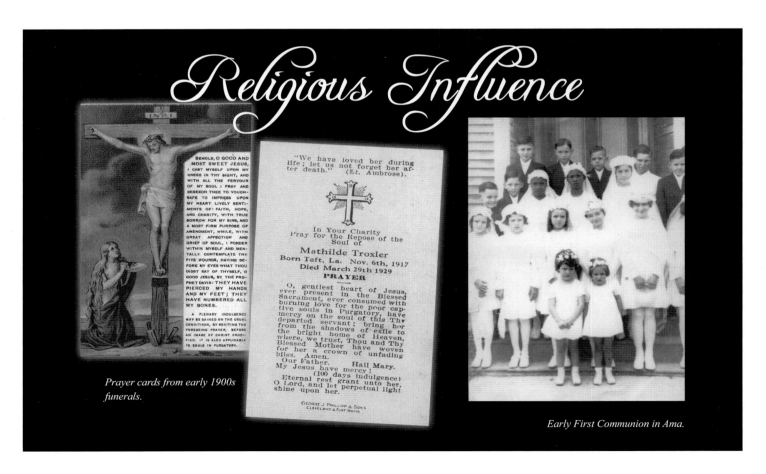

Prayer cards from early 1900s funerals.

Early First Communion in Ama.

One of St. Charles Borromeo Elementary School's graduating classes. (Photo courtesy of Ralph A. Richoux, Sr.)

There have been many priests in residence since the establishment of St. Charles Borromeo in Destrehan. One of the best known is Father John Francis Basty, who arrived on March 10, 1918, and remained until July 1949. He was a visionary who helped restore the spiritual and physical life of the church parish. Father Basty immediately saw the need to improve conditions in his new pastorate and to finance the construction of the new church. He immediately built a new rectory, made repairs, and enlarged the Little Red Church. Under his leadership, the following accomplishments occurred:

1920—Of the 617.68 acres of church property, six hundred acres were sold and seventeen acres were reserved for church, school, and cemetery use.

1921—A new church was built from the sale of church lands.

1924—St. Isidore the Farmer's Chapel at Montz was erected.

1929—The rectory of the Red Church was remodeled by elevating the existing building and closing in the ground level. The two-story building and other original buildings remain in place today.

1929—A two-story combination elementary school and convent was built, opening the first parochial school between New Orleans and Baton Rouge on the east bank.

1929—The Sisters of the Congregation of the Immaculate Conception were solicited to operate the elementary school. Sister Margaret Mary, C.I.C., was the first principal.

1939—A combination auditorium-classroom unit was erected.

1942—Two lots in Norco were acquired and the old St. Matthias Church of New Orleans was rebuilt as the Sacred Heart Mission Chapel.

1947—The Christian Brothers religious order was sought to operate a projected high school.

1948—A private, parochial high school, St. Charles Borromeo High School, opened under the direction of the Sisters of the Immaculate Conception.

1949—Contracts were put in place for the building of a new convent.

The Little Red Church facility remained on the grounds of St. Charles Borromeo for years after the new church was constructed. It was later torn down. Parishioners recall attending plays and other events in the building. A replica is on display on the church grounds.

Father Basty's legendary flock of sheep roamed the grounds of the church and schoolyard. Wool from the sheep was bundled and sold to the parishioners for quilt making. Despite speculation or the belief that Father Basty was the first pastor of St. Charles Borromeo to have sheep, 1747 records reveal a partnership: "Jean Rommel and the Reverend Father Pierre form an act of partnership whereby Rommel agrees to look after twenty-five sheep and five rams belonging to the Reverend Father for one-half the profits." ✤ ✤ ✤

The new St. Charles Borromeo Church was dedicated on January 25, 1922. In the 1978 restoration and expansion of the church, the old Stations of the Cross were restored and the solid cypress pews were used as paneling and the balcony railing. St. Charles Borromeo Church continues to serve Catholic parishioners in the twenty-first century and is the second oldest church parish in the Archdiocese of New Orleans. Support of clergy and laity over the years has contributed to the preservation of the integrity of this historic landmark.

Following the departure of the Immaculate Conception order in May of 1960, the Sisters of the Most Holy Sacrament came to the school to continue the education program. In 1979, St. Charles Borromeo High School closed. The archdiocese opened a new Catholic high school in LaPlace. In the twenty-first century, St. Charles Borromeo Elementary is the largest private parochial school in the parish.

Father John F. Basty.

*Top right: School and convent combined–1929.
Middle right: School auditorium. The expansion
of the educational program reaches its conclusion
with the opening of the high school (bottom right)
in 1948. Sister M. Valerie, C.I.C. (below) was its
first principal and guided it with a strong sense of
purpose, exceptional educational credentials, and
a firm religious faith. Her presence contributed
to the success of the high school. (Photos from
the 250th Anniversary Celebration of St. Charles
Borromeo Parish, Destrehan, Louisiana, 1723–
1973 booklet. Copyright 1973.)*

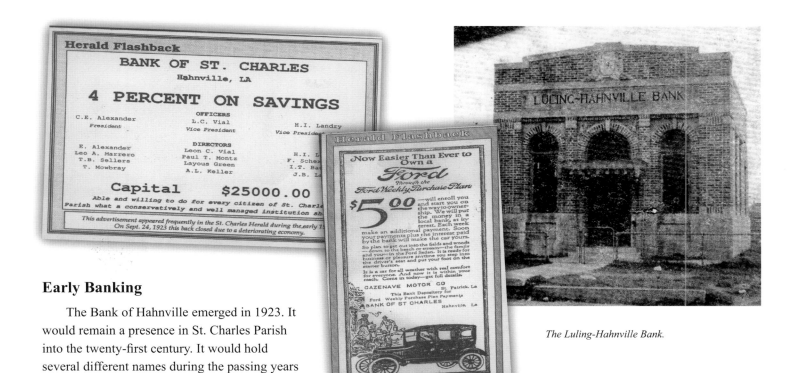

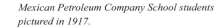
The Luling-Hahnville Bank.

Early Banking

The Bank of Hahnville emerged in 1923. It would remain a presence in St. Charles Parish into the twenty-first century. It would hold several different names during the passing years and exist in several locations.

1923—Bank of Hahnville

1925—Luling-Hahnville Bank

1939—Luling-Hahnville Norco Branch

1955—Bank of St. Charles and Trust

1989—First American Bank and Trust Company. (First American was chartered as the Bank of Vacherie in 1910 and assumed its current name in 1978.)

The Luling-Hahnville Bank was established to "meet the needs of industrial and agricultural St. Charles." The original bank building stands across from the courthouse in Hahnville and is the site of a law firm.

Public Education

With the arrival of the petroleum industry in the early 1900s, a major shift took place in the public school district. These major industries would not only begin to provide tax revenues which would help to bolster public education, but would also promote better schooling for their employees' children. Because of their keen awareness of the importance of education, schools were established on some of the industry sites. Mexican Petroleum in Destrehan demonstrated its commitment to the school system, specifically higher education, by donating three and one half acres of its property to the school board for the construction of a high school. On August 7, 1923, the school board president accepted the donation and also authorized the purchase

Mexican Petroleum Company School students pictured in 1917.

Montz's Grammar School in 1927. (Source: The Refinery, *the Destrehan High School yearbook, 1927)*

St. Rose School. (Source: The Refinery, *the Destrehan High School Yearbook, 1927)*

The 1927 school "transfers" are lined up and ready to roll. (Photos courtesy of Patrick Yoes)

The Bayou Gauche school boat owned by Willie E. Dufrene. (Photo courtesy of Opal Dufrene)

Teachers–DHS Faculty. (Source: The Refinery, *the Destrehan High School yearbook, 1927)*

The Teacherage at Destrehan High School in 1924 provided a place for unmarried educators to live. Similar housing was available at Hahnville High School. Housing was also available on the campus for the principals and their families.

Destrehan High School opened in 1924.

of Keller property for the construction of a west bank high school in Hahnville. Mexican Petroleum was recognized by the school board for their support of the bond issues, which financed the construction. This was an early example of industry/school cooperative efforts, which would exist throughout the years that followed. In 1923, the superintendent was authorized to open a Negro school at Shell Mound as a direct result of a petition by the African American residents of the area. Destrehan High School was dedicated on September 15, 1924, and Hahnville High School on the west bank was dedicated the same year.

The Hahnville High School in 1924. The parish courthouse is in the background.

Soon after their openings, the two schools were lauded for their accomplishments in a front-page photographic layout in the *Times Picayune* rotogravure supplement. Opening of the two high schools in 1924 dramatically changed the way white students would be schooled in the parish. Before this time, students had to seek higher education at other venues such as Leon Godchaux High School in Reserve. This was supplemented by funds provided by St. Charles Parish. Some went to

The Hahnville High School dedication in 1925.

The Hahnville High School eleventh grade graduating class in 1929.

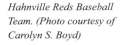

Hahnville Reds Baseball Team. (Photo courtesy of Carolyn S. Boyd)

live with relatives or attended schools in the city or surrounding parishes. Secondary public educational opportunities for African American students continued to be meager.

Flooding—A Constant Springtime Concern

The Great Flood of 1927 is considered one of the worst disasters in American history. One million people lost their homes and hundreds of thousands relocated. More than five hundred people along the Mississippi River were killed as the levees broke at thirteen places including one between Montz and LaPlace. This low-lying area of bottomland is still referred to as "The Slew." The town of Montz was once a vibrant town with its own post office, train station, several groceries, and a garage. Although there had been a Flood Control Act passed in 1917 as a reaction to the Hymelia, Bonnet Carré, and other crevasses, the 1927 flood prompted the authorization of the Mississippi River and Tributaries Project in the Flood Control Act of 1928. The "levees only" policy of the past was discarded since it had failed to sufficiently protect those living along the Mississippi.

A levee inspection takes place during the Flood of 1927. (Photo courtesy of Joan Weaver Becnel)

Water reaches a critical stage before the Flood of 1927. (Photo courtesy of Joan Weaver Becnel)

Above: A levee near Good Hope is shored up as a protective measure. (Photo courtesy of Joan Weaver Becnel)

Above right: The levee is being repaired at New Sarpy in late 1927. (Photo courtesy of Joan Weaver Becnel)

The Corps of Engineers adopted a new approach based on improved levees plus floodways, including a spillway to divert water into Lake Pontchartrain above New Orleans. The site chosen was the spot which had been affected by the nineteenth-century Bonnet Carré Crevasses and the area recommended by John McDonogh. Between 1849 and 1882, four major crevasses had occurred at this location. During the flood of 1849, a seven-thousand-foot-wide crevasse at Bonnet Carré flowed for more than six months.

Workers try to protect threatened levees before the 1927 flood. (Photo courtesy of Joan Weaver Becnel)

Bonnet Carré Spillway Construction

The Bonnet Carré Spillway is just one element of a comprehensive U.S. Corps of Engineers flood control plan in the Lower Mississippi Valley. The construction of the Bonnet Carré Spillway not only provided employment to thousands of workers but ultimately "put Norco on the map." Unfortunately, Delhomme, Roseland, Hermitage, and Myrtle Land plantations, as well as many residences and family cemeteries, fell

victim to the construction of the spillway. President Franklin Delano Roosevelt paid a visit to the site in April 1937, following an earlier dedication in December of 1935. The design and construction of the spillway was completed in just two and a half years. Today, the spillway, managed by the U.S. Army Corps of Engineers–New Orleans District, remains as it was originally

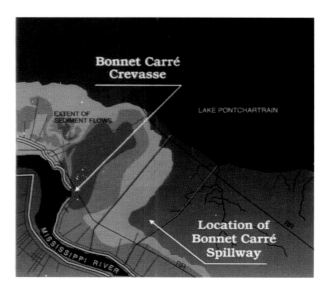

Between 1849 and 1882, the Bonnet Carré Crevasse left a large, fan-shaped imprint on the landscape. (Map from the New Orleans District U.S. Army Corps of Engineers Brochure on the Bonnet Carré Spillway)

A view from the levee shows the Sellers neighborhood affected by spillway construction. The upper end of the weir section is seen in the extreme left over the housetops. (Photo courtesy of Patrick Yoes)

A photo taken on March 19, 1930, near the center line of the spillway weir section shows the Stephens Brothers and Miller Hutchinson Construction Company at work. (Photo courtesy of Patrick Yoes)

A view from the levee shows completed piers and the upper part of the Bonnet Carré Spillway weir section, which was taken on March 19, 1930. (Photo courtesy of Patrick Yoes)

It works! The spillway opens in 1937.

Hundreds turned out for the spillway opening in 1937.

constructed; no significant modifications to the structure have been needed. In addition to its primary purpose, the spillway area is a popular recreation destination for locals and visitors from around the state and nation. Park rangers are on the scene in both a supervisory capacity as well as to provide educational services. It is listed on the National Register of Historic Places.

The Great Depression, 1929–39

It has been said by some that the St. Charles Parish area may not have been as profoundly affected by the Depression as the rest of the nation because many German Coast residents were still living in less than desirable conditions having never fully recovered from the Reconstruction period. However, there were adverse effects. The "little" man was particularly affected by the hard times of the Depression. Teachers, for instance, were often paid reduced salaries, many times in "script." School terms were shortened. Many people relied on the American Red Cross for assistance. Members of benevolent societies were often dependent on their group for basic needs. PTA's were known to open school cafeterias to prepare food for those in need.

The Trepagnier Plantation in Sellers, now Norco.

There were signs of hope, however. An influx of industry began to occur. People also had access to farmland, hunting grounds, and fishing areas. In 1935, the federal government stepped in with several programs designed to put people to work. The Works Progress Administration (WPA) was formed. It was responsible for constructing highways, hospitals, parks, and in St. Charles Parish, sidewalks some of which are still visible along the River Road throughout the parish and in older subdivisions. The Historical Records Survey conducted by the Louisiana State University was part of the Federal Writers' Project of the WPA. The objective of the survey in Louisiana was the preparation of complete inventories of the records of the state, including each parish, city, and other local governmental units. The projects in St. Charles Parish were listed as No. 45 and were published in November 1937.

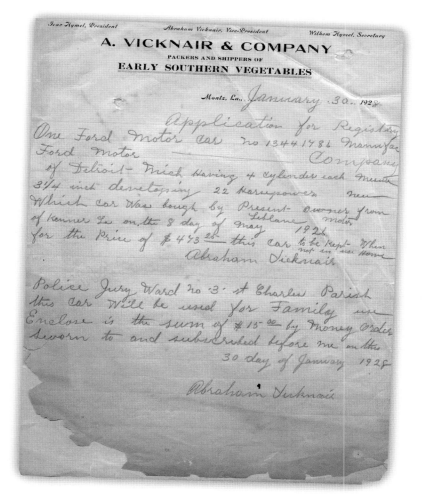

Also established was the Civilian Conservation Corps (CCC), under the jurisdiction of the Departments of Labor, Agriculture, War, and Interior, which paid young men thirty dollars a month and provided food, clothing, and shelter in exchange for their work in the nation's forests and parks. In St. Charles they worked on the construction of several roads, such as the "CC" Road along the perimeter of the spillway in Montz, which is still in use at the start of the twenty-first century.

The open spillway attracted many visitors to the site. According to the March 29, 1937, *Shell Bulletin*, "thousands of automobiles choked the highway from New Orleans to Norco one way, and Baton Rouge to Norco the other carrying the curious to see 'Old Man River' take a short cut to the sea. Nearly every state was

The spillway became a tourist attraction.

An oil rig stands tall in the waters of Bayou Gauche. (Source: St. Charles Parish Resources and Facilities publication, 1947)

represented when license plates were counted one Sunday afternoon. A by-stander checked thirty-two different state tags on autos parked on or near the Spillway bridge."

In addition to the major industries opening and supportive smaller businesses coming onto the scene, another area of commerce emerged as the twentieth century progressed. West bank oil fields were being discovered in rapid succession:

1938—Bayou Des Allemands Field
1939—Paradis Field
1940—Lake Salvador Field
1942—Bayou Couba Field

President Franklin D. Roosevelt

In April 1937 President Franklin D. Roosevelt, accompanied by the mayor of New Orleans and Governor Richard Laiche, rode through the streets of Norco on his way to visit the newly dedicated Bonnet Carré Spillway. His open-air vehicle gave all those along the

way a chance to see his characteristic broad smile. The *Shell Bulletin* reported in its May 3 issue that his route was lined with waving schoolchildren and Norco and vicinity residents. He kept his hand raised high in greeting. He inspected the spillway project thoroughly, spending fully forty minutes on his tour. He then retraced his route back to New Orleans where thousands waited for him in City Park.

A picture from a 1930s Shell Bulletin *shows the crowds waiting on the levee for the president.*

President Roosevelt rides through the streets of Norco.

The Little Red Church on the River *by Clarence Millet, 1940 (Courtesy of The Historic New Orleans Collection, Acc.#1999.118.8)*

Springtime Comes to The Mississippi *by Clarence Millet, 1955 (Courtesy of Collections of Louisiana State Museum URL 1997 20.2.001.)*

Spotlight on Renowned Native Son

Clarence Millet was born in Hahnville in 1897. Although he would later receive acclaim as a popular artist, he began his working career as a store clerk in New Orleans. He was encouraged to pursue a career as an artist because of his apparent talent. Millet went on to study art in New York City. His works were shown at the New York World's Fair of 1939 as well as at the Art Institute of Chicago. He opened a studio in the French Quarter of New Orleans where he became an active and respected member of the New Orleans Art League and the Southern States Art League, among others. He was accepted into the National Academy of Design in 1943. Millet was commissioned by the federally sponsored WPA as an easel painter. He became a prolific painter whose works gave insight into the lifestyles of the people in his area. He was quoted as saying, "I paint the things I know, see, and feel." His art became widely appreciated in the twenty-first century. Clarence Millet died suddenly on August 23, 1959, and is buried in St. Louis Cemetery No. 3 in New Orleans.

"In Front of the Fireplace," Norco, 1938; unidentified photographer. Nearly everyone had to struggle to make ends meet. Nearly everyone had to make sacrifices. Yet, no real change in the way of life seemed to occur. "Not in Louisiana," it is said, "not like it was in the North." The picture in this photo essay was taken by a photographer working under the auspices of two New Deal federal programs—the Resettlement Administration (RA), which in 1937 became the Farm Security Administration (FSA)—and depicts this country's most dramatic economic collapse and documents the trials and the triumphs of the human spirit under most adverse circumstances. ⚜ ⚜ ⚜

Shell Arrives in the Parish

New Orleans Refining Company, which gave the town of Norco its identity, was purchased in 1929 by Shell Petroleum Company, a forerunner of Shell Oil Company. It assumed the name Shell Norco Refinery. Its presence in the community expanded as did the employee village, which had been created by New Orleans Refining Company. Some employees and their families lived in the Shell village while

An early view of Shell Petroleum.

Shell's entrance gate circa 1940s.

A social gathering for African American employees circa 1940s.

Company Town—Norco 1940s.

Cistern. (Courtesy of Janis Blair)

others had access to the plant site amenities. These eventually included such things as a movie house, golf course, baseball fields, bowling alley, gymnasium, swimming pools, and tennis courts. Social activities and sporting events were a source of entertainment for the broader community.

Change! How Things Would Continue to Change!!

The transition of public roadbeds from dirt to clam shell to gravel to asphalt or concrete in the first half of the twentieth century facilitated the establishment of new businesses, industries, and residential developments. Major changes occurred in the everyday life of the citizens of St. Charles Parish!

Natural gas contracts with private companies and an electricity franchise with Louisiana Power and Light Company were approved by parish officials. In the 1930s natural gas, then electricity, became available to most residents. Wood or coal burning stoves for heating and cooking could then be replaced with natural gas heaters and stoves. Houses would be wired to receive electricity with a meter and a connection to the power company's main lines running to the edge of residential property lines. Oil and kerosene lamps would be replaced with electric light fixtures and lamps.

Cisterns were used at residences in St. Charles Parish as a rainwater reservoir from earliest colonial times until about the middle of the twentieth century. They were usually made of cypress boards with metal straps; later, some were made of metal. Rainwater used for drinking, cooking, and bathing was channeled by gutters into the cistern. Cistern tops and screens were eventually required for health purposes to eliminate breeding grounds for mosquito larvae and to prevent small animals from entering. Many people also had ground wells, pumping water for animal consumption. The establishment of public waterworks systems in the 1940s usually eliminated the need for cisterns and wells although some continued to be maintained for agricultural purposes.

Outhouses in St. Charles Parish were small stand-alone structures usually built around a "pit" and were used as outdoor toilets or privies at residences from colonial times until about the middle of the twentieth century. The pits were not attached to any sewer system. Outhouses were eventually replaced with indoor plumbing in bathrooms when running water, either piped from wells or received from public water systems, allowed flushing of waste into a yard cesspool. Most outhouses still standing today are President Roosevelt's WPA structures built in rural areas during the Great Depression. Legend says the crescent cutout in the door was for use by ladies, the star cutout for gentlemen. However, the main purpose of the door cutout was to allow light into the otherwise dark structure. Public sewer systems were constructed in Luling, Norco, and Good Hope in the 1950s and a parish-wide sewer system was completed in the 1980s. Exceptions to these residential situations existed in the industry villages of Mexican Petroleum in Destrehan, Shell in Norco, Cities Service in St. Rose, and General American in Good Hope, where residents living in company houses from 1918 enjoyed heat, electricity, running water, indoor plumbing, and many other amenities courtesy of the company's systems.

Outhouse. (Courtesy of Janis Blair)

Medical advances in the first decades of the twentieth century would not only improve the longevity statistics of residents in St. Charles but would make life healthier and happier on the German Coast. Improving primitive water and sewer treatment also helped to eliminate illness. Who can forget President Roosevelt's promotion of the March of Dimes program to stop polio, or how the introduction of sulfa drugs, penicillin, and later other antibiotics, would change lives? Life would become easier on the German Coast, and future generations would never experience the hardships dealt with for over two hundred years from the earliest settlers to the twentieth century. Crevasses, dirt roads, dreaded disease, cisterns, outhouses, and coal burning stoves would all become a thing of the past in a few short decades.

Roadways in St. Charles Parish

From its earliest beginning as a muddy path along the Mississippi River, the Great River Road had been a vital transportation link to other parts of the state and the country. On the east bank, in later years, it was the sole overland route between New Orleans and Baton Rouge until the completion of U.S. LA Highway 61—the Airline Highway—in 1935. To travel the eighty miles between Baton Rouge and New Orleans as the crow flies required a day's drive along River Road, a 120-mile dirt highway winding along the banks of the Mississippi River. Airline Highway, a straight concrete road linking Baton Rouge and New Orleans, reduced the trip to less than two hours. The highway earned its name from being straight as an airport runway.

The Great River Road was first a muddy path, then graveled before hard surfacing.

Built in 1922, the St. Rose Tavern site has been a bar, hotel, restaurant, and barbershop over the years. As a hotel, it was used to house construction workers building the Airline Highway during the 1930s. This picture was taken in 2007.

U.S./La. Highway No. 61-65 to New Orleans. In the background is Moisant International Airport (early view), used by the citizens of St. Charles Parish. (Source: St. Charles Parish Resources and Facilities publication, 1961)

"Who will ever forget the perils and the inconveniences and the nightmarish experiences of that 120–mile drive?" (The New Louisiana) ⚜ ⚜ ⚜

Airline Highway remained a two-lane road north of the Bonnet Carré Spillway until the mid-1950s. It was not until the Huey P. Long Bridge was completed in 1935 that the west bank of St. Charles Parish became "connected" with New Orleans for both rail and vehicular traffic.

Dr. John Earle Clayton, born in 1892, was involved in medicine and politics most of his life. He retired from politics in 1968 after serving as coroner from 1944. He was known by his peers as the "Dean of St. Charles Politics." In a 1979 *River Parish Focus* article, Henry E. Yoes III stated that Dr. Clayton was known for three things: (1) his ability to diagnose illnesses; (2) his political acumen; and (3) Claytonia. He lived his last years in LaPlace.

Built in 1935, "Claytonia," the home of Dr. John E. Clayton, was a showplace on Airline Highway in Norco. It was destroyed by Hurricane Betsy in 1965. (Photo courtesy of Carolyn Cambre Alleman)

"Dr. & Mrs. Clayton were honored by St. Charles Parish officials in 1969. Dr. Clayton was presented with a plaque proclaiming him 'Dean of St. Charles Politics.'" Standing left to right were Julius Sellers, Dr. Earl Alleman, State Senator George Oubre, State Representative Ralph Miller, daughter Earline, Clerk of Court Eddie Dufresne, and Sheriff John O. St. Amart. (Source: River Parish Focus, 1979)

School Days

In 1930, during the tenure of Superintendent J. B. Martin, the passage of a bond election provided the funds to build or expand public schools across the parish.

Allemands Elementary School
Allemands, Louisiana

Allemands Elementary School, 1931–74. (Photo courtesy of Mrs. Stanley Dufrene)

Norco Primary School on Apple Street, circa 1930s. Were these students awaiting the arrival of Franklin D. Roosevelt on his way to the spillway in 1937? Perhaps the WWL station wagon was there for the same reason. This photo remains a mystery.

Supt. Martin Of St. Charles Fetes Jubilee

By L. A. PICOU, JR.

DESTREHAN, April 26.—The St. Charles parish teachers sponsored a Silver Jubilee luncheon for Superintendent of Public Schools Johnny B. Martin The affair commemorated 25 years of continuous service in the field of public education.

Superintendent Martin was totally unaware of the celebration in his honor until his arrival at the Luling school. Principal A. A. Songy of Destrehan High, president of the Parish Teachers' association, served as master of ceremonies, and did well at concealing the fact that a surprise luncheon was in the offing.

As Superintendent Martin walked into the school, expecting a teachers' meeting, about 100 teachers began singing Auld Lang Syne.

Miss Jeanne Peyregne, oldest teacher in the service, having served some 25 years, presented Mr. Martin with a silver bowl. Julius Sellers, one of the youngest teachers, presented him with a silver cigarette box to adorn his desk. Both gifts were presented on behalf of the parish teachers.

Principals E. J. Landry of Hahnville High school, and A. A. Songy of Destrehan, sang "Swing Low Sweet Chariot."

Among the guests present were Dr. J. M. Foote, statistician for the state department of education; Dr. F. H Miller of L. S. U.; Mrs. J. M. Foote, and school board members P. N. Schexnayder and Flavin Keller.

Relating some of the happy and historic incidents in the life of Mr. Martin, Dr. Foote told the

SUPERINTENDENT MARTIN

group that he recalled standing on the levee in 1915 and taking a picture of Superintendent Martin in a model A Ford. The characteristic cigar was in his month. A copy of this picture is in the files of the state department of education in Baton Rouge. Included in one of the pictures is one of the old schools. "What a contrast," declared Dr. Foote, "to this wonderful structure of brick, mortar and iron we are seated in on this happy occasion. Surely the fruits of the superintendent's labor answer the

question: 'Is he a success?'" Dr. Foote said that the superintendent and the St. Charles parish school system were "well thought of in the state department of education, and were in the front ranks in the field of education in Louisiana."

Principal E. J. Landry delivered an address on the "Leadership of J. B. Martin." Mr. Landry related some of the highlights in Mr. Martin's career. He told the story of the large building program under the incumbent's administration. The group was informed that Mr. Martin had been a leader in the health movement even before the state department took the matter over in an extensive manner. Mr. Martin was one of the first superintendents in the state of Louisiana to produce a school band, said Mr. Landry. Under Mr. Martin's superintendency St. Charles has been a pioneer in the audio-visual field. Both high schools in the parish, Destrehan and Hahnville, are using the very last word in the line of teaching . . . the motion picture machine.

Superintendent Martin has been largely responsible for the success of the South Central Athletic association. He has fought, and not without success, to imbue coaches in the district with the philosophy of "participation" rather than "competition."

Dr. Miller complimented Superintendent Martin on his achievements and faithful service. Dr. Miller said: "We respect your ability; we admire your courage, and we love Johnny Martin." .

St. Charles Parish School Day, April 30, will be dedicated to Mr. Martin's silver jubilee.

J. B. Martin, superintendent of St. Charles Parish Public Schools from 1913 to 1944, is called "the Father of St. Charles Parish Schools." Martin was born in 1881 and was the great-grandson of Jean Baptiste LaBranche. He attended local schools but finished high school in New Orleans and graduated from Louisiana State University. It has been said that many of the great advances made in education in St. Charles Parish can be attributed to the determination and conscientious work of its first professional superintendent, J. B. Martin. J. B. Martin Middle School in Paradis is named in his honor. (Source: Times Picayune *newspaper)*

Raymond K. Smith, teacher, principal, supervisor of colored schools, and assistant superintendent of schools, was keenly aware of the value of education and did all he could to see that the students under his care had what was necessary for them to succeed. For his contribution to education, the Raymond K. Smith Middle School in Luling opened in 2006 and was dedicated in his honor.

Pictured in 1924, Allemands Elementary was moved down the bayou and back up to Des Allemands. It was later converted to an American Legion Home. (Photo courtesy of Mrs. Stanley Dufrene)

The Fashion School in Hahnville. (Photo courtesy of Patrick Yoes)

The Good Hope School was one of nine opened following the 1930 bond election.

Mr. Albert Cammon was a hero in the battle for fair education for all. Although not an educator himself, he nonetheless promoted education as a valuable commodity. His efforts brought about the opening of a high school for black students on the east bank, Bethune High School. Albert Cammon Middle School in St. Rose was named in his honor. The painting shown hangs in the school. (The artist is unknown; used with the school's permission.)

Gloria Robottom Cureau, pictured in 1939, was the principal of Hahnville Colored School and the daughter of Henry Robottom, whose family ran the first mortuary in St. Charles Parish. She was one of several people selected by J. B. Martin to assist in the development of a school system. She was a devout Catholic but attended schools in black Protestant churches until the school system provided buildings. In 1939 Gloria and her brother Harry Robottom headed Hahnville Colored School.

Harry Madison "Prof" Hurst arrived at Destrehan High in 1930 and remained for thirty-six years. He served as a teacher and coach before being appointed principal. Mr. Hurst is remembered as a quiet, dignified gentleman. A school named in his honor, Harry M. Hurst Middle School, is located on the site of the original Destrehan High School—his workplace and his home for so many years.

Eual J. "Teeny" Landry, Sr., teacher and principal at Hahnville High School, was recognized as an innovator who produced positive results and advancements in education during his forty-five years of service. His use of motion pictures as teaching tools was considered progressive and ahead of its time. He served in the military in World War II, was elected parish delegate for the 1974 Louisiana Constitutional Convention, appointed a member of the 1976 Home Rule Charter Commission, and appointed a member of the St. Charles Parish Police Jury for several years. Eual J. Landry, Sr. Middle School in Hahnville was named to honor his achievements. (Source: Times Picayune newspaper)

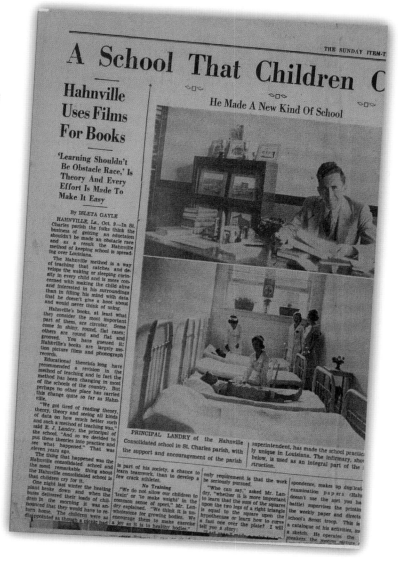

Ethel Schoeffner, teacher and principal at St. Charles Parish Public Schools from 1917 to 1965, set the standard for exemplary primary schools. She cared for her students on both a professional and personal level. Her years of outstanding service were acknowledged by the naming of an elementary school in her honor. She was the first female educator so recognized.

Ama School students prepare to raise the flag, circa 1940s. (Photo courtesy of Ernestine Kappel)

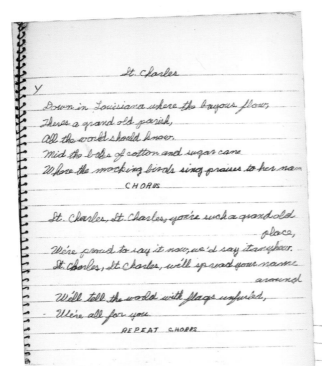

St. Charles

Down in Louisiana where the bayous flow,
There's a grand old parish,
All the world should know.
Mid the bolls of cotton and sugar cane
Where the mocking birds sing praises to her name

CHORUS

St. Charles, St. Charles, you're such a grand old
place,
We're proud to say it now, we'd say it anywhere.
St. Charles, St. Charles, we'll spread your name
around
We'll tell the world with flags unfurled,
We're all for you.

REPEAT CHORUS

A school stage curtain, circa 1940s, reflects community business and industry support for education through the purchase of advertisements.

St. Charles Parish in song, from Ralph D. St. Ament's student notebook, 1939.

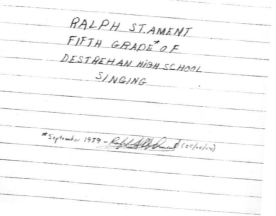

RALPH ST. AMENT
FIFTH GRADE OF
DESTREHAN HIGH SCHOOL
SINGING

September 1939

Women workers at Shell Norco.

Source: St. Charles Herald *newspaper*

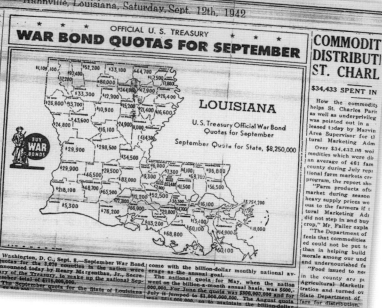

World War II

As early as the middle of 1939, the *St. Charles Herald* ran stories reflecting the unrest around the world. World War II would live up to its name before it ended in August of 1945 with the surrender of Japan. Battles were fought across the globe—in the Pacific, Europe, Africa, and beyond. The U.S. was on the fringe until the bombing of Pearl Harbor on December 7, 1941, by the Japanese Army. Already a call had gone out in the local paper for recruits to fight the war. After Pearl Harbor, the U.S. declared war on Japan and the recruitment effort intensified. War-related editorials and cartoons suddenly moved to front pages. A weekly article on page one of the *St. Charles Herald* called "With Our Men in Service" featured brief stories about the local men and women serving their country. Calls to buy war bonds went out. Gasoline and food rationing was the norm. Many other necessities, such as shoes, were in short supply. The Civilian Conservation Corps established during the Depression began looking for "unemployed young men" to fill needed positions in the community. Women went to work as never before. After their involvement in such groups as the American Red Cross, they left home in large numbers to shore up businesses whose workforces had been depleted by the war. They managed both homes and workplaces reminiscent of women

War Ration Book Four

of earlier times. Following the war, most service men and women returned home but others remained in the service having had their lives redirected by this "war to end all wars." Many never returned having sacrificed their lives for their country.

Here at home citizens volunteered to be "civilian airplane spotters" with the Army/Air Force Ground Observers Corps. Over a million Americans across the country participated. In the river parishes, spotters were also encouraged to look out for anything suspicious along the river. The citizenry was particularly concerned about German submarines working their way upriver, as many were responsible for damage to U.S. ships around the mouth of the Mississippi River. ❧ ❧ ❧

The courthouse area served as the site of a German prisoner of war camp. ❧ ❧ ❧

It was reported in the *Herald* newspaper that more than 125 U.S. Army anti-aircraft infantrymen were sent to St. Charles Parish after the Pearl Harbor bombing to guard facilities at Shell, Pan American, GATX, Cities Service, along with other plants and the Bonnet Carré Spillway.

World War II Veteran Anthony (Antonio) Portera, a naturalized citizen.

The Great Outdoors

For centuries in St. Charles Parish, the rivers, bayous, swamps, and lakes provided the citizens with unlimited fish and game for recreation as well as commerce for those individuals who preferred working in the great outdoors.

A trapper dries muskrat pelts in the sun. The St. Charles marshland is a fertile area for trapping muskrats and other fur-bearing animals. (Source: St. Charles Parish Resources and Facilities publication, 1947)

Sports fishermen pull in a nice catch of bream. (Source: St. Charles Parish Resources and Facilities publication, 1947)

Bayou Gauche serves as a base for commercial fishermen and trappers. (Source: St. Charles Parish Resources and Facilities publication, 1947)

Shrimp packers busy with the day's catch at Des Allemands. (Source: St. Charles Parish Resources and Facilities publication, 1947)

Nora Zeringue and John Lehmann display a catfish catch from the Mississippi River. (Photo courtesy of Chip Zeringue)

An early 1900s photo of hunters in St. Charles Parish.

P. A. Torres is a typical river shrimp fisherman.

Percy Alleman and Paul Richard show off their duck hunting results. (Photo courtesy of Merrill Richard Zeringue)

Shrimping on the Mississippi River in New Sarpy. (Photo courtesy of Suzanne Friloux)

156

Music Legends and Lesser-known Musicians

Music has always been a part of everyday life in St. Charles Parish. From within the home to within the community and beyond, the ability to play a musical instrument or perform with a singing group has received high praise. For some, musical ability reached its peak in a school band. For others, talent was shared with the community at such local venues as the Hahnville Concert Hall in the 1870s.

The St. Charles Borromeo Guitar Band in the 1940s.

The Hahnville High School Band in the 1940s.

(Left) Sherman Washington, a resident of Boutte, and the Zion Harmonizers Contemporary Music Legends, were internationally recognized gospel recording stars. (Source: Music Legends of St. Charles Parish Booklet prepared by St. Charles Historical Foundation.)

The First Brass Band of St. Charles Parish in the 1920s.

Susie's Kitchen Band was comprised of family members of the New Orleans Refinery Company Band, circa 1920s.

The first black school band in St. Charles Parish, circa 1951. Some musicians reached a higher level of proficiency. (Photo courtesy of Carolyn S. Boyd)

(Left) The Eight Tones Orchestra in the 1950s was formed by Raymond K. Smith, musician, educator, and civic leader. He was aware of the value of music in a person's life and he promoted the art with his students. He later served as assistant superintendent of schools in St. Charles Parish. The Eight Tones was organized as a rhythm and blues and rock band as students moved into the new Carver High School. Later the band played for Shell dances, on college campuses, and for fraternities at Ole Miss, Tulane, and LSU.

(Right) In the early 1920s, the Norco Refining Company Band provided entertainment for the refinery.

Entrepreneur Extraordinaire

Henry "DeDe" Friloux was educated in Ama schools and attended Soule' Business College in New Orleans before arriving in Norco in 1924 to begin working for New Orleans Refining Company. In 1931, he acquired Norco Cleaners and Laundry so that Shell workers could have starched and pressed white shirts for their weekend social activities. The cleaning business needed a steady supply of natural gas, so Friloux arranged with a pipeline company to tap their line. Learning of the interest of other parish residents to have natural gas, in September of 1931 Friloux and his investors quickly organized Norco Gas

and Fuel, Inc., to distribute natural gas to east bank residents. He served as chairman of the board and president of the company for decades, and his sons Henry, Jr., and Nash joined him in the business in later years. The success of Norco Gas led Friloux to organize South Coast Gas Company and the Dixie Gas Company. Norco Gas and Dixie Gas were sold to Louisiana Gas Service and eventually became Atmos Energy, which continues to have a presence at the original site in Norco. Of all the utilities enjoyed today by parish residents (natural gas, electricity, water, telephone, garbage pick-up, sewer, cable), Henry Friloux's natural gas distribution was the "first of its kind" utility in the rural community. Henry Friloux's entrepreneurial spirit would not only help small businesses but would begin to change the lives of ordinary citizens in St. Charles Parish much like Henry Ford's wheels brought change to America.

In 1924, Leon Preston Madere, Sr., son of former Sheriff Anthony "Tony" Madere, opened his garage on River Road in Hahnville. Madere would soon own a Chrysler, Dodge, Plymouth automobile dealership and continued to serve the river parishes area until the recession of 2009 when Chrysler eliminated many of its franchises. Originally owned by Madere Sr., eventually his son Preston, Jr., daughter Mildred, and his son-in-law Frank Pizzolato, Sr., became co-owners. The garage is

Miss Lettie Smith weds Henry Friloux in January 1938 at the Smith home in Gramercy.

Madere's Garage, 15042 River Road in Hahnville across from the St. Charles Parish Courthouse, opened in 1924. (Photo courtesy of David Pizzolato, Sr.)

Shoppers pictured in front of the Mamzelle Store in Destrehan.

The Tom in 1925 was used to deliver goods up and down the river. (Photo from St. Charles Library Collection, courtesy of Miss Francis Lorio)

currently owned by Preston, Sr.'s youngest son, Jan Madere and grandsons David and Michael Pizzolato. Leon Preston Madere, Sr., served for many years as a member of the parish police jury. He had twelve children and today the Madere family, of German descent, is a large and prominent west bank family whose ancestors have been traced back to Natchitoches in the 1700s where Jean "Matere" and his German Coast wife, Marie Marguerite Materne, lived.

Entrepreneurial Spirit Abounds

Although major industries dominated the headlines during the early part of the twentieth century, all across St. Charles Parish small businesses were also popping up to meet the needs of the ever growing population. It was not unusual to have "peddlers," selling everything from brushes to jewelry, go door-to-door with their wares stored in the trunk of their cars. If the customers couldn't go to them, the merchants went to their customers. These merchants were known as drummers. Insurance salesmen visited customers at home. Ice houses were located

The W. L. Bergeron Machine Shop and Garage on Paul Maillard Road in Luling was moved from Cousin's Lumber Camp and the building is still standing today as Quality Wholesale and Janitorial. (Photo courtesy of Mrs. J. B. Nicholas)

The Bossier Store.

Wesco Paints was located on Wesco Road between Good Hope and Norco.

Bouvier's Drug Store in Destrehan, 1923–24.

The Bossier Store in Norco.

Alfred Levesque's Store in Des Allemands/Comardelle.

Laura Robottom Smith and Joseph Smith were the owners of Smith's Grocery in Hahnville. (Photo courtesy of Carolyn S. Boyd)

The Colonial Dairy Farms in Taft opened in 1935 and became one of the largest dairies in Louisiana.

The Des Allemands Store was across the bayou from the sawmill. (Photo courtesy of Opal Dufrene)

Richard's Department Store in Norco was located at the corner of Apple Street and River Road.

The Norco Pharmacy on the River Road in Norco provided a workplace for Pharmacist Ned Lowry and Shell Oil Company Physician Dr. Paul Landry. The soda fountain was a favorite. In the 1930s, the upstairs was a boarding house for Shell workers. The building is still in commerce in the twenty-first century.

at various sites in the parish, but the "ice man" also made the rounds of the neighborhoods. Children would run after the truck shouting, "a chip, a chip." Many merchants allowed their customers to use the "on credit" system. As items were purchased, the sale was recorded, often in small receipt books kept on a rack behind the counter in the store, with payment due on "payday." Physicians made "house calls," sometimes receiving goods for services.

The Vitrano Store in Killona was the site of the murder of Sheriff Lewis Ory in the late 1800s.

Numa Zeringue's Mamzelle Store was built in 1875 on the River Road in Destrehan where the Capital One Bank is today. Notice the wheel ruts in the road. The family home was located behind the store. (Photo courtesy of Chip Zeringue)

Smith's Grocery on the River Road in Hahnville, 1921–98.

Dufrene's Garage in Montz.

Banquer's Store, Falcon's Apartments, and Migliore's Food Store on the River Road in New Sarpy.

The St. Charles Pharmacy in Norco was owned by Pharmacist Percy Alleman. For a time it also served as the office of his brother Dr. Earl Alleman and Dr. Posey Landeche, DDS.

Bar-None Ranch Riding Facility and Social Club. (*Source:* St. Charles Parish Resources and Facilities publication, 1961)

Haydel's Appliance Store employees. (Photo courtesy of Harold Haydel)

Haydel's Appliance Store on Apple Street in Norco is still in business at the same location. (Photo courtesy of Harold Haydel)

The Royal Theater on River Road in Norco, circa 1945. (Photo courtesy of Joan Weaver Becnel)

Robottom's Mortuary on the River Road in Hahnville, a family business since the early 1900s, was the first mortuary in St. Charles Parish. Owned by Mr. Henry Robottom and P. D. Lorio, Sr., services were offered to both white and black families. Robottom's Mortuary is still in operation in Hahnville under the direction of third generation family members.

Robert J. Anderson is pictured in the Country Store in Norco.

Sharkey's Bar in Norco. The building remains in 2010.

A Lobdell Bakery truck makes a delivery in 1939.

Richard's Department Store in Luling. (Photo courtesy of Patrick Yoes)

The Cobbler Shop

Patriarch of the Medina family in Luling, Francisco Medina came to St. Charles Parish as a railroad employee from Querato, Mexico, to work under railroad stationmaster Laurent J. Labry. As a side job, young Francisco apprenticed under Luling cobbler Ben Paul learning the artistry of shoe repair. Francisco's family has owned and operated the Cobbler Shop for decades, mending boots, shoes, purses, belts, and other leather goods. Second and third generation Medina members, Joe and daughter Carolyn, carry on the family business in Luling on Paul Maillard Road.

Business district of Destrehan with St. Charles Borromeo School in the background. (Photo courtesy of Chip Zeringue)

During the Great Depression, there were 120,000 cobbler shops operating in the nation. There are now only 7,000. ⚜ ⚜ ⚜

Luling landmark, Vial's Bar (the Corner Bar) also housed the Cobbler Shop, a barbershop, and a bus depot in the back. (Watercolor courtesy of Sylvia Corbin)

Louis Armstrong New Orleans International Airport

As early as the mid 1930s it was apparent that expanded airport facilities would be needed to serve the city of New Orleans' growing air transportation needs. In 1940, the city of Kenner was selected as the site of the new airport. The land was designated as Moisant Field in honor of John B. Moisant, an early daredevil aviation pioneer. Construction was delayed when the United States became involved in World War II in December 1941. The land for Moisant Field was taken over by the U.S. government for use as an air base. In 1946, the government returned the land plus 295 adjacent acres to the City of New Orleans. Commercial air service began at Moisant Field in May of 1946. The official name of the airport was changed in 1960 to New Orleans International Airport. In August 2001, the name was changed to Louis Armstrong New Orleans International Airport in honor of the famous jazz musician on the one hundredth anniversary of his birth. In May of 1992, the east-west runway was reopened with the new extension into St. Charles Parish. The airport played a major role in rescue efforts for victims of Hurricane Katrina in 2005.

A scene in front of the airport in its early days. (Photo courtesy of Louis Armstrong New Orleans International Airport)

Mid-century Changes

As the 1950s rolled around, other economic engines were starting up. The Delta Match Corporation opened in St. Rose in 1952 on the old Frellson Plantation, and Lion Oil Company (Monsanto) construction began in 1952 in Luling on the old Ellington Plantation. Delta opened as the first large, wooden match manufacturing plant in the South, eventually becoming the largest of its kind in the world. In 1955, Shell Chemical opened a plant in Norco on the site of the old Diamond Plantation.

In 1958, the parish would experience a loss of commerce with the closing of one of its first major industries, the American Oil Company in Destrehan. Hundreds of workers were left jobless. White-collar workers were given options to move to other company locations. Intervention by parish officials resulted in cooperative efforts with the company to help the unemployed workers find jobs.

Bunge Grain Elevator, Destrehan.

The first unit of the Little Gypsy Power Plant in Montz was activated by the Louisiana Power and Light Company in 1960. And, as in the past, new opportunities were just around the corner. A new type of industry was being actively pursued by parish officials. Two grain elevators started up in Modoc: Bunge Grain Elevator in 1961 and the St. Charles Grain Elevator in 1968. On the west bank, the Farmers' Export Grain Elevator opened in 1963 in Ama. Large industrial corporations opened facilities in the sixties, including Union Carbide (Dow), Hooker Chemical in Taft, and Waterford I and II on plantation land formerly used primarily for sugar cane farming. Plans for Waterford III Nuclear Power Plant surfaced in 1970 and commercial operation commenced on September 24, 1985.

Fire Protection for St. Charles

The parish's newest fire station is located on the River Road in New Sarpy.

Since the mid-1950s, groups of men and women have volunteered at fire stations around the parish to respond to fires, accidents, explosions, or a variety of other situations, which might require their expertise. The eleven departments currently have a membership of approximately two hundred volunteers. All departments are members of the St. Charles Firemen's Association. According to an article in the *Times Picayune* of May 3, 1992, the group was formed to improve communication between the various volunteer departments. A one-eighth cent sales tax provides the revenue needed for operation of their respective departments. In addition to the revenue, the sharing of equipment and manpower enhances the quality of services provided.

Two other elements serve to raise the level of excellence of fire protection and public safety. The parish is implementing major improvements to the waterworks system to increase available water pressure across the parish. Secondly, firefighters go through extensive and continuous training. Several are also registered emergency medical technicians. These volunteers can be credited with helping to reduce insurance costs by improving the fire rating of their districts.

This fire truck was issued in the 1950s. It is still in the care of the department. State-of-the-art equipment now takes to the streets.

Locke Breaux Oak in the 1950s. (Photo courtesy of St. Charles Parish Library/Jimmy Westlake)

Locke Breaux Oak

The Locke Breaux Oak, named after a prominent New Orleanian, was originally known as the Providence Live Oak after the plantation that it had watched over for years—Providence Plantation in Taft. At one time declared the world's largest oak, it became the victim of progress.

Margaret L. Herman, right, started the first lending library in Hahnville, opening her own home for this purpose in 1949. She is pictured in this photo with Parish Librarian Mrs. Greeson.

Library Services—Here Comes the Bookmobile!

History indicates that as early as 1872, Governor Hahn "laid out" a library for the parish seat of Hahnville. There is no evidence to indicate this library ever materialized, but the seed for the need of such a facility had been planted. The idea would not come to fruition until much later. In the 1940s, citizens in the community began writing letters of inquiry to the Louisiana State Library. Finally, their persistence paid off. According to an article in the *St. Charles Herald*, the state library agreed to establish a "demonstration library" in Hahnville to help the parish start a permanent system.

In April 1955, Mrs. Charlotte Gaylord was appointed librarian of the St. Charles Parish demonstration library. At long last Governor Hahn's idea had materialized. The "demonstration library" concept was replaced with a permanent library system to operate with the passage of a tax in April 1956.

OIC EXHIBIT—Kirby J. Ducote, center, Chairman of the St. Charles Parish Oil Information Committee, explains the operations of a fractionating column exhibit to Mrs. J. D. Walker, left, Norco Branch Librarian, and Mrs. Charlotte Gaylord, Parish Librarian. The exhibit was on display in the Norco library for two weeks.

In a picture from the Shell Bulletin *October 1957, Norco Branch Librarian Mabel Walker, left, is shown viewing an exhibit with St. Charles Parish Oil Information Committee Chairman Kirby Ducote and Parish Librarian Charlotte Gaylord.*

Early bookmobiles in the 1950s. (Photo courtesy of St. Charles Parish Library)

The East Bank Regional Library in Destrehan.

On August 7, 1955, library branches were opened in Norco and Hahnville. The system soon acquired a bookmobile, which traveled to small isolated communities and neighborhoods. It bore the name "Louisiana State Library" but soon would be replaced with two vehicles, which were the property of the St. Charles system. Since 2006, the system has owned one modern bookmobile, which serves both sides of the river. Although the bookmobile no longer visits schools, library services are taken to nursery schools, nursing homes, senior citizens centers, and private homes upon request.

In the 1970s, with voter approval of a parish bond issue, two parcels of land were purchased and two new regional libraries were constructed. The West Regional Library resources include a nationally recognized planetarium, the Louisiana Room, which houses a portion of parish archived records, and the system's administrative offices. Both East and West Regional Libraries have audio-visual equipment as well as Internet access through computer workstations.

The West Bank Regional Library in Luling.

Educational Update

Another educational component was added to the mix in 1959 when another parochial elementary school, Sacred Heart, opened in Norco. The school remains open in 2010 serving the children of the church parish as well as students from the region.

An early photo of Sacred Heart School in Norco. (Source: St. Charles Parish Resources Facilities publication, 1961)

St. Charles Parish Hospital in 2009.

Health Services Then and Now

Louisiana has one of the oldest healthcare systems in the nation. Early government records in St. Charles Parish reveal the health of the residents of the community was a primary concern for officials. But twentieth-century officials brought healthcare to a new level. In 1959, St. Charles Parish Hospital opened its doors to the community. In 1961, the following evaluation of the health and medical conditions in the parish was presented in a parish-sponsored document published by the St. Charles Parish Development Board: "St. Charles Parish is a healthful parish, due in a large part to the immunization practices that have been instituted. Flood control and greatly improved sanitation have helped to win the fight against communicable diseases. This fight was led by the Parish Health Unit. Today there is a modern general hospital on the west bank and several well equipped clinics located in the parish. Ambulance service is available, as is good ferry service to reach the general hospital. Eleven doctors and six dentists have greatly improved the medical situation reducing the need for going to New Orleans." The hospital became readily available to all residents with the opening of the Hale Boggs Bridge. In 1998, an east bank medical office building was opened by the hospital, and in 2010, a state-of-the-art hospital acute care facility in Luling offers a broad spectrum of medical services.

St. Charles Parish Community Health Center in 2009. (Courtesy of the St. Charles Community Health Center)

Community Health Center

St. Charles Community Health Center opened its doors in 2003 at 843 Milling Avenue in Luling directly behind St. Charles Parish Hospital replacing a state health unit, which had closed. The center's mission is to provide accessible high quality healthcare through collaborative community efforts, to promote prevention and coordinate treatment, and to improve the healthcare status of the community with the emphasis on the underserved and vulnerable populations. The center now has satellite centers in Destrehan, Kenner, and Norco as well as a mobile medical unit.

172

Parish Survives Betsy, but Recovery Will Take Months

St. Charles Parish has a full-time staffed Department of Emergency Preparedness (formerly the Civil Defense Office established in 1977). The late John M. "Ikey" Lucas served as director of both. He remained in the post until 1996.
⚜ ⚜ ⚜

Ikey Lucas, right, shakes hands with celebrity chef Justin Wilson, left, in 1988.

Hurricanes and Stormy Weather

Mother Nature has had a significant effect on the citizens of St. Charles Parish throughout its history. As early as 1722, one of Mississippi's most respected historians, Charles Sullivan, wrote in *Hurricanes of the Mississippi Gulf Coast* that this area had been impacted to varying degrees by hurricanes over the years. Recorded data chronicles the arrival of these storms classified as "Fatal Storms:"

> 1856 Unnamed
> 1893 Unnamed
> 1965 Betsy
> 1969 Camille
> 2005 Katrina

The most intense Atlantic hurricanes on record:

> 1915 "Great West Indian Hurricane"
> 1992 Andrew
> 2005 Rita

Major Hurricanes Passing Within Seventy-five Miles of St. Charles Parish Since 1960

Date	Name	Highest Attained Strength
9/14/1960	Ethel	Category 5
9/28/1964	Hilda	Category 4
8/27/1965	Betsy	Category 4
8/14/1969	Camille	Category 5
9/5/1971	Edith	Category 5
8/29/1974	Frederic	Category 4
8/16/1992	Andrew	Category 4
9/15/1998	Georges	Category 4
9/14/2002	Isidore	Category 4
9/21/2002	Lili	Category 4
8/23/2005	Katrina	Category 5

Chart by the Department of Emergency Preparedness of St. Charles Parish.

Path of the "Great West Indian Hurricane of 1915." This hurricane made landfall at Grand Isle as a Category 4 storm. It brushed St. Charles Parish as a Category 2 hurricane, but the small settlements of Frenier and Ruddock along Lake Pontchartrain in St. John Parish were washed away by the wind and water. Many lives were lost. Twelve miles of Illinois Central double tracks were destroyed. Six thousand men were put to work to restore rail services. (Source: Frenier Beach Hurricane Storm Surge Revisited by Samuel P. Landry, Jr. P.E.)

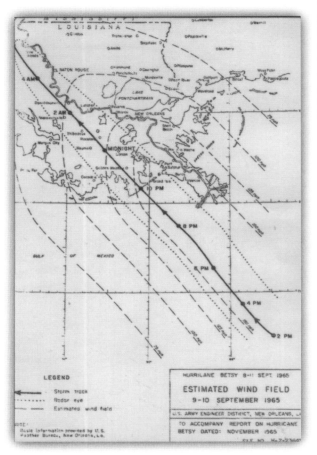

(Source: New Orleans District U.S. Army Corps of Engineers Report on Hurricane Betsy, September 8–11, 1965)

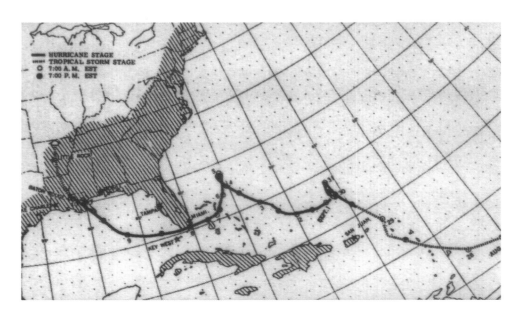

(Source: New Orleans District U.S. Army Corps of Engineers Report on Hurricane Betsy, September 8–11, 1965)

A speaker addresses students during ceremonies for the first and last Hahnville Colored High School graduating class in the spring of 1952. Underclass students transferred to Carver High School (Hahnville) in the fall. (Photo courtesy of Carolyn S. Boyd)

Hahnville Colored High School dedication plaque.

Desegregation of Public Schools

In the early sixties, the parish school system began to plan for desegregation of public schools. The voluntary integration of schools began in 1965–66, but it was not until 1969 that total integration of all schools occurred. Diligent and deliberate preparation by the administrators, faculties, and staffs and the cooperation of the parents and their children facilitated the implementation of integration.

Years later, an incident took place which temporarily threatened the stability of the system. A tragic shooting occurred on the edge of the Destrehan High School campus. One student lost his life, another's life was changed forever, and the lives of many others were greatly affected by the incident. With time and a concerted effort on the part of the school system and the community, Destrehan High and the rest of the schools of the district resumed orderly operations.

The schools of St. Charles Parish, whether public, private, or parochial, have enjoyed excellent reputations over the years. Innovative techniques, sound financing, community support, nationally accredited teachers, strong administrators, as well as parents and students who are engaged in the learning process have all contributed to their success.

Don Raymond, an outstanding student athlete, transferred to Hahnville High School from Carver High in the ninth grade through the "freedom of choice" option. He lettered in four sports and was on the 1968 Class AA football team. His life was cut tragically short due to injuries received in a traffic collision on the River Road in Hahnville. Out of respect for his achievements as an individual, a student, and an athlete, each year the Don Raymond Track and Field Relays are held at Hahnville High School in his honor.

Bethune High in Norco, 1952 (*Source:* St. Charles Parish Resources and Facilities publication, 1961)

Carver High School, 1952 (*Source: Graduation invitation courtesy of Connie Robinson*)

Although limited high school classes were offered for African American students as early as 1947 (west bank only), it was not until the fall of 1952 that new comprehensive high schools were opened on each side of the Mississippi River. Further changes came with the desegregation of schools.

The 1970 *Bunge Explosion*

The Bunge Grain Elevator in Destrehan (Modoc) was rocked by two explosions on a quiet Sunday evening in September of 1970. The grain industry, which had been seen as a redeeming force in the parish's economy in the early 1960s following the closing of the American Oil Company in Destrehan, suffered a setback as a result of this accident. The families of the six employees who were hospitalized as well as the whole community were deeply affected by this event. Many homes and a nearby school were extensively damaged. The fire which erupted burned for almost twenty-four hours and destroyed the elevator. The safety concerns of the neighborhood were brought to a sobering reality. The elevator was eventually rebuilt and put back into commerce.

Bottom left photo courtesy of the Times Picayune. *Remaining three photos courtesy of the* St. Charles Herald.

Story of a Newspaper

In 1969, Allen Lottinger, a newspaper publisher in Houma, was approached by a west bank businessman looking for a place in which to advertise. He suggested the need for a newspaper to serve west bank communities. Lottinger toured the area and decided the project had possibilities. Allen and his wife Collette established an office for the publication of a newspaper in Boutte in the building previously occupied by the Raven, a popular nightclub on Highway 90. In August 1969, the *West St. Charles Guide* was published for the first time. The circulation grew over the years. It became a paid publication in 1979. The entire Lottinger family has been involved in the enterprise. The business, which expanded to include other forms of publications, remains in Boutte in the original location. The *Guide* merged with the *St. Charles Herald* (Yoes Family) in 1993 and the name was changed to the *St. Charles Herald Guide*. In 2006, Pat and Gail Yoes agreed to sell their half of the company to the *Guide* group, known as Louisiana Publishing, Inc. In 2010, Tony and Anne Lottinger Taylor continue to operate the *Herald Guide* and also publish six magazines including the *Louisiana Sportsman*.

Flooding in Hill Heights is depicted in this 1973 view. (Photo courtesy of Fay Walker Louque.)

An aerial view of Hill Heights, Destrehan, shows flooding in 1973. (Photo courtesy of Fay Walker Louque)

Flooding in St. Charles Parish

Although the Bonnet Carré Spillway has controlled the waters of the Mississippi River, flooding from rainfall and tides continued to take its toll on St. Charles Parish. In the latter part of the 1900s—1973, 1989, and 1995, the parish experienced major flooding caused by heavy rainfalls. Rising tides and rainfall associated with hurricanes also plagued the area.

Still under construction, the East Bank Hurricane Protection Levee is designed to provide a buffer between Lake Pontchartrain and the developed area. On the west bank, similar protection was not yet in place in 2010 although plans are being made to construct a levee system. The ongoing challenge to secure and protect the mainland of the German Coast known as St. Charles Parish continues as erosion plays a role in the increasing vulnerability of the low-lying terrain.

St. Charles Borromeo Church, 1973

St. Charles Borromeo Parish celebrated its 250th anniversary on June 3, 1973. Many church leaders and government officials, as well as parishioners, participated in the day's activities. These included a mass of celebration, a pageant honoring the early German settlers, cajun music, and square dancing. All in attendance enjoyed an outdoor luncheon served under the majestic, historic oak trees on the church grounds.

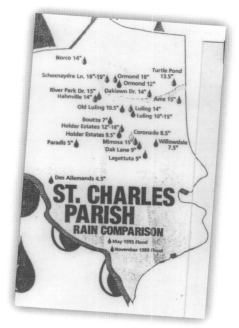

St. Charles Parish rainfall statistics published in a chart presented in a 1995 issue of the Herald Guide.

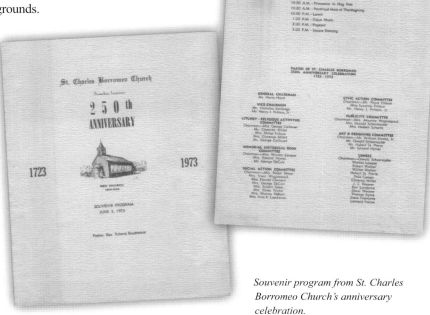

Souvenir program from St. Charles Borromeo Church's anniversary celebration.

Distinguished guests at the 250th anniversary celebration included Fay Walker Louque, Governor Edwin Edwards, and Elaine Edwards.

Evolution of the Courthouse

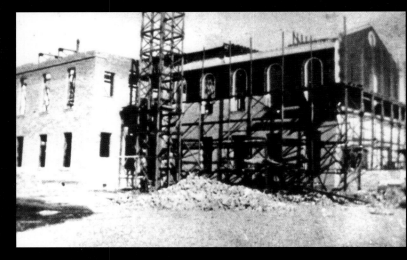

The courthouse undergoes an expansion in 1921.

St. Charles Parish Courthouse in 1826. (Photo courtesy of Gene Yoes)

The courthouse in 1921.

The courthouse is demolished in 1976. (Photo courtesy of the St. Charles Parish Library)

The new St. Charles Parish Courthouse in Hahnville was completed in 1976 at the same site as the former courthouse.

New Schools

Two new public high schools opened in 1976: Destrehan High School in Destrehan and Hahnville High School in Mozella. They continue to serve students at the same sites in 2010. Both schools offer advanced studies programs, as well as art and music. They both are known for their top notch athletic programs. A recently opened Satellite Center in Luling offers specialized courses for juniors and seniors of both schools. These include culinary arts, healthcare, teacher preparation, and TV production.

Hahnville High School (left) and Destrehan High School (right) in 2010.

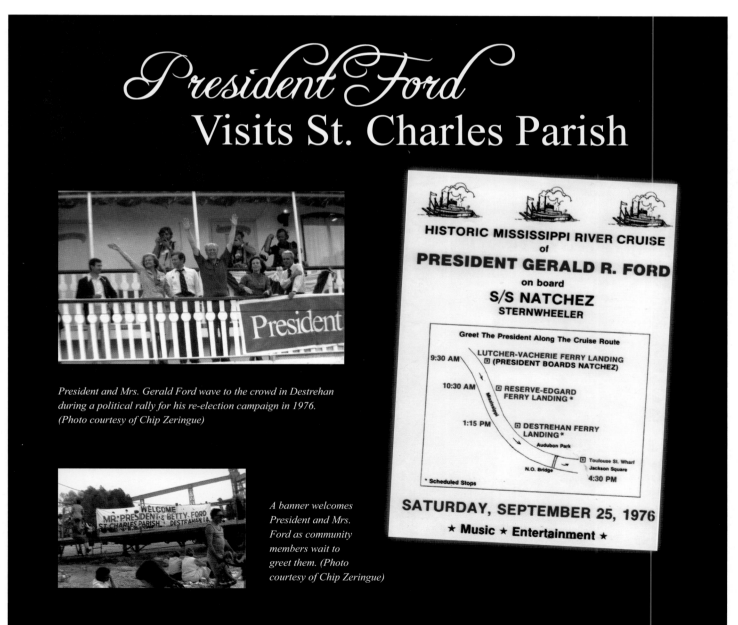

President Ford
Visits St. Charles Parish

President and Mrs. Gerald Ford wave to the crowd in Destrehan during a political rally for his re-election campaign in 1976. (Photo courtesy of Chip Zeringue)

A banner welcomes President and Mrs. Ford as community members wait to greet them. (Photo courtesy of Chip Zeringue)

HISTORIC MISSISSIPPI RIVER CRUISE
of
PRESIDENT GERALD R. FORD
on board
S/S NATCHEZ
STERNWHEELER

Greet The President Along The Cruise Route

9:30 AM LUTCHER-VACHERIE FERRY LANDING
(PRESIDENT BOARDS NATCHEZ)

10:30 AM RESERVE-EDGARD FERRY LANDING *

1:15 PM DESTREHAN FERRY LANDING *
Audubon Park
Toulouse St. Wharf
Jackson Square
N.O. Bridge
* Scheduled Stops
4:30 PM

SATURDAY, SEPTEMBER 25, 1976
★ Music ★ Entertainment ★

Ferry Disaster

The Luling/Destrehan Ferry disaster in 1976 is one of the worst maritime accidents in history. (Photos courtesy of the St. Charles Herald, *Patrick Yoes, and Chip Zeringue)*

(Courtesy of the St. Charles Herald*)*

The George Prince Ferry Memorial was dedicated on October 17, 2009.

Luling/Destrehan Ferry Disaster

The October 20, 1976, collision on the Mississippi River of the *George Prince* ferry and the Norwegian tanker *Frosta* was ranked as the top story of the millennium in the local press. It has been characterized as one of the worst maritime disasters in history. The 120-foot *George Prince* and the 665-foot *Frosta* collided as the ferry made its early morning journey from Destrehan to Luling mainly carrying industry workers as it had done hundreds of times before.

Frantic horn blasts and radio calls from the tanker failed to alert the ferry's pilot to the impending danger. The *Frosta* ran over the smaller boat and flipped it over sending vehicles and ninety-five passengers into the cold, muddy waters of the river. Seventy-seven people perished; nineteen were St. Charles Parish residents and twelve were from St. John. The eighteen survivors fought swirling water, frigid temperatures, and mass confusion as they struggled to escape.

As the news of the collision spread, families and loved ones began to gather on the levee to await news. Rescuers worked valiantly around the clock looking for victims and survivors. Food was brought in for the workers at the temporary headquarters set up on the batture. As bodies were recovered they were transported to the Knights of Columbus Home in Norco and the local fire station. The effort continued until every passenger had been accounted for. An inquiry concluded that the ferry pilot was negligent and his lack of action was the primary cause of the disaster. This judgment could not erase the profound pain and suffering endured by the families and community. A monument to commemorate the tragedy was erected at the East Bank Bridge Park in 2009.

St. Charles Celebrates America's Bicentennial

St. Charles Parish had the first international bicentennial project in the state of Louisiana—a visitor exchange with the town of Breman, Germany. As a result of this project, negotiations began for the establishment of a trade mission in New Orleans. St. Charles Parish, known originally as the German Coast, was one of the earliest areas settled in Louisiana. Beginning in 1719, German families from the John Law Company arrived in St. Charles Parish.

A New Day

Police Jury to Home Rule

St. Charles Parish, one of the most affluent and progressive parishes in Louisiana, became one of the first parishes to adopt a new form of government.

Louisiana's 1974 Constitution provided to the people of a parish their right to establish a home rule form of government. Home rule would give local government the authority to adopt its own laws without regard to state law except in those instances where state law prohibits or denies such authority. In 1977, the St. Charles Parish Police Jury empanelled a Home Rule Charter Commission to study the issue and draft a proposed charter.

Immigration by Professor Waldemar Otto was commissioned by the Breman, West German government as a bicentennial gift to the people of St. Charles Parish in commemoration of the early German settlers. The sculpture, located in the courthouse lobby, was cast in Berlin, Germany, and represents a settler breaking with the past (leaving Germany) and going into the future (going to America). Wording on the base of the sculpture reads: "A project of the United States Bicentennial Celebration, 1776-1976, St. Charles Parish Bicentennial Committee, Exchange Visits with the German Port City of Breman, Germany."

Edward A. Dufresne, Jr., "Father of the St. Charles Parish Home Rule Charter," attorney since 1963, and chairman of the Home Rule Charter Commission, was instrumental in drafting the first parish constitution. He worked tirelessly for its passage and assisted parish officials for years with implementation of the provisions. Dufresne was elected unopposed to the offices of clerk of court, Twenty-ninth Judicial District judge, and appellate judge of the Fifth Circuit Court of Appeal for the Third District, serving as chief judge since 2001. Judge Dufresne has been appointed numerous times to sit on the Louisiana Supreme Court and has served continuously for over forty-five years as an elected official of the parish.

On March 1, 1977, the Clerk of Court and Charter Commission Chairman Edward A. Dufresne, Jr., left, gives instructions to the newly empanelled Home Rule Charter Commission. Charter Commission member Eual Landry, Sr., right, listens to Dufresne. A former principal of Hahnville High School, Landry also served as St. Charles Parish's representative for the 1974 Constitutional Convention.

Voters overwhelmingly supported the proposition for home rule. The charter became effective on January 7, 1978. The provisions of the charter were implemented, but the structure and organization of the new government would not be put into place until June 1980 as police jurors were allowed to serve their terms until that time.

As first parish president, Kevin M. Friloux's mission and approach to organize the new government laid the foundation and groundwork for a modern, progressive government, which carried the parish into the new millennium.

Members of the Home Rule Charter Commission sign and certify the proposed new home rule form of government on August 24, 1977. The charter draft was accepted by the police jury and a special election was held Saturday, December 3, 1977, for the voters to consider a home rule charter proposition. Pictured are back row, left to right: Harry M. Hurst, Dulce Guidry, John Landry, Jr., Allen J. Braud, and Benjamin Parquet; front row: Eual J. Landry, Sr., H. A. LeBlanc, Jr., Edward A. Dufresne, Jr., Irma Green, and Norman Pitre. Rev. Robert C. Kitchell is not pictured.

The proposed home rule charter was signed and certified on August 24, 1977.

The first parish president, Kevin M. Friloux, is surrounded by members of the first parish council in June 1980. Pictured left to right: Clayton Faucheux, Sr., Leonce "Tut" Clement, Cecil Dufrene, Kevin Friloux, Welton "Check" Aupied, Bill Hubbs, Charles Stirling Melancon, Warren Landry, Donald Hogan, and Bruce Rodrigue.

Charles Stirling Melancon, first chairman of the St. Charles Parish Council, also served as the last president of the police jury.

Albert D. Laque (far right), second parish president, served one term from 1988 to 1992 and was re-elected to serve two more terms from 2000 to 2008. A lifelong public servant, he is remembered most for his cooperative leadership.

Chris A. Tregre, third parish president, served two terms from 1992 to 2000 and will best be remembered for leading citizen opposition to a riverboat casino in St. Charles Parish based on the belief that local government should have the right to determine how its land should be zoned and utilized. A landmark Louisiana Supreme Court decision upheld the parish's right to legislate in this regard.

In June 1976 the last full-term elected police jurors were sworn into office in the Old Schexnaydre IGA Building in Taft. Pictured, left to right: Leonard LeDoux, A. J. Faucheux, Steve DeBenedetto, Harney Hooper, and Roosevelt Dufrene. Not shown are Frankie Pizzolato and Freddie Giangrosso. Crowded conditions in the old courthouse forced the police jury to spend several years in the Schexnaydre Building.

Destrehan High School Fire

On June 1, 1977, a fire destroyed the old high school which was being used for other school and government offices. Arson was suspected in the destruction of the grand old building, which had graced the River Road in Destrehan since 1924. A mural by Louisiana muralist Rodney Lewis depicting the school has been painted on the exterior wall of the old cafeteria. Funds were provided by a grant from the River Region Arts and Humanities Council in association with United Way of St. Charles.

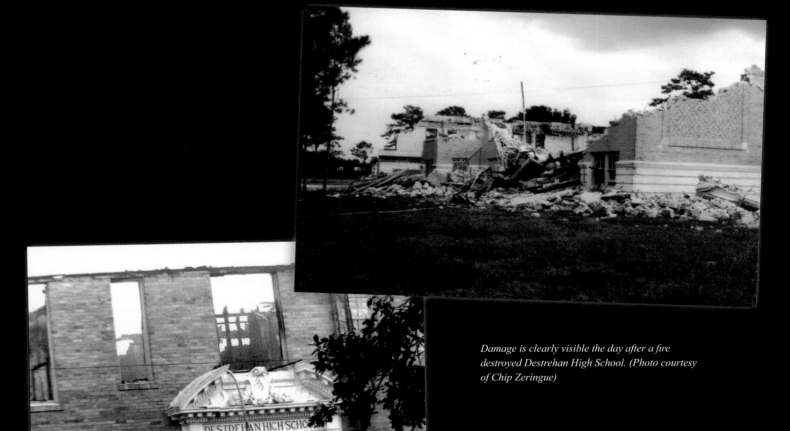

Damage is clearly visible the day after a fire destroyed Destrehan High School. (Photo courtesy of Chip Zeringue)

New Private School Opens on the West Bank

Faced with the desire to make more choices available for students, Boutte Christian Academy began operating as an elementary school in the 1980s. In 2010, its Highway 90 campus continues to serve area students.

The Good Hope Refinery

In 1983, Good Hope Refinery bought out the residential and commercial property of the town of Good Hope in order to expand its operations. The once so-called "Wonder Town" of the 1920s ceased to be a town at all on September 5, 2000, with the passage of parish legislation establishing town boundaries. It is now within the boundary of the town of Norco. The refinery eventually closed and a series of companies purchased the site over the years. In 2003, the refinery and property were acquired by Valero, a Fortune 500 diversified energy corporation and was renamed Valero St. Charles Refinery. The far-reaching resources of the parent company have allowed it to become a major part of the industrial community of St. Charles.

Luling/Destrehan Bridge

On October 6, 1983, life as St. Charles Parish citizens had known it for over 250 years changed forever with the opening of the Luling/Destrehan Bridge. It was hailed as one of the biggest events of the millennium. The new link it provided between the east and west banks of the river spurred residential and economic growth and offered opportunities for cultural and social interaction.

A postcard aerial view.

The Luling/Destrehan Bridge was under construction on October 20, 1976, when the George Prince *ferry accident occurred. (Photo courtesy of Chip Zeringue)*

PROJECT	COST	CONTRACTOR
Substructure	$42,506,392	Massman Johnson Construction Co. Kansas City, Missouri
Superstructure	$41,800,000	Williams Brothers Construction Houston, Texas
South Approach	$16,390,911	Boh Brothers Construction Co. New Orleans, Louisiana
North Approach	$16,343,522	Atlas Construction Co. Kenner, Louisiana
North Approach	$7,184,475	Key Constructors, Inc. Jackson, Mississippi

DESIGNERS

All five construction projects listed above were jointly designed by the firms of Modjeski and Masters of Harrisburg, Pa. and New Orleans, La. and Frankland and Leinhard of New York.

PROJECT ENGINEERS

Since construction began on the Luling-Destrehan Bridge substructure in July, 1974, five Department of Transportation and Development engineers have served as Project Engineers. They are Willie T. Taylor, Jr., Stuart McCardle, A. V. Flotte, Naim Afis, and Osmond "Ozzie" Hansen.

Statistics show the cost and personnel involved in the construction of the bridge. (Source: Dedication Brochure)

Residents from both sides of the river attended the bridge's opening ceremonies.

A water spray on the river was part of the celebration activities.

Governor David Treen and other dignitaries were on hand for the official opening of the bridge.

Bridge area prior to East Bank Bridge Park development.

(Publication courtesy of the American Society of Civil Engineers)

LULING-DESTREHAN BRIDGE — LOUISIANA
THE OUTSTANDING CIVIL ENGINEERING ACHIEVEMENT

AWARDED IN A NATIONAL COMPETITION · 1984
BY THE AMERICAN SOCIETY OF CIVIL ENGINEERS

In 1984, the bridge was recognized as the Outstanding Civil Engineering Achievement of 1984 by the American Society of Civil Engineers for its unique design. It was the third major cable-stayed bridge in the United States. As of 2010, it is the only bridge in the United States that is cable-stayed with an orthotropic deck.

Land under the bridge has been leased by the parish from federal and state governments for public use. East and west bridge parks provide walking and jogging paths; tennis courts; playground areas; baseball, softball, and football fields; pavilions for family gatherings; concession stands; and space for fairs and festivals as well as other community events. Bike paths with scenic overlooks on the Mississippi River levee connect St. Charles Parish with adjacent parishes. The paths are enjoyed by walkers, joggers, and cyclists.

West Bank Bridge Park.

Beautification Task Force Rendering,
East Bank Bridge Park.

Charles Troxler of Taft and friends in 1936 on the Shell skiff. Many citizens used similar vessels to criss-cross the Mississippi River from east to west banks and vice versa!

Ferry boat leaves many fond memories

The Bridge will deprive many future St. Charles parish residents of the glories of riding the ferry boat. Anyone who has not spent many wonderful hours playing ferry boat roulette has missed half his life.

In recent years, some of the pleasure of ferry boating has been lost because, with two boats working, passengers didn't get to fully enjoy sitting on the levee observing the wonderous life of the river.

Because there was little to complain about, people just naturally complained about the ferry boat.

Many wonderful friendships began and were nourished by the sometimes lengthy waits for the boat to arrive. People became neighbors in the ferry boat line.

Now they will wave to each other on The Bridge, waving for the river and they preferred to let the St. Charles fend for itself. The wind and the wall of water drove the ferry boat upriver. It beached itself on the back of the river – in front of Mike Brown's home.

The Housselle was as much a part of the St. Charles as its rudder, its pilot wheel. He had no radar. In dense fog today, pilots be up to the dock and make passengers wait. Doe waded the St. Charles when he couldn't see the deck. He would call to them with orders to cast off and Doe would set his course. He could smell the landings on the opposite sides of

Doe Rousselle, Mike Brown, Cal Callahan, Nelson Eugene, the whistle tooting commander of the deck.

For many years, the pleasure of a stop at the Ferry Inn atop the levee on the West Bank has been a memory. But The Bridge helps one recall the good times there and the memory of Louis Vitrano and those who are a part of a wonderous era of St. Charles history.

The Bridge.

It's supposed to bring miracles. It will never produce the miracles that the St. Charles created.

the river. He would always you across the river sometimes you felt like were halfway up the levee was hard to make a soft landing when you couldn't see the deck.

Felled by a massive heart tack he was doomed by medical science to live out his life like a vegetable. The lure of the Charles became his therapy. His right side was gone, couldn't talk, he couldn't walk.

With the St. Charles therapy, he squeezed a rubber ball until he got a grip back in his hand. He mumbled words that nobody could understand until everybody could understand. Riding a bike he made a daily trip down to the Charles and rode his ferry. The vegetable became a man again and he was soon a frequent visitor to US Coast Guard headquarters trying to get back his pilot's license. Finally he did

"It's about time"

A headline article in the Herald Guide *marked the end of ferry service in the parish.*

The End of Ferry Service

The opening of the new bridge over the Mississippi River brought an end to ferry service in St. Charles Parish. Since the 1800s, when minimal ferry service was provided by private citizens until later years when the state/parish made ferry service available on a regular basis, crossing the river on the "ferry boat" was a time consuming and often times dangerous ritual which tried the patience of all. In October of 1983, the service was discontinued.

Hale Boggs Bridge

In March of 1985, the Mississippi River Bridge between Luling and Destrehan was renamed the Hale Boggs Bridge. Governor Edwin Edwards, U.S. Representative Lindy Boggs (Mrs. Hale Boggs), and numerous state and local public officials gathered to dedicate the bridge to the late congressman who was instrumental in having it built.

Thomas Hale Boggs, Sr., was a Democratic member of the United States House of Representatives for District 2, which included St. Charles Parish. Representative Boggs served in the House from 1941 to 1943, becoming the house majority leader. Following an unsuccessful re-election bid, he joined the U.S. Navy in 1942 as an ensign and served the remainder of World War II. Boggs returned to politics in 1946 and

Early ferry service in the 1930s wasn't always an easy crossing, especially in the spring when the river rose and the river was filled with driftwood.

Automobile and pedestrian ferry over the Mississippi River at Luling. Vehicles could cross the river here and at Destrehan, while pedestrians also used a small boat going between Norco and Hahnville. (Courtesy of The Herald*)*

The pedestrian free ferry on the Mississippi River. (*Source:* St. Charles Parish Resources and Facilities publication, 1961)

was re-elected thirteen times. In October of 1972, while he was still majority leader, the twin-engine airplane in which Congressman Boggs and Congressman Nick Begish were traveling disappeared over a remote section of Alaska. The airplane presumably crashed and was never found. They were declared dead on January 3, 1973. His wife Corinne Claiborne "Lindy" Boggs (born March 13, 1916), by a special election, filled the vacancy which occurred from the death of Congressman Boggs. She was re-elected to eight succeeding Congresses from March 20, 1973 to January 3, 1991. Congresswoman Boggs served as United States Ambassador to the Vatican from 1997 to 2000.

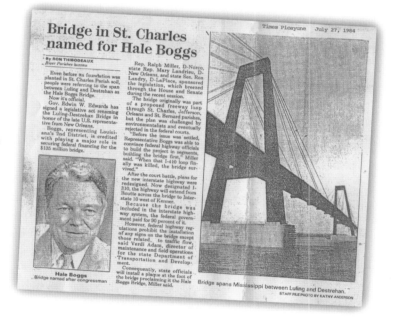

Bridge in St. Charles named for Hale Boggs

By RON THIBODEAUX
River Parishes bureau

Even before its foundation was planted in St. Charles Parish soil, people were referring to the span between Luling and Destrehan as the Hale Boggs Bridge.

Now it's official.

Gov. Edwin W. Edwards has signed a legislative act renaming the Luling-Destrehan Bridge in honor of the late U.S. representative from New Orleans.

Boggs, representing Louisiana's 2nd District, is credited with playing a major role in securing federal financing for the $135 million bridge.

Rep. Ralph Miller, D-Norco, state Rep. Mary Landrieu, D-New Orleans, and state Sen. Ron Landry, D-LaPlace, sponsored the legislation, which breezed through the House and Senate during the recent session.

The bridge originally was part of a proposed freeway loop through St. Charles, Jefferson, Orleans and St. Bernard parishes, but the plan was challenged by environmentalists and eventually rejected in the federal courts.

"Before the issue was settled, Representative Boggs was able to convince federal highway officials to build the project in segments, building the bridge first," Miller said. "When that I-410 loop finally was killed, the bridge survived."

After the court battle, plans for the new interstate highway were redesigned. Now designated I-310, the highway will extend from Boutte across the bridge to Interstate 10 west of Kenner.

Because the bridge was included in the interstate highway system, the federal government paid for 90 percent of it.

However, federal highway regulations prohibit the installation of any signs on the bridge except those related to traffic flow, said Verdi Adam, director of maintenance and field operations for the state Department of Transportation and Development.

Consequently, state officials will install a plaque at the foot of the bridge proclaiming it the Hale Boggs Bridge, Miller said.

Times Picayune July 27, 1984

Hale Boggs
Bridge named after congressman

Bridge spans Mississippi between Luling and Destrehan.
STAFF FILE PHOTO BY KATHY ANDERSON

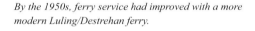

By the 1950s, ferry service had improved with a more modern Luling/Destrehan ferry.

(Courtesy of the Times Picayune*)*

The Ferry Inn offered some comfort to the thousands who waited patiently for "the next ferry." (Photo courtesy of Ruby Reeves)

Early cane harvesting.

Sugar Cane to Nuclear Power—Waterford

Sugar cane production has been a constant presence in the parish since the 1700s. Although it continues on a limited basis in 2010, some of the prime land originally used for sugar cane crops became the site of homes, businesses, and industries in later centuries. One such property was the Waterford Sugar Cooperative, which was located on land first owned by Karl Darensbourg who served as the first German Coast commandant. The land changed hands several times. In 1897, Richard A. Miliken, a native of Ireland, purchased the land and called it Waterford after his hometown. The Waterford Company was liquidated in 1950.

A look at the Waterford III site formerly the Waterford Sugar Cooperative located on the west bank at Killora. (Photo courtesy of Carol Ford)

Sugar cane is inspected in the fields sometime during the sixties. St. Charles is one of nineteen parishes still producing cane.

Louisiana Power and Light purchased the property in the 1970s and it is currently the site of two electrical generating plants and a nuclear power, steam electric generating plant. Commercial operation of the plant commenced at 12:01 a.m. on September 24, 1985. Its opening was heralded as "one of the most significant boons to the parish treasury" of that time. Not without controversy, the "nuclear element" of the project caused some concern to the citizenry. Company employees went out into the community early in the process to meet and inform the residents about nuclear energy to lessen their concerns.

The Waterford Plantation bell is on display in front of the administrative offices of Entergy in Taft. ❖ ❖ ❖

In 2006, a worker prepares the fields for the next sugar cane crop. (Photo courtesy of Lenny Gray)

Lost Treasures Discovered

In 1987, the journal and fifty-three watercolor paintings of Father Joseph Michel Paret, artist and pastor of St. Charles Borromeo Catholic Church in Destrehan from 1848 to 1869, were "discovered" by historian and writer Marcel Boyer who learned of their existence through correspondence with a Louisiana family (Pages 67–74 contain color images of eleven of Father Paret's paintings). The journal and paintings were in the possession of Paret's relatives in France. The aged paintings were color-corrected to reveal their original clarity. They provide a unique and unparalleled look at life in prosperous St. Charles Parish only two years before the beginning of the Civil War. Most of the plantations and other buildings depicted did not survive the Civil War or the ravages of time. Excerpts from the journal provide a further glimpse into life on the German Coast from 1848 to 1869.

In 2001, a book entitled, *Plantations by the River,* featuring twenty-eight out of fifty-three of the watercolors as well as portions of the journal, was published by LSU Press. The Paret journal had been published earlier in France in 1993. In the preface to the book, Mary Louise Christovich gave her evaluation of the importance of the publication, "Father Paret's watercolors have a Janus-like effect, looking back toward the eighteenth century when agricultural empires were rested from raw landscapes and forward to a time when these same properties only suggest a recollection of Louisiana's enduring architectural legacy."

Father Joseph Paret.

Interstate 310 provides a link to the interstate system (I-10) as well as other major federal/state highways. (Source: Dedication Brochure)

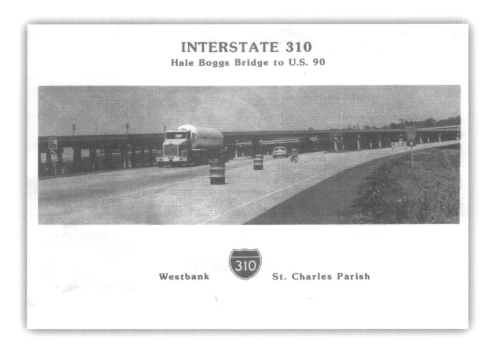

INTERSTATE 310
Hale Boggs Bridge to U.S. 90

Westbank   **310**   St. Charles Parish

In 1990, with the passage of Public Law 10-398, the United States Congress created the Mississippi River Corridor Study Commission that resulted in the creation of Louisiana's Mississippi River Road Commission and the development of the Mississippi River Road Master Plan, a blueprint for the River Road's future. In 1991, the National Trust for Historic Preservation designated the historic Mississippi River Road Corridor between Baton Rouge and New Orleans one of the nation's eleven most endangered historic properties. It is a legacy worth preserving! ❧ ❧ ❧

Public officials cut the ribbon officially opening the west bank I-310 roadway to U.S. 90 on March 23, 1988.

New to the commerce scene in the fourth quarter of the twentieth century has been the development of business parks where a wide variety of businesses share common facilities and land space. The east bank is home to three: James Business Park, Plantation Business Center, and Riverbend Business Park. There are also three on the west bank: Dufresne Business Park, St. Charles Industrial Park, and Taft Industrial Park. They bring a new type of business opportunity and environment to the citizens as well as enhance the economy. The economy remains strong in 2010.

Parish Activities
in the 80s and 90s

An article in the Times Picayune *in May 1993 marked the opening of the I-310 linking St. Charles Parish to the interstate system.*

This segment of Interstate 310, which opened Wednesday, may lead to an economic boom on St. Charles Parish's west bank.

STAFF PHOTO BY S. ANDREW BOYD

Road puts St. Charles in fast lane for growth

By MATT SCALLAN
River Parishes bureau

Dot Woodiel, left, and Marilyn Richoux, right, welcome Republican delegates to the Destrehan Plantation grounds. (Photo courtesy of Marilyn Mayhall Richoux)

St. Charles Parish
Proudly Welcomes the
1988
Republican National Convention

to a

Day at Historic
Destrehan Plantation

St. Charles Borromeo Catholic Church celebrated the 250th anniversary of its patron saint on November 4, 1990. (Source: Dedication Brochure)

We, the people of St. Charles Borromeo, cordially invite you to join in celebrating the two hundred and fiftieth year with St. Charles Borromeo as our Patron Eucharistic Celebration Eleven o'clock a.m. Sunday, the fourth of November Nineteen hundred and ninety Archbishop Frances B. Schulte, Celebrant Dedication of the Memorial Shrine and luncheon will follow St. Charles Borromeo Church on the historic River Road Destrehan, Louisiana

R.S.V.P 764-6383
by October 15, 1990

On October 17, 1988, Republican National Convention delegates, meeting in New Orleans, visited St. Charles Parish and spent a day at Destrehan Plantation. (Source: 1988 Republican National Convention event brochure)

Special Events

St. Charles Historical Foundation members, along with Parish President Chris A. Tregre and Richard Keller, hosted a visit by Lieutenant Governor Kathleen Blanco at Home Place Plantation on May 18, 1999.

School children cheer the arrival of the Olympic Torch as it passes through St. Charles Parish on the way to Atlanta in 2001. (Photo courtesy of Suzanne Friloux)

The Olympic Torch run continues down the River Road in New Sarpy. (Photo courtesy of Suzanne Friloux)

Davis Pond Freshwater Diversion Project

The Davis Freshwater Diversion Project was authorized by the Flood Control Act of 1965 (PL 89-298), the Water Resources Development Act (WRDA) of 1974 (PL 93-251), WRDA 1986 (PL 99-622), and WRDA 1996 (PL 104-303). Construction began in January 1997. Located on the west bank of the Mississippi River in St. Charles Parish near the town of Luling, the project diverts freshwater, with its accompanying nutrients and sediments, from the Mississippi River into the Barataria Basin to reduce saltwater intrusion and establish favorable salinity conditions in the area. These diversions also increase commercial and recreational fish and wildlife productivity, enhances vegetated growth for a healthier estuarine ecosystem in the Barataria Basin, and reduces coastal wetland loss from erosion. The project dedication ceremony was held on March 26, 2002.

September 11, 2001 Terrorist Attacks

Terrorist attacks paralyzed the nation on September 11, 2001, when airplanes flew into the twin towers of the World Trade Center in New York City as well as the Pentagon in Washington, D.C. In St. Charles Parish, security measures increased dramatically at refineries and in particular at the nuclear power plant.

Retired Air Force Lieutenant Colonel Robert Hymel.

9/11 Pentagon Casualty is Norco Native

Retired Air Force Lieutenant Colonel Robert (Bobby) Hymel, son of Sidney and Elsie Gourgues Hymel, was born in Hahnville, grew-up in Norco, and was a graduate of St. Charles Borromeo Elementary and High School (1964) and the University of Southwestern Louisiana at Lafayette. On September 11, 2001, he was killed in the terrorist attack at the Pentagon. Hymel was working as an analyst for the Defense Intelligence Agency. Thirty years prior, in 1972, Hymel was the lone survivor of the crash of his B52 aircraft attempting to land at a base in Thailand after it was hit by two surface-to-air missiles near Hanoi. Lieutenant Colonel Hymel is buried in Arlington National Cemetery.

The Gumbo Krewe were members of Vic Bradley's family and friends who spearheaded humanitarian trips to New York City following 9/11. Community support was widespread.

Louisiana Purchase Bicentennial

In 2003, in conjunction with the Louisiana Purchase Bicentennial Celebration in St. Charles Parish, the St. Charles Historical Foundation developed several projects to commemorate that special occasion.

State Representative Gary Smith, Jr., portrayed the explorer LaSalle at the bicentennial celebration.

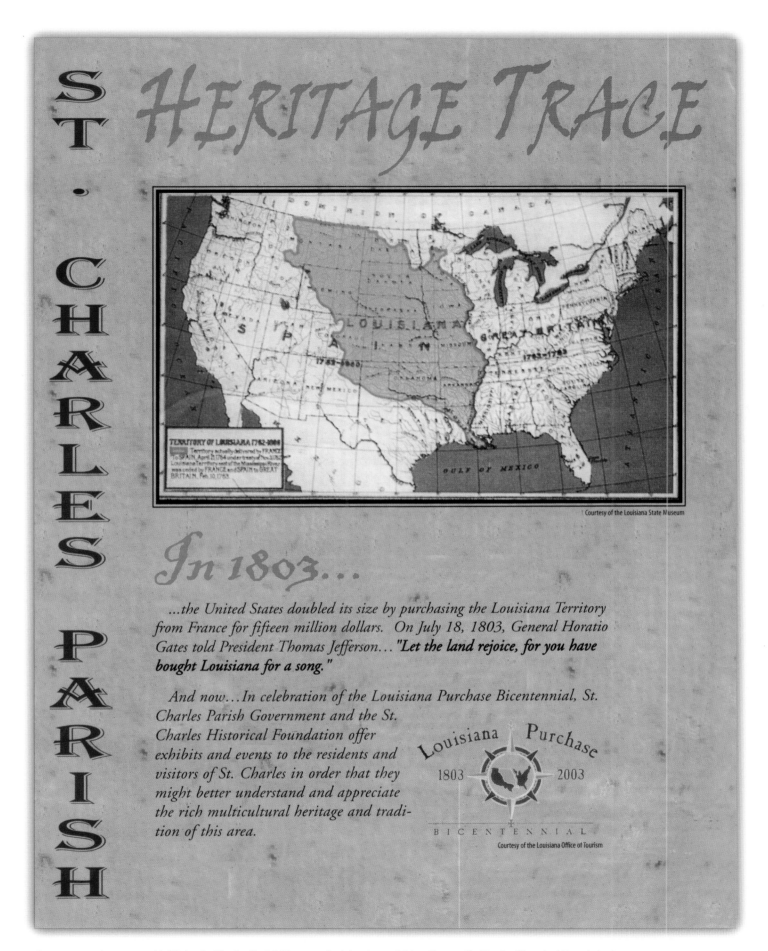

ST. CHARLES PARISH

HERITAGE TRACE

Courtesy of the Louisiana State Museum

In 1803...

...the United States doubled its size by purchasing the Louisiana Territory from France for fifteen million dollars. On July 18, 1803, General Horatio Gates told President Thomas Jefferson... **"Let the land rejoice, for you have bought Louisiana for a song."**

And now...In celebration of the Louisiana Purchase Bicentennial, St. Charles Parish Government and the St. Charles Historical Foundation offer exhibits and events to the residents and visitors of St. Charles in order that they might better understand and appreciate the rich multicultural heritage and tradition of this area.

Louisiana Purchase
1803   2003
BICENTENNIAL
Courtesy of the Louisiana Office of Tourism

A commemorative program highlights St. Charles Parish history and celebration activities. (Source: St. Charles Historical Foundation)

Hurricane Katrina, 2005

Hurricane Katrina had a profound effect on St. Charles Parish and the entire region. Life changed dramatically after the storm and did not return to "normal" for quite some time. Many citizens evacuated and did not return for weeks or in some cases months. The event was front page news locally and across the nation. Local author Patrick Yoes published his personal Hurricane Katrina experiences in a book entitled *Chest Deep and Rising*.

(Courtesy of the Herald *Guide)*

Complimentary Hurricane Issue II

St. Charles Herald Guide

www.heraldguide.com — SERVING ST. CHARLES PARISH SINCE 1873

WEDNESDAY SEPTEMBER 14, 2005 — VOL. 132 NO. 71

TO HELL AND BACK
LOCAL SWAT TEAM RESCUES LULING NURSE, HOSPITAL EVACUEES

SWAT TEAM MEMBERS organized by St. Charles Parish Sherrif Greg Champagne included: From Left: Captain Patrick Yoes, Lt. Rodney Madere, Dep.. Ryan Ordner, Dep.. David Erhmann, Captain Jonathan Walsdorf, Sgt. Roscoe Brewer, Gary Martin, St. Charles School Systems Chief Deputy Joseph Cardella, Staff Sgt. Rob L'Huillier, 1/244th CAB, Alpha Co., La. Army National Guard, Lakefront Airport (not pictured), Deputy Douglas Carter (not pictured), Sgt.Wayne Joseph (not pictured), Staff Sgt. Dan Beier, 1/244th CAB, Alpha Co., La. Army National Guard, Lakefront Airport (not pictured),Wayne Lee (not pictured), Detective Steve Gonzales (not pictured).

BY COLETTE LOTTINGER

The scene at the Ernest J. Morial Convention Center, viewed through the eyes of the television camera, horrified the nation. But while most St. Charles residents sat and watched the nightmare unfolding, one local nurse was living it.

On Saturday night as Hurricane Katrina was approaching, Renee Riddick of Luling went to work at Memorial Hospital in New Orleans where she is employed as a newborn nurse.

The usual practice during a storm is to allow a nurse and her family to go in and be housed there in the secure hospital. Instead, her husband David decided he would take their three children, ages 11, 7 and 2, to his sister's house in Austin, Texas.

Katrina came and went and Riddick worked along with the others in tireless fashion. Then the waters came up Wednesday

Memorial Hospital Nurse Renee Riddick and the group of 28 hospital workers and family members relax after harrowing time at convention center.

morning and everyone had to be evacuated from the hospital. Some groups went to Baton Rouge and some went to Thibodaux. Renee's group, drawing the unlucky lot, was taken to the convention center. "They told us that we would be catching a bus there," said Riddick, who, along with 27 other Memorial employees, was

RESCUE ON PAGE 14

School begins Thursday, system preparing for student influx

BY ERIC LEBLANC

After announcing that school will resume on Thursday for students enrolled in St. Charles Parish schools before Katrina, the school system is making preparations for the influx of new students.

"We are making sure our infrastructure is in place before we start classes for new students," said Communications Coordinator Regina McMillan.

The only change to the regular schedule so far is that Friday was a faculty study day. That will not be taking place and Friday will be a full day for all schools.

Parents of students who were displaced and are now living in St. Charles have until Wednesday to fill out a data collection form to begin the process of registering for school.

As of Monday, the school system has received about 1,150 data collection forms.

Also, Monday was the first day back for teachers and the turnout was very high.

"We had about a 90 percent turnout for our teachers on Monday," said McMillan. "And there are still some that will be back that have not made it back to parish yet."

The school board received 344 applications for new teacher positions and were holding a job fair on Tuesday. Candidates were screened and then invited to the fair to interview with principals from different schools.

The school will decide when to allow displaced students to begin classes once all data collection forms are turned in and the school finds out how many current students are leaving because of parents moving.

School officials also stated that they are working diligently to ensure that lunch will be available when classes resume tomorrow.

Parish continues climbing to normal

BY BLAKE M. PETIT

Two weeks after Hurricane Katrina's devastating rampage through the Gulf South, St. Charles Parish has gotten back on its feet.

Tab Troxler, head of the department of emergency operations, says that his department has held regular meetings with government and industry leaders alike, beginning even before the storm

struck on Aug. 29. By Friday he reported that the Valero refinery in Norco was back in operation, and the Motiva refinery would soon join it.

Troxler said he urged all parish public works employees to return as soon as possible once the storm passed so they could begin the work of cleaning up and restoring St. Charles. "You can take such a hit after a disaster like that," he said.

Troxler said he is continuing work to establish a FEMA center in St. Charles Parish, but the parish's quick recovery has taken the feds by surprise. "I don't think they realized that we were trying to get things going," he said.

Corey Faucheux, director of economic development and tourism, stressed that all residents who work in St. Charles Parish should check in with their employers and return to work as

soon as possible. "It's important for the local economy," he said. "It's more important than ever."

The parish's website, www.stcharlesgov.net, has been running a list of commercial operations in the parish as they re-open, but Troxler said they may discontinue that as more businesses are open. As of Friday, he estimated that 60 to 65 percent of the parish's businesses were back in operation.

Volunteers package meals for families affected.

Emergency response workers prepare for evacuees.

The Louisiana National Guard was stationed in St. Charles Parish to assist with aftermath.

Trees were toppled and power outages lasted for weeks.

Hurricane Katrina had a devastating impact on the Zion Baptist Church.

Local Notables

Miss Teen USA 2004 Shelley Catherine Hennig of Destrehan is pictured with Parish President Albert Laque, left, and St. Charles Public Schools Superintendent Rodney Lafon, right.

Senator Joel T. Chaisson president of the Louisiana Senate. Joel T. Chaisson II, a lifelong resident of St. Charles Parish, is a 1977 graduate of Destrehan High School. He obtained his undergraduate degree in business in 1980 from the University of New Orleans followed by his juris doctorate degree in 1983 from the Louisiana State University Law Center. Upon obtaining his law degree, Chaisson sought and won an at-large council position on the St. Charles Parish Council becoming the youngest parish-wide elected official in Louisiana at that time. In 1991, Chaisson was elected to the Louisiana House of Representatives where he represented St. Charles Parish for eight years. Chaisson was elected to the Louisiana Senate in 1999 and was re-elected without opposition in 2003 and again in 2007. On January 14, 2008, Chaisson was elected by his colleagues to serve in the Louisiana Senate's highest leadership post, president of the Senate. In addition to his political career, Chaisson has established a well-respected legal practice in the river parishes and has been very successful as a real estate investor and developer. He and his wife, Sandra Stage Chaisson, reside in Destrehan and have one daughter, Martine Marie Chaisson. He is the oldest of Judge Joel and Bobbie Chaisson's nine children.

Judge Mary Ann Vial Lemmon serves on the United States District Court for the Eastern District of Louisiana since her appointment to that position by the president of the United States in 1996. Prior to that appointment, she served as a district judge in the Twenty-ninth Judicial District Court in St. Charles and St. John the Baptist parishes, the first woman to be elected judge in either of those parishes. Previously, she practiced law in Hahnville with her husband, Harry Lemmon and her father, James P. Vial. In 2005, she was chair of the National Conference of Federal Trial Judges and in 2007 was elected to the Hall of Fame of Women in Government. Judge Lemmon worked with school officials to establish a court school for behavior-disordered children on probation. She also spearheaded a Zero Tolerance Program to handle violent behaviors on school campuses. In an effort to comfort and advise domestic violence victims, she hired and trained a special court officer to work with these individuals. Judge Lemmon is the granddaughter of former Sheriff Leon C. Vial, Sr. (Photo by Timeless Images)

Nancy Tregre Wilson, retired schoolteacher (thirty-eight years), historian, and author, is president of the Louisiana Gourmet Enterprises, a family-owned food manufacturing company headquartered in Hahnville. The enterprise was the first to introduce Cajun foods to the grocery market as convenience foods (Mam Papaul Brand). Nancy has written several books including a cookbook, which details her German-French heritage. In 1976, she wrote the history of St. Charles Parish as a bicentennial project. Nancy and Charles Wilson reside in Hahnville.

Curtis Johnson, Jr., wide receivers coach, joined the New Orleans Saints in 2006 after forging a reputation for developing top-flight targets on the college level for over two decades. His Saints team defeated the Indianapolis Colts in the 2010 Super Bowl. In February of that year, Curtis was honored for his accomplishments with a weeklong exhibit of his memorabilia at the St. Charles Museum on the grounds of Destrehan Plantation. At opening ceremonies, he received salutations and commendations from federal, state, and local officials. Born in New Orleans, he is a kindergarten through high school graduate of St. Charles Borromeo School in Destrehan. Curtis is the son of late Councilman Curtis Johnson, Sr., of St. Rose.

Justice Harry T. Lemmon served on the Louisiana Supreme Court from 1980 through 2002. He served on the court of appeals for the Fourth Circuit from 1970 to 1980. Prior to becoming a judge, he practiced law in Hahnville with his father-in-law, James P. Vial. He grew up in Morgan City, Louisiana, the son of Gertrude Blum and Earl Lemmon, both teachers. He served as education chair of the National Conference of Appellate Judges for ten years. In 2002, he was selected Outstanding Jurist by the Louisiana Bar Foundation. (Photo by Timeless Images)

Hahnville folk artist Lorraine Gendron and her husband Louis have created a thriving art industry featuring Mississippi mud. Her mud sculptures have appeared in prestigious venues, fine art museums across the South, and in international collections. Lorraine is also known for her vivid acrylic paintings and whimsical wood cutouts. Her work was featured at the White House in 2001 and is currently hanging in the State Capital in Baton Rouge.

Library Celebrates Fiftieth Anniversary

Celebrating its fiftieth anniversary in 2005, the library system continue to provide services needed to enrich, enhance, and educate not only the students of the area but all citizens of St. Charles Parish. In 2006, the library system operated from five locations including the two regional libraries, which opened in the 1970s. A new East Regional Library was constructed in Destrehan in 2009 and opened in 2010.

East Bank Regional Library, 2010.

Main Lobby

Saving the Wetlands

In 2006, cypress forests and their management became front-page news. Today's debate is not about the value of the wood but the "woods" and the role they play in maintaining a buffer against tides and winds. According to a *Times Picayune* October 16, 2006 story, "extensive cypress logging has occurred in recent months around Lac Des Allemands in St. Charles Parish," in spite of the concern being raised about continuing to do so. Overall, the cypress swamps area has dwindled from 2.2 million acres in the 1800s to the only 845,000 acres today because of clearing, cutting, and lack of re-growth.

Wetland Watchers

For over forty years, environmentalist Milton Cambre of Norco has been a vigilant guardian of the wetlands. He has studied, explored, and offered solutions to wetland problems. His work has been acknowledged and honored at the local, state, and federal levels including being designated as one of President George H.W. Bush's "Thousand Points of Lights." In 2010, Mr. Cambre was recognized for his work at the Gathering of Elders at the twenty-first annual National Service Learning Conference. He was one of only five people from around the United States to be so honored. In recent years, he has been joined by Barry Guillot, a teacher at Harry Hurst Middle School and founder of Wetland Watchers, who along with his "Wetland Watcher" students has furthered the cause of wetlands preservation. The group is featured in the 2010 publication entitled Heroes of the Environment—True Stories About People who are Helping to Protect Our Environment. ❧ ❧ ❧

Louisiana cypress swamps may be a fading sight.

Fairs and Festivals

Annual fairs, festivals, and parades have been occurring in the parish for decades, one for over a century. Many take place in churchyards, on school grounds, at bridge parks, and at plantations and are eagerly anticipated by locals and visitors alike.

An early Catfish Festival brochure welcomes visitors to Des Allemands.

Mr. Alligator greets his fans at an early Alligator Festival.

The Alligator Festival fairgrounds as pictured in 1977.

St. Charles Borromeo Fiesta, 1953.

The Destrehan Plantation Fall Festival crowd in 2006.

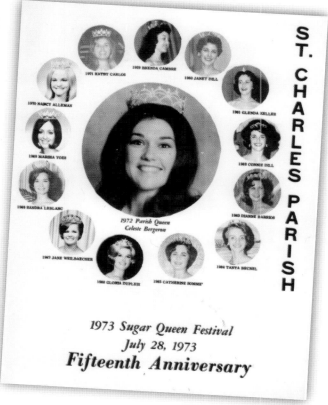

(Source: St. Charles Parish Sugar Festival Brochure, 1973)

The Norco Christmas Parade Fire Chief salutes the crowd in 2009.

A Red Church festival brings families out to enjoy carnival rides and activities.

The Norco Christmas Parade in 1974 featured a visit from Santa just as it does today.

Des Allemands Parade

The St. Charles Parish Sheriff's Department rides in the Des Allemands Parade.

The St. Charles Hospital float in the Krewe of Des Allemands Parade.

Mother's Day Parade

Sponsored by the Hahnville chapters of the Grand United Order of Odd Fellows and its women's auxiliary, the Household of Ruth, the Mother's Day Parade in Hahnville still takes place in the twenty-first century. Odd Fellows Lodge 2842 was founded in 1887 and its parade was organized soon after. Shown are photos from the 1946 parade. (Photos courtesy of Carolyn Smith Boyd)

Luling Parade

The first Luling Parade in 1978 highlighted King and Queen "Papa John" and Jennie Bushalacchi.

Hahnville High School Band Director David Rosenthal has marched in every parade since the Krewe of Lul began. He retired in 2009—the year this picture was taken. (Photo courtesy of Debbie Dufresne Vial)

In 2007, St. Charles Parish celebrated its two hundredth anniversary. (Photo courtesy of St. Charles Historical Foundation)

Speeches, pageantry, demonstrations, sweet treats, and camaraderie were highlights of the parish's bicentennial celebration.

200
BiCentennial
1807 ST. CHARLES 2007

Birthday Celebration
March 31, 2007

Sheriff Greg Champagne and his wife Alice enjoy the bicentennial.

Tri-Parish Bicentennial Celebration

St. Charles, St. James, and St. John Parishes joined together to celebrate the bicentennial. The River Region Arts and Humanities Council presented "Herons in the Hall" on June 2, 2007, at San Francisco Plantation in Garyville, Louisiana.

Senator Joel Chaisson, left, and Judge Robert Chaisson, right, are pictured at the tri-parish celebration.

Tri-parish residents enjoy visiting with each other during the bicentennial celebration.

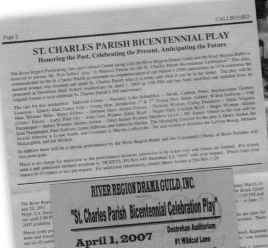

Uniquely decorated herons were on display at the celebration event.

Artist George Rodrigues served as one of the heron judges.

Quality of Life

Community Chorus of the River
   Parishes
Community Band of St. Charles/
   Community Jazz Band
Louisiana Artist Association
St. Charles Art Guild
River Region Drama Guild
River Region Ballet
River Road Historical Society
St. Charles Museum and Historical
   Association
River Region Arts and Humanities Council
St. Charles Women's Club

German-Acadian Coast Historical and
   Genealogical Society
German Coast Farmers Market
St. Charles Humane Society
American Legion and Auxiliaries
Lions Clubs
St. Charles Rotary Club
Civic Associations
Benevolent Societies/Church
   Organizations
Veterans of Foreign Wars (VFW)
School Associations
Krewe of Lul

Krewe of Des Allemands
St. Charles Council on Aging
Retired Senior Volunteer Program
Garden Clubs
Homemaker Clubs
Recreation Booster Clubs
Daughters of the American Revolution
Patriotic Organizations
Boy Scouts/Girl Scouts
4-H Clubs
The ARC of St. Charles
Beautification Task Force

Into the Future

Following the bicentennial celebrations in 2008, the parish moved forward anticipating the future. The 2007 election of a new parish president and council set in motion plans for continued growth and the ever-changing way of life on the German Coast—St. Charles Parish.

St. Charles Parish President V. J. St. Pierre.

Fourth Parish President
Distinguished Vietnam War Veteran
Past Police Jury President
Former local businessman
Promoter of parish unity and comprehensive growth
through progressive leadership

St. Charles Parish President and Council, left to right: Marcus M. Lambert, Dennis Nuss, Carolyn K. Schexnaydre, Paul J. Hogan, V. J. St. Pierre, Terry Authement, Wendy Benedetto, Billy Raymond, Sr., Shelley Tastet, and Larry Cochran.

Conclusion
The Breadbasket Continues…

When morning arrives in St. Charles Parish in southeast Louisiana and as the sun rises, our quiet community begins doing the work that serves our entire nation—

The grain that is loaded today in St. Charles Parish will soon make its way to the breakfast tables of families all along the east coast—60 percent of America's grain moves through our port—

Before midwest farmers can irrigate and harvest their crops, the tractors will be filled with the fuel that was produced right here in St. Charles Parish. We produce 3 percent of America's daily crude oil—500,000 barrels per day—

When doctors and nurses reach for vital surgical supplies, we know that the largest port in the country, located in St. Charles Parish, helped put those supplies in the proper hands. We have the largest tonnage port in the Western Hemisphere—50,000 barge movements logged annually—

For generations, we have proudly nurtured our fading wetlands to share fish, shrimp, crab, alligator, and crayfish with the finest restaurants in the world—

It is a lifestyle and a livelihood that serves our entire country and extends around the world.

So, the breadbasket continues…

And yet, every year we live with the threat of losing it all!
In one day, with the force of Mother Nature bearing down on our fragile ecosystem:
fuel supplies could be shut down;
ships could be dry-docked for months;
sugar and grain could be lost in the flooded fields;
and we, St. Charles Parish and America, could be changed forever.

Railway, crude oil, grain, petro chemicals, trucking, seafood, shipping…all would be affected!

We live with the threat that could be devastating to St. Charles Parish but all of America will suffer too.
We are the providers of food, fuel, and energy that keeps America growing.
When we are productive, America is productive!

Three hundred years later, the German Coast continues to be a breadbasket for America!

(Permission for use of concluding content received from Melanie Worrall and Renee Allemand Simpson, St. Charles Parish Government.)

Epilogue

The Catholic Church in St. Charles Parish

For over a century, St. Charles Parish was predominantly Catholic. Capuchin missionary priests from France serving the Church of St. Charles were relentless in their pursuit of converting settlers in the colony. The first church to appear was a tiny chapel named St. Jean des Allemands, built in 1723 near present-day Killona and attended by Capuchin priests. St. Jean predated the St. Louis Cathedral and was one of Louisiana's earliest churches. Unfortunately that church is no longer in existence. Tradition holds that in 1740 the church parish was relocated to the east bank and renamed St. Charles. A log church served parishioners for many years until it burned in 1806. A new wood-framed church painted red replaced it in 1806 and became known as "The Little Red Church." Historians believe that in 1770 General Alexander O'Reilly expropriated a large plot of river frontage for the Germans to be used for a church and cemetery. A new Catholic church was established in 1868 as *L'Eglise Notre Dame du Rosaire* Chapel in Taft (Our Lady of the Holy Rosary Church). An arsonist set the St. Charles Church rectory on fire in 1877 and most of the church records dating back to colonial times were destroyed. Holy Rosary established many mission chapels: St. Anthony of Padua, a mission in 1877, became a chapel in 1902, and a church parish in 1961; St. Mark, in 1898 in Ama, became a church parish in 1974; St. Gertrude the Great, in Des Allemands in 1900, became a church parish in 1955; St. John the Baptist Catholic Church in Paradis was established in 1970. Holy Family Catholic Church, first established as a mission chapel of St. Anthony of Padua

in 1978, became a church parish in 1980. St. Charles Borromeo Church Parish also established mission chapels. St. Isidore the Farmer was established as a mission chapel in 1924 in Montz. Sacred Heart of Jesus was established as a mission chapel of Borromeo in 1942 and became a church parish in July 1959. Holy Rosary was relocated from Taft to Hahnville in 1965. Hurricane Betsy destroyed St. Isidore Chapel in 1965. The first Protestant church was established in 1859, altering 136 years of Catholic Church domination in St. Charles Parish.

Appendix I

Newspapers in St. Charles Parish

The history of Louisiana newspapers dates back to the establishment of *Le Moniteur de la Louisiana* on March 3, 1794. This newspaper lasted at least until 1814. The local press over the years has provided an up-close and unique look at the news of the area. In the twenty-first century, many other sources of information are available, but the local newspaper endures as one of the primary and comforting sources of area news. The following is a list of newspapers published in and primarily for the St. Charles Parish citizens:

L'Avant Coureur
January 29, 1853–77
Weekly on Sunday
Editors: Prudent D'Artlys (1853–57); Ernest Le Gendre and Eugene Dumez (1857?–May 15, 1858); Eugene Dumez (May 22, 1858–73?)

A spinoff newspaper of *LeMeschacebe* was published in Lucy, which was at that time the parish seat of St. John the Baptist Parish. Publication apparently was not permitted between mid-1862 and January 1866.

St. Charles Republican Pioneer
186?–72
Editor: Senator Mortimer H. Smith (Edgard)

St. Charles Herald
February 15, 1873–May 27, 1993
Weekly
Editors: Marsellus Vallas (1873–79), T. H. Ryan (1879–81), H. T. Henry (1881–82), Bennett Hinton (1882), Beatrice Hinton (1883), Joseph N. Carew (1883–90), O. B. Baque-publisher, J. C. Triche & Company–editor and business manager (1890–1903), J. B. Martin (1903–13), J. Clem Triche, Jr. (1913–17), W. A. Brady (1917–19), J. C. Triche, Jr. (1919–29), Triche children including L. Taft Triche, Polymenia Troxler, Mrs. O. Triche Troxler (1929–August 19, 1954), Henry E. Yoes, Jr. (August 19, 1954–?), Patrick Yoes

St. Charles Mirror
February 20, 1876–77
Editor: Horace Vallas

Paradis Sentinel
(1906, two issues)

Paradis Times-Hustler
August 15, 1912– June 7, 1914
Monthly
Editor: J. Lahroy Slusher

Paradis Enterprise
January 6, 1914–21
Weekly on Saturday
Editor: Dr. Luther A. Youngs

Norco News

Good Hope News
September 2, 1929–October 11, 1930
Weekly
Publisher and business manager: R. L. Crager; Editor: T. B. Mayer
Correspondents: Good Hope—Inez

Bourg, Marie Guillot; Destrehan—
Pauline Warfield, Ethel Picou, Edna
Seale Delaune, Lucy Weaver, Elta
Haydel Miller; Norco—Estelle Menuet,
Mrs. R. L. Gray, Marguerite L. Cooper,
Ruth Schexnailder; St. Rose—W. G.
Knobloch; Hahnville—Ella Baudoin,
Helen Martin; Luling—Jean DeBoker,
Mary E. Lussen; Kenner—Loretta
Louviere, Marguerite Dutreix; Modoc—
Ethel Rome; New Sarpy—Mrs. Herbert
Lauderbaugh; Des Allemands—Alverta
Dufrene.

St. Charles News
January 7, 1938–February 9, 1940
Weekly on Friday
Publisher: Lamar Jones; Editor: Rodney
P. Woods, Jr.
(Merged with *St. James Voice* in
Convent and *St. John Herald* in LaPlace
to form *River Parishes Journal* on
February 9, 1940)

River Parishes Journal
February 16, 1940–67
Editors: Rodney P. Woods, Jr. and later
Joseph P. Lucia, Sr.
(Formed from merger of *St. Charles
News*, *St. James Voice*, and *St. John
Herald*. Later merged with the *News-
Examiner* in Lutcher.)

Voice of St. Charles
March 19, 1964–November 12, 1964 (?)
Weekly—Democratic
Published by "The State-Wide Service
Inc." Reputedly financed by Edward
Dufresne, Jr., Melvin Barre, George
Delaune, Eric Fleming

West St. Charles Guide
August 27, 1969–June 30, 1976
Weekly on west bank
Publisher: Allen Lottinger, Jr.
Began as free-circulation weekly

River Parishes Guide
July 7, 1976
Weekly (Paid circulation became semi-
weekly on September 4, 1983)
Publisher: Allen Lottinger, Jr.
Merged with *St. Charles Herald* on
June 3, 1993

The Guidepost
November 1970–June 1972
Free-circulation weekly on east bank
Editor: Evon Stevens

The River Road Press
October 20, 1973–74
Editor: Henry Wolfe, Jr.
First black-centered newspaper in parish

The Gazette
December 2, 1985–February 1986
Free-circulation weekly on east bank
Publisher: Henry E. Yoes, Jr.

St. Charles Herald-Guide
June 3, 1993–present
Semi-weekly to 2005 and returned to
weekly
(Formed from merger of *St. Charles
Herald* and *River Parishes Guide*)

Magazines:

River Parishes Focus
June 1978–October 1979
Monthly
Editor: Henry E. Yoes III;
Associate Editor: Edith Vicknair

River Region Pride
February 1997–February/March 1998
Editor: Scott Madere

Louisiana Sportsman
(five other sport magazines)
Editors: Tony and Ann Lottinger Taylor

St. Charles Historical Foundation

Project History

Along the way, foundation members determined that elements of our mission and vision to establish a museum could be achieved by creating a "Museum Without Walls." This was done by using our libraries, churches, courthouse, plantation houses, restaurants, airport, and other sites to put exhibits in place. General membership meetings were held at historic sites. Those in attendance were provided historic perspectives by guest lecturers or board members.

The following list includes most of the many projects and exhibits that the St. Charles Historical Foundation either initiated, sponsored, completed, assisted with, or assumed supportive roles in preservation efforts:

Louisiana Purchase Bicentennial Celebration in 2003:
Evening With the Notables—Destrehan Plantation
Framed Louisiana Purchase Documents—Presented to Schools

Heritage Trace Projects of the Louisiana Purchase Bicentennial:
Heirloom Sewing Exhibit—Ormond Plantation
1811 Slave Revolt Exhibit—Ormond Plantation
Annual Historical Scavenger Hunt—A Look Beyond the Obvious
Louisiana Italians—Folkways and Food—St. Rose Tavern
Historical Walkway—West Bank Bridge Park
Atlatl Demonstration—West Bank Bridge Park
Rural Life Exhibit—Esperanza Restaurant
Mardi Gras Exhibit—Esperanza Restaurant
Governor Georg Michael Hahn Exhibit—Courthouse Lobby
Music Legends of St. Charles Parish Exhibit—Louis Armstrong New Orleans Int'l Airport
Historic Cypress Luggers Denver and Champion—Brochure—Ormond Plantation

Miscellaneous Projects:
Oral Histories—Bethune and Old Norco Elementary
Lecture Series—Women of the 19th Century—Destrehan Plantation
Establishment of Historic Districts and Areas—Legislation and Implementation
Annual Scavenger Hunt
Preservation of Home Place—Hahnville
Preservation of Dugas House—Ama
Preservation of Davis Nicholas House—Hahnville
Preservation of Taft Triche Kitchen—Taft (now at Home Place)

Preservation of Oscar Gervais House Artifacts and Station—Boutte
Preservation of Richard Taylor Residence at Fashion Plantation—Hahnville (now on Highway 90)
Preservation of Elfer House—St. Rose
Preservation of Old Des Allemands School
Preservation of Killona School Artifact (Lintel) and Vintage Bricks
Preservation of Good Hope and Paradis Depot
Preservation of Denver and Champion Luggers
Preservation of Bethlehem Baptist Church History and Artifacts—Hahnville
Rotating Exhibits (Two Exhibit Cases)—Courthouse Lobby
Annual Atlatl Demonstration and Contest
Early American Indian Exhibit—Rotating Exhibit—Courthouse
Parish Archival Preservation
St. Charles Borromeo Conservation Plan
Historic Designation—Placement of Plaques and Markers
Early German Village Exploratory Thermograph Flyover
Initiation of St. Charles Parish Bicentennial Committee and Member Representation
Pictorial History Book Project for Parish Bicentennial
Lt. Governor Mitch Landrieu's Visit to Discuss Cultural Economy Initiative
Louisiana Department of Culture, Recreation and Tourism Partnership
Fiscal Agent—Beautification Task Force—Old DHS Buy-A-Brick Program
Historic DHS Mural
Fiscal Agent—German Coast Farmers' Market
German Coast Farmers' Market
Initiating Parish Proclamation: Gallet as *Official Fry Bread* of St. Charles
Time Capsule—Courthouse
Historic Lighting—Mile of History—Destrehan
Sale of Pursuit of Excellence Books—History of Education in St. Charles
Note Cards Depicting Historic Sites/Structures
Cypress Lumber Stored at Old Des Allemands School
Enhancement—Historic DHS Film
"Mile of History" Official Parish Designation
Liaison with German Cultural Center in Gretna

Historical Markers
in St. Charles Parish

Les Allemans—Site of first German settlement in St. Charles
Located in Killona on La. 18 (River Road) at the St. Charles/St. John boundary line

L'Anse Aux Outardes (Bustard's Cove)—First east bank settlement site
Located in New Sarpy on La. 48 (River Road)

St. Charles Borromeo—"Little Red Church"—
Famous Mississippi River landmark
Located in Destrehan on La. 48 (River Road)

Destrehan Manor House— Originally constructed for Robert de Logny
Located in Destrehan on La. 48 (River Road)

Home Place Plantation—Built in 1790s
Located in Hahnville on La. 18 (River Road)

LaBranche Plantation Dependency House—
Only remaining building from the original plantation
Located in St. Rose on La. 48 (River Road)

Skirmish of Boutte Station—Civil War site
Located in Boutte on US/LA 90

Fashion Plantation—Home of General Richard Taylor
Located in Hahnville on La. 18 (River Road)

Battle of Des Allemands—Site of Civil War battles
Located in Des Allemands on US/LA 90

Flagville—Letter left at this site by Tonti for LaSalle
Located in Hahnville on La. 18 (River Road)

Historical Marker Information

Les Allemands

German immigrants led by Karl Darensbourg in 1722 joined other settlers on Law's concession in the Villages of Hoffen, Augsburg, and Mariental. The chapel was erected by 1724. These industrious German farmers saved New Orleans from famine. (Erected by German-Acadian Coast Historical & Genealogical Society)

L'Anse Aux Outardes (Bustard's Cove) 1722

Settled by Canadians and the French. Bienville came here in 1699 from Lake Pontchartrain using small waterways, portage. LeSuer and Canadians used the route and were met here by Iberville and Tonti on February 24, 1700. It became part of the "Second German Coast" about 1730. (Note: Some west bank settlers moved to this east bank site in 1722.) (Marker missing in 2010)

St. Charles Borromeo—"Little Red Church"

First constructed of logs about 1740. Burned and rebuilt in 1806. Famous riverboat landmark, twenty-five miles from New Orleans where boat captains traditionally paid off their crew. Again burned and rebuilt about 1921. (Note: New white stucco Spanish mission-style church was built in 1921 and the 1806 wooden church was torn down later. Oldest German cemetery in the South. Church, cemetery, and school complex built on the original 1770 Spanish land grant.) (Erected by Louisiana Department of Commerce and Industry in 1964.)

Destrehan Manor House

Constructed in 1789–90 for Robert de Logny. Inherited by Jean Noel d'Estrehan in 1800. Bought from heirs of Pierre A. Rost in 1914 by Mexican Petroleum Company. Donated in 1972 to River Road Historical Society by American Oil Company. (Note: Purchased by Jean-Nöel Destrehan from deLogny estate. Site of Rost Home Colony following Civil War. Named by River Road Historical Society for Louisiana Statesman Jean-Nöel Destrehan.) (Erected by St. Charles Parish Police Jury and St. Charles Bicentennial Committee in cooperation with Louisiana Tourist Division of the Department of Commerce.)

Home Place

Built in the 1790s, this French Colonial raised cottage is of West Indies bousillage construction. Owners included LaBranche, Fortier, and Gaillaire, with the Keller family ownership since 1885. (Note: A National Historic Landmark and is listed on National Register of Historic Places.)

(Erected by St. Charles Parish Police Jury and St. Charles Bicentennial Committee in 1975 in cooperation with Louisiana Tourist Division of Department of Commerce.)

LaBranche Plantation Dependency

This late eighteenth–early nineteenth century Creole house is of statewide significance because of its exceptional Federal woodwork and its rarity as a plantation dependency. Listed on National Register of Historical Places.

Battle of des Allemands

Le district des Allemands, settled by Germans about 1720, the scene of numerous skirmishes between Confederate guerillas and Union forces, 1862–63. Most famous skirmish resulted in capture of an entire detachment of Union soldiers on September 4, 1862.

Skirmish of Boutte Station

Union train with sixty men ambushed by Confederate force of Louisiana militia and volunteers on September 4, 1862. Train escaped to New Orleans. Fourteen Union soldiers killed and twenty-two wounded in the skirmish. (Erected by St. Charles Parish Police Jury and St. Charles Bicentennial Committee.)

Fashion Plantation

Home of General Richard Taylor, son of Zachary Taylor, Louisiana statesman and member of 1861 Secession Convention. Commanded Louisiana District, 1862–64; defeated Banks at Battle of Mansfield, 1864. Federals plundered home in 1862. (Erected by Louisiana Department of Commerce and Industry in 1961.) (Marker missing in 2010)

Flagville

Named for O. J. Flagg in 1870; now a part of Hahnville. Letter left here by Tonti in 1686 with Quinipissa chief for LaSalle. Taensa Village, 1713. De Veuve, French Concession, 1718. Site included grant to Joseph Roi de Villere, 1765. (Erected by Louisiana Department of Commerce and Industry in 1962.)

Notes following historical marker information reflect supplemental or corrected information pertinent to the site. Historical markers were manufactured by Sewah Studios in Marietta, Ohio.

Historical Settlements
in St. Charles Parish

Allemands—named for the Germans, became Des Allemands

Ama—named for the daughter of Alice Plantation owner (means "to love" in Greek).

Bayou Gauche—gauche means left or left-handed. Bayou Gauche is the left and smaller fork of Bayou des Allemands.

Boutte—named for Tisaphane Boutte and his son, J. L.

Des Allemands—French name for the Germans; was Allemands

Destrehan—named for the Destrehan family

Elkinsville—named for Palmer Elkins; became a part of St. Rose

Flaggville—named for Orthello Flagg; became a part of Hahnville

Good Hope—named for Good Hope Plantation (included an area known as "The Island"); became a part of Norco in 2000

Hahnville—named for Georg Michael Hahn

Killona—Gaelic for Church of St. John (named by Richard Millikin from Ireland).

LaBranche—named for the LaBranche family (it was located on the shores of Lake Pontchartrain and destroyed by a hurricane in 1915).

Luling—named for Florenz A. Luling

Moberly—named for the Cumberland-Moberly Lumber Company in Taft

Modoc—named for Modoc Plantation; now a part of Destrehan

Montz—named for the Manz (Montz) family

Mozella—named for Mozella Plantation

New Sarpy—named for Leon Sarpy; site of second Sarpy Plantation

Norco—acronym for New Orleans Refining Company (formerly Sellers and Diamond; also included an area known as Wesco)

Paradis—named by developer and railroad builder Eduardo Paradis

Sarpy—named for Leon Sarpy; became Sellers then Norco

Sellers—named for Colonel Thomas Sellers; became Norco

Taft—named for lumber baron Charles Taft, President William Howard Taft's brother.

St. Rose—named for St. Rose Plantation

*Settlements remaining in the twenty-first century

Cemeteries
in St. Charles Parish

Ama
Mount Pilgrim Cemetery
Mount Zion Cemetery

Boutte
Mount Airy Memorial Park Cemetery
Mount Zion Baptist Cemetery
Saint Mary Cemetery
Young Cemetery

Des Allemands
Bayou Gauche Cemetery
Mennonite Cemetery
Saint Gertrude Cemetery
Sunset Cemetery

Destrehan
Saint Charles Borromeo Cemetery

Hahnville
Bethlehem Baptist Church Cemetery

Killona
Killona Rest Haven Cemetery

Luling
Dufresne Family Cemetery
Saint Charles Cemetery

Montz
Providence Baptist Church Cemetery

New Sarpy
New Sarpy Cemetery

Norco (Bonnet Carré Spillway)
Kenner Cemetery
Kugler Cemetery

Paradis
Antioc Baptist Church Cemetery
First Baptist Church Cemetery
Paradis Cemetery
Shell Mound Cemetery

St. Rose
Jefferson Memorial Gardens
Saint Rose Cemetery

Taft
Green Hill Cemetery
Holy Rosary Cemetery

Glossary

Allemands: Germans

anse: Cove

arpent: Old French measurement of land; slightly less than one acre

Blessed Sacrament: Consecrated host (bread) received by Christians as the body of Jesus

bonnet carré: English for square bonnet

broadsides: Posters

Cannes Brulee: Burnt reeds or cane; area covering Tchopitoulous Coast to St. Charles Parish boundary

carpetbagger: Person from the North who traveled to the South following the Civil War to seek political and/or financial gain

circa: About; in approximate dates

circular order: An instruction of a highest federation or land authority.

Code Noir: Set of Louisiana laws governing the conduct of slaves

colony: A settlement far away from the country which governs it

commandant: Person in charge of a colonial government entity

Compagne des Indies: Originally led by John Law, this company had a twenty-five-year management contract and trade monopoly with France to establish the Louisiana Colony.

concession: Large tract of land used for agricultural purposes to feed the colony

concessionaires: Citizens awarded government grants

cote: French word for coast

crevasse: French for deep crack or crevice, as in a levee

delta: Triangle-shaped area of land at the mouth of a river

demonstration library: Pilot program for the library system

diocese: Church territory under the jurisdiction of a bishop

ecclesiastical: Of the church or clergy

El Puerto des Alemanes: Spanish for the "coast of the Germans"

engages: settlers to farm the land for the concessionaires (legally between free men and slaves)

German Coast: Area today referred to as the Parishes of St. Charles and St. John the Baptist; settled by the Germans

home rule: Local form of government

indigenous: Occurring naturally in an area

integration (school): Various parts of the system made into one

interdiction: Punishment by which the faithful remaining in communion with the Church are forbidden certain sacraments or prohibited from performing certain sacred acts

L'anse aux Outardes: Cove of the bustards; site of the first east bank settlement in New Sarpy.

land grant: Piece of land granted to an individual or group by the government

Le premier ancien village allemand: First old German village

Les Deaux Freres: Name of German pest ship, translates to "two brothers;" first ship to arrive in Biloxi with Germans in 1721

levee: Dike used to restrain Mississippi River from spreading over the land during high water seasons

Little Red Church: 1860 frame church painted red which became a landmark on the east bank of the Mississippi

Mississippi Bubble: General reference to John Law's Company of the Indies' financial plan for reviving the French economy through his new world Mississippi company. So called because it continued to grow in size.

monstrance: Church vessel used for displaying the consecrated host

mulatto: Person of black and white ancestry

ouragan: Hurricane

parish: Division of local government similar to county; was derived from the French "paroisse" and the Spanish "parroquia;" the ecclesiastical division under the charge of a curate

pest ship: Ship filled with disease and unbearable conditions, which delivered the Germans to the Biloxi shores

police jury: Form of local government since after the Louisiana Purchase

port: City with a harbor where ships can anchor

Portefaix: Ship which carried Karl Fredrick Darensbourg to shores of Old Biloxi

progenitor: Originator of a line of descent

Reconstruction: Period after Civil War during which the government was rebuilt

scalawags: Southerners who supported the federal plan of reconstruction

secession: Withdrawal from an organization, group, or union

Sieur: Old French title of rank or respect; sir

"Troop of Horse:" Military unit's name during the War of 1812

Union forces: Forces from the North

Bibliography

Andrist, Ralph K. *Steamboats on the Mississippi.* New York: American Hertiage Publishing Company, Inc., 1962.

Arguides, Mrs. J., trans. "The Old Red Church and Its Cemetery." *L'Observateur Louisianais*, (January 4, 1896) 496–509.

Barry, J. *Rising Tide: The Great Mississippi Flood of 1927 and How It Changed America.* New York: Simon & Schuster, 1997.

Baudier, R. *The Catholic Church in Louisiana.* New Orleans, 1931, 1939.

Billings, W., and E. Haas. *In Search of Fundamental Law.* 1993.

Blume, H. *The German Coast During the Colonial Era, 1722-1803.* Destrehan: The German-Acadian Coast Historical and Genealogical Society, 1990.

Booth, Andrew B. Commissioner Louisiana Military Records, compiler. Military Records of Louisiana Confederate Soldiers and Louisiana Confederate Commands, Vol. 1, 1920.

Borne, F., Jr., compiler. *Remembering Hurricane Betsy on Her 40th Anniversary.* Jefferson History Notebook, Jefferson Historical Society of Louisiana, Volume 9, No. 2, 2005.

Boyer, M. *Mon Journal D'Amerique, 1853.* Joseph Michel Paret, Marcel Boyer Publisher, 1993. Boyer, M., *Plantations by the River, Watercolor Paintings from St. Charles Parish, Louisiana by Fr. Joseph M. Paret.* Baton Rouge, LA: Louisiana State University Press, 2001.

Brasseaux, Carl A., Glenn R. Conrad, and R. Warren Robison. *The Courthouses of Louisiana.* Lafayette, LA: Center for Louisiana Studies, University of Southwestern Louisiana, 1977.

Caldwell, E. *Deep Delta Country.* New York: Duell, Sloan & Pearce, 1944.

Calkins, Carroll. "The Story of America." *Readers Digest*, 1975.

Campbell, A. and W. Marston. *Louisiana: The History of an American State.* Atlanta, GA: Clairmont Press (1999) 8, 148, 282, 348.

Carlson, R., N. Keisman, and Lakewood Elementary School students. *Old Luling on the River.* Luling, LA, May 2003.

Carpenter, A. *The New Enchantment of America.* 1967, 1978.

Casey, Powell A. *Encyclopedia of Forts, Posts, Named Camps, and Other*

Military Installations in Louisiana, 1700-1981. Baton Rouge: Claitor's Publishing Division, 1983.

Cavendish, M. *Celebrate the States, Louisiana*. Tarrytown, NY: Benchmark Books, 1997.

Chambers, J. *The Mississippi River*.1968.

Chompomier, P. A. Statement of Sugar Made in Louisiana in 1844. Louisiana Genealogical Register (*Louisiana's German Coast: A History of St. Charles Parish*) December 1965.

Conklin, P. "Framing a Century." *Louisiana Cultural Vistas*. (Spring 1994) 40–41.

Conrad, Glenn R. ed. *A Dictionary of Louisiana Biography*. New Orleans: The Louisiana Historical Association, 1988.

Conrad, Glenn R. *The German Coast: Abstracts of the Civil Records of St. Charles and St. John the Baptist Parishes, 1804-1812*. Lafayette, LA: Center for Louisiana Studies, University of Southwestern Louisiana, 1981.

Conrad, Glenn R. (edited and annotated). *Historical Journal of the Settlement of the French in Louisiana*. Translated by Virginia Koenig and Joan Cain. Copyright University of Southwestern Louisiana, Lafayette, LA, 1971.

Conrad, Glenn R. *St. Charles: Abstracts of the Civil Records of St. Charles Parish 1700-1803*. Lafayette, LA: University of Southwestern Louisiana, 1974.

Cortada, James W. *Pierre Rost and Confederate Diplomacy: A reevaluation*. Louisiana Historical Quarterly, Summer–Fall 1971.

Costain, T. *The Mississippi Bubble*. Landmark Books, 1968.

Culinary Traditions of the Crescent City. An exhibit by The Historic New Orleans Collection, January 16–July 7, 2007.

Curry, M., ed. *Remembering Hurricane Betsy on Her 40th Anniversary*. Jefferson Parish, LA: Jefferson Historical Society of Louisiana, October 2005.

D'Oliveira, L., H. Harvey, and K. Roger, *Legacy of Old Louisiana, Destrehan and Harvey Families*, 1983.

Dart, B. *Constitution of the State of Louisiana and Selected Federal Laws*. Indianopolis: Bobbs-Merrill Co., 1932.

Davis, E. *Louisiana, A Narrative History*. Second Edition, Nashville, TN: Benson Printing Co., 1961, 1965.

Davis, E. *Louisiana: The Pelican State*. Baton Rouge: LSU Press, 1959, 1961, 1969, 1975, 1983.

Davis, E. *The Story of Louisiana*. Vol. II, New Orleans, 1960 (*Louisiana's German Coast: A History of St. Charles Parish*).

Deiler, J. Hanno. *Settlement of the German Coast of Louisiana and the Creoles of German Descent*. Baltimore: Genealogical Publishing Co., 1975.

Divine, Breen, Fredrickson, and Williams. *America, The People and the Dream*. Scott Foresman Publishers, 1991.

Dormon, James H. *The Persistent Specter: Slave Rebellion in Territorial Louisiana*. Louisiana History, Fall 1977.

Eyraud, Rt. Rev. Msgr. Jean M., and Donald J. Millet, comp. and ed. *A History of St. John the Baptist Parish with Biographical Sketches*. Marrero, LA, 1939.

Farrell, J. *The Great Depression*. San Diego, CA: Lucent Books, Inc., 1996.

Forsyth, A. and Earline Zeringue, compilers/translators. *German Pest Ships 1720-1721*. New Orleans: The Genealogical Research Society of New Orleans, Limited Edition, 1969.

Fortier, Estelle M. *The Fortier Family and Allied Families*. Cochran, 1963.

Franks, H., J. Yakubik, J. Treffinger, C. Goodwin, and P. Armstrong. "Cultural Resource Inventory of the Montz Freshwater Diversion Project Corridor, St. Charles Parish, Louisiana." U.S. Army Corps of Engineers, New Orleans, 1986.

Genealogical Register, Land Grants at the German Coast of Louisiana, Volume VIII, No. 3. Translated and edited by S. J. Gianelloni, Jr., Baton Rouge, LA: Louisiana Genealogical and Historical Society, 1961.

Gianelloni, E., compiler. *Calendar of Louisiana Colonial Documents, Volume III, St. Charles Parish. Part One: The Darensbourg Records 1734-1769*. Baton Rouge, LA: Louisiana State Archives and Records Commission, 1915.

Giraud, M. *A History of French Louisiana, The Reign of Louis XIV, 1698-1715*. Volume One. Translated by Joseph C. Lambert. LSU Press, 1953.

Good Hope News. Various issues from 1929 and 1930.

Hart, B. L. and B. Pitt (eds). *World War II: An Illustrated History*. Great Britain: Purnell and Sons Limited, 1977.

Harvey, Horace H. and Katherine Harvey Roger. Completed by D'Oliveira, Louise Destrehan Roger. *To Reach Afar*. Clearwater, FL: Hercules Publishing Company, 1974.

Heurtin, S. *J.B. Martin, Superintendent, St. Charles Parish*, "A Prospectus Presented to The Class of Education 501, Nicholls State University." July 1971.

Historic New Orleans Collection Culinary Traditions of the Cresent City, The. 2007 Exhibition.

Inventory of the Parish Archives of Louisiana, prepared by the Historical Records Survey, Division of Women's and Professional Projects, Works Progress Administration, No. 45. St. Charles Parish. November 1937.

Johnson, M. *Louisiana Why Stop, A Guide to Louisiana's Roadside Highway Markers*. Texas: Gulf Publishing Company, 1996.

Joseph, D. *A Teachers Guide to Louisiana*. Baton Rouge: LSU Press, 1964.

Kane, Harnett T. *Deep Delta Country*. Louisiana edition. New York: Duell, Sloan & Pearce.

Kane, Harnett T. "Plantation Parade." 1945.

Knight, M. "The Rost Home Colony, St. Charles Parish, Louisiana," *Prologue* Magazine. College Park, MD: National Archives and Records Administration, Volume 33 #3, Fall 2001.

Kondert, Charles. *Frederick D'Arensbourg and the Germans of Colonial Louisiana*. Lafayette, LA: University of Southwestern Louisiana, 2008.

Kondert, R. *The Germans of Colonial Louisiana 1720-1803*, Stuttgart, Germany: Academic Publishing House, 1990.

L'Avant–Coureur newspaper.

LaHarpe, J. B. *Historical Journal of the Settlement of the French in Louisiana*. Lafayette, LA: University of Southwestern Louisiana, 1971.

Landry, Stuart Omer, ed. *Louisiana Almanac and Fact Book*. New Orleans, 1949.

Landry, S., Jr., consultant. "Frenier Beach Hurricane Storm Surge Revisited."

LeConte, Rene. *The Germans in Louisiana in the Eighteenth Century, Louisiana History,* Winter 1967.

Leeper, Clare D'Artois. Private Correspondence.

Lerner, S. *Diamond: A Struggle for Environmental Justice In Louisiana's Chemical Corridor*. MIT Press, 2005.

Les Voyageurs. A publication of the German-Acadian Coast Historical and Genealogical Society. Vol. XXVII, No. 1, March 2006.

Levatino, M. *Past Masters-The History and Haunting of Destrehan Plantation*. New Orleans: Dinstuhl Printing and Publishing, 1991.

Louisiana Almanac. (2007) 218.

Louisiana Cultural Vistas Magazine, "Richard Sexton's River Road," Vol. 10, No. 4, New Orleans, Winter 1999-2000.

Louisiana Department of Public Works, Planning Division. St. Charles Parish. *Resources and Facilities, survey by St. Charles Development Board.* Louisiana State Archives, Calendar of Louisiana Colonies Documents.

Merrill, E. *Germans of Louisiana*. Gretna, LA: Pelican Publishing Co., Inc., 2005.

Mexican Petroleum. Pan American Petroleum & Transport Company, New York, 1922.

Morgan, Cecil. *The First Constitution of the State of Louisiana*. Baton Rouge: LSU Press, 1975.

Nolan, C. A. *History of the Archdiocese of New Orleans*. Editions du Signe, France. 2000.

Ormond Plantation Tourist Brochure.

Oubre, E. Vacherie. *St. James Parish, Louisiana: History & Genealogy*. Desktop Publishing, 2002.

Our Lady of the Rosary Church Memorial Book, 1977. Hackensack, NJ: Custombook, Inc.

Peacock, J. *Reconstruction: Rebuilding after the Civil War*. Mankato, MN: Capstone Press, 2003.

Pena, C. *Touched by War: Battles Fought in the Lafourche District*. Thibodaux, LA: C. G. P. Press, 1998.

Phillips, Susan. *A Study of Place Names in St. Charles Parish, Louisiana*. Thesis, University of New Orleans, Department of English, 1979.

Prichard, Walter, ed. *A Tourist's Description of Louisiana in 1860*. The Louisiana Historical Quarterly, October 1938.

Prologue, the Quarterly of the National Archives and Records Administration. Fall 2001, Vol. 33, No. 2.

Richard, Carl. *The Louisiana Purchase, Louisiana Life Series, No. 7*. Lafayette, LA: Center for Louisiana Studies, University of Southwestern Louisiana, 1995.

River Current Magazine by L'Observateur Newspaper, LaPlace, LA, Vol. 3 No. 6, December/January 2000.

Robichaux, A., Jr. *German Coast Families*. Rayne, LA: Hebert Publication, 1997.

Robison, R. *Louisiana Church Architecture*. Lafayette, LA: University of Southwestern Louisiana, 1984.

Ross, S. *Causes and Consequences of World War I*. Austin, TX: Steck-Vaughn Company, 1998.

Samuel, Ray, Leonard Huber, and Warren Odgen. *Tales of the Mississippi*. New York: Hastings House Publishers, 1955.

Scarpaci, V. *A Portrait of the Italians in America,* Charles Scribner's Sons, United States. 1982.

Sexton, R. *Vestiges of Grandeur*. San Francisco: Chronicle Books, 1999.

Shell Bulletin. "Flood Water Through Norco." Norco, LA. Vol. 1, No. 1, March 29, 1937.

Shell Bulletin. Norco, LA. Vols. 1–2, 1937–38.

St. Charles Borromeo Church, 250th Anniversary. Hackensack, NJ: Custombook, Inc. Limited Edition, 1973.

St. Charles Herald. Various issues of the publishers and St. Charles Parish Library, 1873–1972.

St. Charles Herald Guide. Luling, LA, April 12–18, 2007.

St. Charles Herald Is 100 Years Old. Vol. 100, St. Charles Parish Libary, 1973.

St. Charles Parish Resources and Facilities, "A Survey by St. Charles Parish Development Board." 1947, 1961

St. Gertrude the Great Catholic Church Golden Jubilee Edition, 1955–2005.

Sternberg, Mary Ann. *Along the River Road*. Baton Rouge: Louisiana State University Press, 1996.

Sullivan, C. *Hurricanes of the Mississippi Gulf Coast, 1717 to Present*. Gulf Publishing Company.

Taylor, J. *Louisiana, A Bicentennial History*. New York, NY: W.W. Norton & Company, 1976.

Thompson, M. *The Story of The States: The Story of Louisiana*. Boston, MA: D. Lothrop Company, 1888.

Thrasher, A. *On to New Orleans, Louisiana's Heroic 1811 Slave Revolt*. New Orleans: Cypress Press, 1996.

Times Picayune newspaper. New Orleans: The Times Picayune Publishing Company.

Todd, L., and M. Curti. *Triumph of the American Nation*. Florida: Harcourt Brace Jovanovich, Inc. 1986.

U.S. Army Corps of Engineers. *Bonnet Carré Spillway*. New Orleans, LA: U.S. Corps of Engineers.

Vogel, C. *The Capuchins in French Louisiana (1722-1766), Franciscan Studies No. 8*. New York: Joseph F. Wagner, Inc., 1928.

Wall, Bennett, L. Cummins, J. Taylor, W. Hair, M. Carleton, and M. Kurtz. *Louisiana: A History*. Arlington Heights, Illinois: Forum Press, Inc., 1984, 1990.

White, H. *The Freedman's Bureau in Louisiana*. Baton Rouge: LSU Press, 1970.

White, William W. and Joseph O. Baylen. *Pierre A. Rost's Mission to Europe, 1861-1863*. Louisiana History, Vol. II, No. 3, Summer 1961.

Wilson, N. *Louisiana's Italians, Foods, Recipes and Folkways*. Gretna, LA: Pelican Publishing Company, 2005.

Wilson, N. *St. Charles Parish...A Brief Look at the Past*. 1976.

Wilson, S. *The Architecture of Colonial Louisiana*. Compiled and edited by Jean M. Farnsworth and Ann B. Masson. Lafayette, LA: University of Southwestern Louisiana, 1987.

Yoes, Gene, Jr. *The Pursuit of Academic Excellence*. St. Charles Parish School Board, Luling, 1991.

Yoes, Gene III. *Louisiana's German Coast, A History of St. Charles Parish*. Racing Pigeon Digest Publishing Company, Inc., 2005.

Yoes, Henry E. *A History of St. Charles Parish to 1973*. Norco, LA: St. Charles Herald Publishers, 1973.

Index

H

Hahn, Georg Michael, 82, 89, 92

Hahnville, 4, 15, 16, 17, 19, 38, 39, 41, 45, 46, 47, 48, 51, 62, 63, 68, 74, 82, 84, 85, 86, 89, 92, 94, 95, 98, 102, 105, 137, 139, 145, 150, 152, 159, 161, 163, 166, 170, 171, 175, 178, 189, 196, 200, 201, 202, 207, 215, 222, 223

Hahnville Colored High School, 175

Hahnville Courthouse, 83

Hahnville High School, 139, 179

Hale Boggs Bridge, 185, 186, 187, 188, 189

Hampton, Wade, 48

Harvey Canal, 51,52

Harvey, Horace, 52

Harvey, Joseph Hale, 51

Harvey, Louise Destrehan, 51, 52

Henderson, Stephen, 49

Henderson, Zelia Destrehan, 49

Henning, Shelley Catherine, 200

Herman, Margaret, 170

Hermitage Plantation, 70

Hiddleston, 101

Hill Heights, 177

Highway 90, 75

Hoffen, 23, 24, 221

Hogan family, 55

Home Place Plantation, 36, 38, 39, 56, 89, 220, 221

Home Rule, 181, 182

Hooker Chemical, 169

Huber, Jacob, 52, 53

Huey P. Long Bridge, 75, 112

Hurricane Katrina, 198, 199

Hurricanes, 173

Hurst, Harry Madison, 152, 182

Hymel, Robert, 196

Hymelia Crevasse, 77, 99, 114, 115, 116, 117, 118, 119

I

Iberville, Pierre le Moyne, 16, 19, 20, 100, 221

Interdiction, 41, 134

International Matex Tank Terminals, 91

Interstate 3-10, 192

Intracoastal Waterway System, 52

Island Refinery, 124

Italians, 86

J

Jackson & Great Northern Railroad, 58

Jackson, "Stonewall", 80

Jean Louis Endowment, 20, 31

Jefferson Document, 44

Jefferson, Thomas, 43, 44, 45, 49

Johnson, Curtis, Jr., 201

Johnson, Fountain, 85

K

Karlstein, 17, 25, 26, 30, 31

Kemper and Leila Williams Foundation, 74

Kenner Cemetery, 69, 84

Kenner, H., 101

Kenner, Martha, 69

Kenner, P. M., 101

Kenner, William, 69

Kinler family, 75

Klondike Store, 75

Kugler Cemetery, 70

Kugler, George Frederick, 70

L

L.S.U. Press, 67

L'Anse Aux Outardes, 20, 25, 220

LaBranche, 24, 25

LaBranche Dependency House, 83, 220, 221

LaBranche Plantation, 17, 36, 37, 41, 68, 72, 83, 220, 221

LaBranche, Alexandre, 34, 48, 49, 50, 68

LaBranche, Brice Similien, 69

LaBranche, Cyprien, 72

LaBranche, Edgar, 57

LaBranche, Euphemond, 72

LaBranche, Jean Baptist, 37, 50, 72, 129

LaBranche, Jean Louis Plantation, 72

LaBranche, Jean, 17, 25, 37

LaBranche, M. O., Plantation, 68

LaBranche, Marie Trepagnier, 72

Labry, Marie Martin, 129

Lafitte, Jean, 50

Lafitte, Pierre, 50

M

About the Authors

Fay Walker Louque (deceased 2008) was born in Norco and graduated from St. Charles Borromeo Elementary and High School (1957). Fay retired from the St. Charles Parish Library System after twenty-one years of public service and served as a parish election commissioner for over forty-three years. As an historian and genealogist, Fay was the founder of the German-Acadian Coast Historical and Genealogical Society, serving as president for five years, vice-president for fifteen years, and as a board member. She was a member of the Daughters of the American Revolution, United Daughters of the Confederacy, River Road Historical Society, and founder and historian (for over twenty-five years) of Destrehan Descendants Guild, organizing the Destrehan Family Reunion 1989 and 1999. She was also an active member of St. Charles Borromeo Church. Fay lived in Destrehan with her husband of over fifty years, Warren Louque. She was the mother of Kim and Hollie Louque Ericksen and grandmother of Ashley and Matthew Ericksen.

Marilyn Mayhall Richoux is a resident of St. Charles Parish and a graduate of Destrehan High School and Meadows Draughan Business College. After retiring from co-owning and managing a retail bridal and formal wear shop and coordinator of community education, she became actively involved in historical preservation and founded the St. Charles Historical Foundation, serving as president for twelve years. She is a board member of the St. Charles Museum and Historical Association, former member of the St. Charles Parish Planning and Zoning Commission, and a member of the St. Charles Parish Master Plan Steering Committee. She serves as president of the German Coast Farmers' Market, is a member of the Ladies Leukemia League, St. Charles Borromeo Church choir, and civic and community organizations. She and husband Ralph have three sons, one daughter, and eight grandchildren and reside in Destrehan.

Suzanne Friloux is a graduate of St. Charles Borromeo High School and LSU Baton Rouge (B.S., MEd.). She is a retired teacher/administrator from St. Charles Parish Public Schools, an active participant in several civic and social groups, and is also involved in church activities. Sue is a board member of the St. Charles Museum and Historical Association and River Region Arts and Humanities Council. She is a member of the Ladies Leukemia League, River Road Historical Society, St. Charles Humane Society, Retired Teachers' of St. Charles Parish, and St. Charles Borromeo Church.

Joan Weaver Becnel, direct descendant of one of the pioneers, the first families of the German Coast, was born in 1943 and is a native of Destrehan. She graduated from St. Charles Borromeo Elementary and High School and the University of Southwestern Louisiana at Lafayette. Joan worked in the oil and gas industry in New Orleans, Lafayette, and New Jersey prior to employment with the St. Charles Parish Government. She served as the parish council secretary until retirement in 2000 after twenty-five years of public service. She is a member of Our Lady of the Most Holy Rosary Catholic Church. Joan has a son, Greg, and a daughter, Jenny, and six grandchildren. She resides in Hahnville with her husband, Roland.

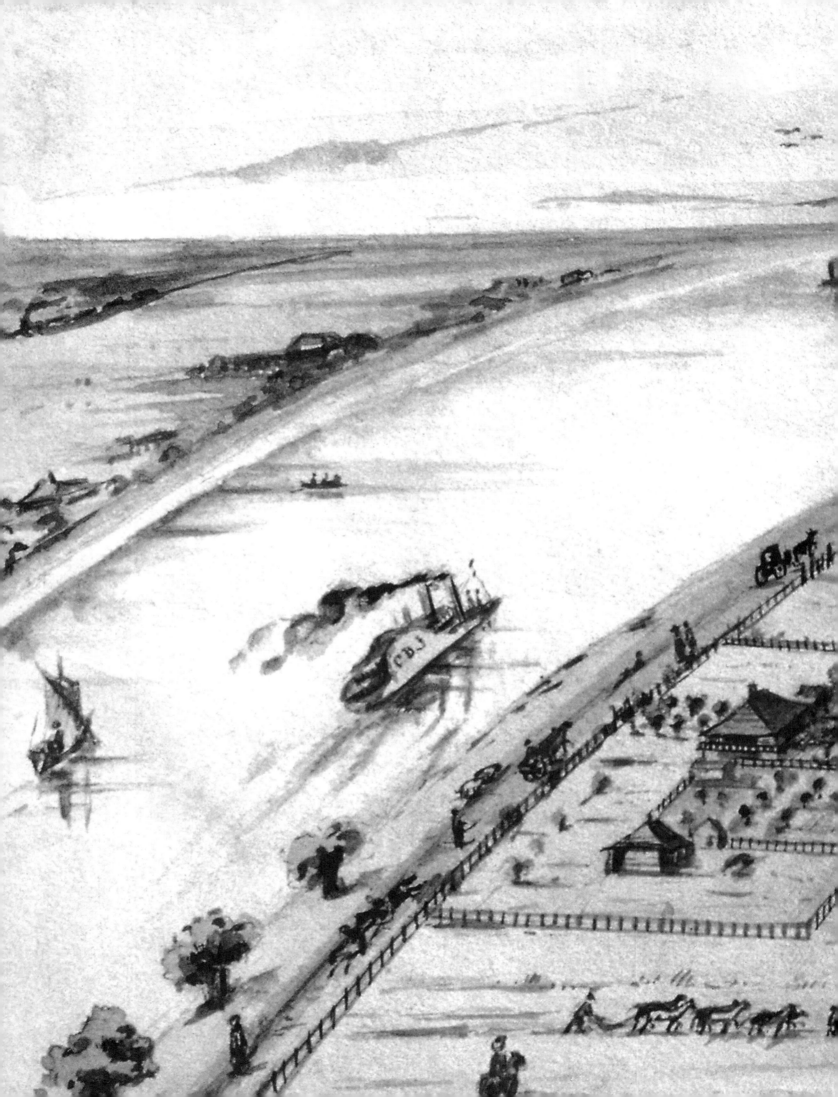